Why Did Jesus, Moses, the Buddha, and Mohammed Cross the Road? Christian Identity in a Multi-Faith World

"[Brian McLaren] actually believes that Jesus and his followers can change the world. This book is no exception—he starts with a joke but quickly you realize just how serious he is about doing what Jesus teaches us to do. Helpful, timely, and really, really inspiring."

—**Rob Bell**, author, *Love Wins*

"A one-man army for decency, compassion, and common sense... McLaren takes our yearnings for peace and turns them into optimism about a new Christian path through which all religions can become a force for human liberation." —**Frank Schaeffer**, author, *Crazy for God*

"This is a major work in every sense of the word—so major, in fact, that it would be impossible to exaggerate either its importance or its worth to the current conversation about religion and religions..."

—**Phyllis Tickle**, lecturer on religion in America and author, *Emergence Christianity*

"...Groundbreaking, redefining religious pluralism for the twenty-first century. It is a 'must read' for Christians and followers of other faiths or no faith."

—**John L. Esposito**, university professor, founding director of the Center for Muslim-Christian Understanding, Georgetown University, and author of *The Future of Islam*

"Brian has resisted the temptation to create an all-you-can-eat buffet of religions, where you can pick and choose what you want. Instead, he curiously explores what it looks like to be unashamedly Christian and still be nice to people who aren't...I am deeply grateful for thinkers like Brian who are helping us discover a Christianity that looks like Jesus again." —**Shane Claiborne**, author, activist, and lover of Jesus

"With wisdom and wit, Brian McLaren courageously explores the contours of his Christian faith in light of his experiences with people from other religious communities. His questions and insights are important contributions to the unfolding interfaith discussion in the United States and beyond."

—**Rabbi Or N. Rose**, director, The Center
for Global Judaism, Hebrew College

"Genuine dialogue with difference has often been avoided by the Christian community because of a fear that it will undermine, weaken, or erode the faith. Here McLaren shows us that, far from being something that is acidic to Christian identity, such engagement is part of its deepest expression."

—**Peter Rollins**, author, *Insurrection:
To Believe Is Human; To Doubt, Divine*

"I think Brian McLaren is a spiritual genius! Not only does he have the courage to say what must and can be said, but he says it with a deep knowledge of both Scriptures and Tradition, and then says it very well besides—in ways that both the ordinary layperson and the scholar can respect and understand. You can't get any better than that."

—**Fr. Richard Rohr**, O.F.M., Center for Action and
Contemplation, Albuquerque, New Mexico

"Brian wants us to have an identity crisis—to ask ourselves what it is about our group identities and the beliefs we profess that causes the addiction to chosenness, to uniqueness, to projecting our fears and insecurities on to the other. The chapter on Christology alone is worth the cover price."

—**Mark Braverman**, human rights activist and author of *Fatal
Embrace: Christians, Jews, and the Search for Peace in the Holy Land*

"Brian McLaren is the most creative Christian theologian and spiritual teacher writing and preaching today in the U.S., yet his universal message is as relevant to people of all faiths and none..."

—**Rabbi Michael Lerner**, editor, *Tikkun*, chair of the Interfaith Network of Spiritual Progressives, author of *Jewish Renewal*, *Spirit Matters*, *The Politics of Meaning*, and *The Left Hand of God*

"...Important and extraordinarily timely...a soothing balm for the searing pain of our times."   —**Huffington Post**

"Brian McLaren is at his best in this book—pastoral, practical, challenging, and thoughtful. As always, he speaks the right words at the right moment, meeting us where we are, but helping us see just around the bend...[I]t will make you a better Christian and a better neighbor."

—**Rachel Held Evans**, blogger and author of *Evolving in Monkey Town* and *A Year of Biblical Womanhood*

"I recommend this new guidebook leading us to better multi-faith understanding 1) because the content is creative, and engaging and 2) because the author has shown the character in his life that qualifies him to direct us in this effort. There are few other books in this genre you will enjoy more..."

—**Randy S. Woodley, Ph.D.**, associate professor of Faith and Culture, George Fox Seminary, and author of *Living in Color: Embracing God's Passion for Ethnic Diversity*

"Brian doesn't shy away from the challenging issues regarding interfaith cooperation. This is a book to cherish, to read over and over, a book that sheds light and warmth on one of the most difficult questions of our era."

—**Eboo Patel**, founder and president, Interfaith Youth Core, and author of *Acts of Faith* and *Sacred Ground*

"I remember the time when I gave my life to Jesus: the tears, the joy, my whole being trembling with possibilities. Only to be told over the years that being a Christian means staying enclosed in what and whom we know. No more. And no fear. To live an open life does not mean playing loose with Christian identity. Quite to the contrary, it turns out that moving outward and rooting deeper is the very same process! With this book Brian McLaren blows the lid off, and after reading it, I tremble again."

—**Samir Selmanovic**, author of *It's Really All About God: How Islam, Atheism, and Judaism Made Me a Better Christian*

"This book is a tremendous and timely contribution both to the Christian faith and to the global community."

—**Dr. Sailesh Rao**, founder of Climate Healers and author of *Carbon Dharma: The Occupation of Butterflies*

"...This is a wonderful exploration of some hints of the great paradigm shift that is coming upon the Christian faith at this time."

—**James Alison**, Catholic priest and theologian

"As a professor of interreligious education, I am delighted that Brian McLaren has provided us with a new book that demonstrates how one can maintain a strong sense of fidelity to one's own tradition while constructively engaging with people of other faith traditions...I am hopeful that Mr. McLaren's work will help us to forge deeper bonds across communities and solve the most dire problems of our time."

—**Najeeba Syeed-Miller**, professor, Claremont School of Theology

Why Did Jesus, Moses, the Buddha, and Mohammed Cross the Road?

Christian Identity in a Multi-Faith World

BRIAN D. McLAREN

JERICHO
BOOKS

New York • Boston • Nashville

Jericho Books
Hachette Book Group
237 Park Avenue
New York, NY 10017
www.JerichoBooks.com

Printed in the United States of America

RRD-H

First trade edition: September 2013
10 9 8 7 6 5 4 3

Jericho Books is an imprint of Hachette Book Group, Inc.
The Jericho Books name and logo are trademarks of Hachette Book Group, Inc.

The publisher is not responsible for websites (or their content) that are not owned by the publisher.

The Library of Congress has cataloged the hardcover edition as follows:

McLaren, Brian D., 1956–
Why did Jesus, Moses, the Buddha, and Mohammed cross the road? : Christian identity in a multi-faith world / Brian D. McLaren. — 1st ed.
    p. cm.
Summary: "Brian McLaren, one of the established leaders of the emerging church movement, invites interfaith dialogue, suggesting tolerance and respect between religions"—Provided by the publisher.
Includes bibliographical references.
ISBN 978-1-4555-1396-3
1. Christianity and other religions.   2. Religions—Relations.
3. Identification (Religion) I. Title.
BR127.M347 2012
261.2—dc23
2012013493

ISBN 978-1-4555-1395-6 (pbk.)

Contents

Part III
The Liturgical Challenge   165

Part IV
The Missional Challenge   221

Grace: ability to laugh at our own imperfections in God's presence.

Chapter 1

The Scene of a Thousand Jokes

Laughter is one of the ways we cope with the discrepancies of our lives. There is a dream we all have for this world, and then there is, well, this world. There are expectations we have of our religions, and then there are our religions....Our capacity to love God, ourselves, people, and all of life grows with our capacity to laugh. We are ridiculous, and not to laugh at our religions, our worldviews, and our philosophies (that is, ourselves), would be a false witness.... This ability to laugh in the midst of our imperfections in the presence of God is what we call grace.

—*Samir Selmanovic*[1]

Why did Jesus, Moses, the Buddha, and Mohammed cross the road?[2]

The question, of course, recalls an old riddle about a chicken. The riddle goes back at least to 1847 when it appeared in a New York

---

1. Samir Selmanovic, *It's Really All About God: How Islam, Atheism, and Judaism Made Me a Better Christian* (San Francisco: Jossey-Bass, 2009), pp. 267–268. Samir is echoing G. K. Chesterton, who said, "It is the test of a good religion whether you can joke about it."

2. Bruce Main asks a similar question in his book *Why Jesus Crossed the Road* (Carol Stream, Ill.: SaltRiver, 2010). His subtitle suggests the energetic direction of his answer: *Learning to Follow the Unconventional Travel Itinerary of a First-Century Carpenter and His Ragtag Group of Friends as They Hop Fences, Cross Borders, and Generally Go Where Most People Don't.*

magazine. By the 1890s, the joke was so well-known that it was generating riffs and variations on the theme.[3]

The original riddle exemplifies "anti-humor"—a joke that is funny because it isn't funny. Anti-humor works by setting up a convention that leads us to expect a joke, and then reverses that expectation in a humorous way.[4] In the nearly countless "Chicken-Joke 2.0" riffs and variations being hatched around the world, jokesters build humor upon the anti-humor, like this:

Why did the chicken cross the road?

GRANDPA: In my day we didn't ask why the chicken crossed the road. Somebody told us the chicken crossed the road to get to the other side, and that was good enough for us.

ALBERT EINSTEIN: Did the chicken really cross the road, or did the road move beneath the chicken?

SIR ISAAC NEWTON: Chickens at rest tend to stay at rest. Chickens in motion tend to cross the road.

A NUN: It was a habit.

HAMLET: That is not the question.

DONNE: It crosseth for thee.

COLONEL SANDERS: Did I miss one?

So, why is it funny to ask about Jesus, Moses, the Buddha, and Mohammed crossing the road? Before looking for a punch line, just for fun try to imagine the scene: four of history's greatest religious leaders...not fighting, not arguing, not damning and condemning one another, not launching crusades or jihads, but walking together, moving together, leading together. Doesn't that already reverse some of our expectations? And doesn't that reversal expose our unspoken

---

3. Like this one, in *Potter's American Monthly*: Q: *Why should a chicken not cross a road?* A: *It would be a fowl proceeding.*

4. We see a great fusion of anti-humor and humor at work in this example: *A pastor, an imam, a rabbi, and a Buddhist monk walk into a bar. The bartender asks, "Is this some kind of joke?"*

expectation—that different religions are inherently and unchange-ably incompatible, disharmonious, fractious, and hostile toward one another?

The image of the four men crossing a road also surprises and inter-ests us because it puts the four in a similar situation, in a common predicament. Whatever the answer will be, it will be the same for all of them, perhaps even rendering them companions rather than com-petitors. ✓ That possibility makes claims on all of us who follow them.

If you're a Christian like me, of whatever sort—Catholic, Prot-estant, or Eastern Orthodox; conservative, liberal, or moderate; traditional or whatever—if you love Jesus, if you know and have con-fidence in him as Lord, Savior, Son of God, Son of Man, God incar-nate, Word made flesh, and more, let me ask you to seriously consider this: *how do you think Jesus would treat Moses, Mohammed, and Sid-dhartha Gautama (the Buddha) if they came to a crosswalk together?* ✳ *lovingly*

Would Jesus push Moses aside and demand to cross first, claim-ing that his ancestor's failed religion had been forever superseded by his own? Would he trade insults with Mohammed, claiming his crusaders could whup Mohammed's jihadists any day of the week, demanding that Mohammed cross behind, not beside him? Would Jesus demand the Buddha kneel at his feet and demonstrate submis-sion before letting him cross? Or would he walk with them and, once on the other side, welcome each to a table of fellowship, not demand-ing any special status or privileges, maybe even taking the role of a servant—hanging up their coats, getting them something to eat and drink, making sure each felt welcome, safe, and at home?

If his three counterparts reached out their hands in friendship, it's pretty hard to imagine that "the friend of sinners" would cross his arms or turn his back, refusing to reciprocate.[5] It's much more likely

---

5. Jesus was criticized by his more puritan critics for being too friendly with "the wrong sort" of people. See Luke 7:34.

Jesus saw value, not flaws

4 • Why Did Jesus, Moses, the Buddha, and Mohammed Cross the Road?

he would embrace them with open arms and without hesitation, proving himself over time to be the best friend they ever had. It's pretty hard to imagine Jesus cursing or "smiting" them, but entirely natural to imagine him blessing them and "doing unto others" as he would want them to do for him. I have no doubt that Jesus would actually practice the neighborliness he preached rather than following our example of religious supremacy, hostility, fear, isolation, misinformation, exclusion, or demonization.

After all, according to the four Gospels, Jesus had extraordinary insight into human character. He saw value where others saw only flaws. He saw the love of a sinful woman who anointed his feet with tears at a banquet, the spiritual thirst of an oft-married woman at a well in Samaria, the big seed of hope in a little chap named Zaccheus, the undeniable faith of a Syrophoenician mother, the flinty strength of loudmouth Peter, and the deep and spunky wisdom of Mary of Bethany. With that track record in mind, we can only imagine what he would see in Mohammed, Moses, or the Buddha, not to mention Confucius, Lao Tsu, Nanak, or Wovoka.[6]

It seems ridiculous to imagine that he would be insecure among them, considering them his rivals, or that he would find it necessary to extract from them explicit agreement on fundamental doctrines before condescending to cross a road with them. It's unthinkable, if one of them came to confer with him by night like Nicodemus, or in broad daylight like the rich young ruler, that he would intimidate them, threaten them, call down fire upon them, patronize them, or

---

6. For a good introduction to some of these religious leaders, I'd recommend for Mohammed, *No God but God* by Reza Aslan (New York: Random House, Updated edition, 2011); for Moses, *A History of God* by Karen Armstrong (New York: Ballantine, 1994); for the Buddha, *One Dharma* by Joseph Goldstein (New York: HarperOne, 2003); for Wovoka (or Jack Wilson), *Neither Wolf nor Dog* by Kent Nerburn (Middle Island, N.Y.: New World, 2002). One of the best Christian resources introducing world religions is Adam Hamilton's *Christianity and World Religions* (Nashville, Tenn.: Abingdon, 2005). Also essential reading for Christians is *Who Speaks for Islam*, by John Esposito and Dahlia Mogahed (New York: Gallup Press, 2008).

humiliate them. Maybe his followers would pull out a sword and slash off their ears, or herd them and their followers into ghettoes, concentration camps, or reservations where their influence could be limited. But never Jesus. Never.

And if you know anything about Mohammed, Moses, and the Buddha, how do you think they would approach Jesus, and one another, if they encountered one another along the road? Is it a joke to think they would respect one another and be drawn toward one another as friends, allies, collaborators? Isn't it more ridiculous to imagine any other outcome? I can't help but think of recent scenes of Archbishop Desmond Tutu and the Dalai Lama, a Christian and a Buddhist, almost giddy in their friendship and mutual regard.

So why might Jesus, Moses, the Buddha, and Mohammed cross the road?[7] Imagine if the answer were, "To go to a bar." That answer wouldn't be funny, and many, in fact, would find it offensive.[8] But wouldn't that open the way for another joke that would begin, "Jesus, Moses, the Buddha, and Mohammed walk into a bar..."

Walking into a bar, of course, is the scene of even more jokes than crossing a road. So we might expect a chuckle as Mohammed orders a Wahabi cocktail—a mixed drink of warm milk, sugar, and hot tea (since alcohol is officially forbidden to Muslims, and the Wahabis are known for their strictness on such matters). We might expect a smile as the Buddha makes a sage comment about the mindful breaking of the Fifth Precept, after which he orders a mojito, then makes a toast "to moderation in all things, including following the Fifth Precept."[9]

---

7. One answer might be to escape from a mob of their angry, hypercritical, and hypo-critical followers.

8. It is indeed ironic that some would be furious about their religious leaders being seen walking into a bar together, but are not so scandalized by the fear, prejudice, hatred, and violence promoted and defended in the name of their religions.

9. Buddhists are required to follow ten precepts that are sometimes compared to the ten commandments of Judaism. (Monks of the Theravada tradition agree to follow over two hundred precepts.) In addition to abstaining from "intoxicating drinks and

And perhaps there would be outright laughter if Moses were to part his margarita and Jesus were to order water and then, with a wink, turn it into a fine Stellenbosch pinotage.

Like the road waiting to be crossed, the bar is quintessential comedic space, indeed. It is also prime secular space, a place for the imbibing of spirits rather than Spirit. It's the place of profanity, not sacredness; levity, not liturgy; and relaxation, not reverence, right? What could the pub possibly have in common with the narthex?[10]

The scarily brilliant Romantic poet and visionary William Blake dared to say what many of us have perhaps thought but kept to ourselves: "A good local pub has much in common with a church, except that a pub is warmer, and there's more conversation."[11] Blake had a keen eye for irony. He knew how easily congregations can become cold, hostile places where we Christians intoxicate ourselves on unholy spirits. He knew how, drunk on dogmatism, we can say and do shockingly profane and unholy things. So for Blake the church can become profane and the bar can become sacred, as he portrayed in his poem "The Little Vagabond." A precocious and innocent child speaks to his mother:

> *Dear mother, dear mother, the Church is cold,*
> *But the Ale-house is healthy and pleasant and warm;*

---

drugs causing heedlessness" (the Fifth Precept), Buddhists are to abstain from "harming living beings (1); taking things not freely given (2); sexual misconduct (3); false speech (4); taking untimely meals (6); dancing, singing, music and watching grotesque mime (7); use of garlands, perfumes, and personal adornment (8); use of high seats (9); and accepting gold or silver (10)." (See http://www.thebigview.com/buddhism/precepts.html.)

10. The narthex, the lobby or porch area of a church, is itself a fascinating theo-architectural concept. Historically, it was built so outsiders—the unbaptized or excluded—could "eavesdrop" on the service, thus serving as a liminal space between exclusion and inclusion.

11. This quote is widely attributed to Blake, but the precise source is unknown. It may be a conclusion drawn from the poem that follows in the text, "The Little Vagabond."

Besides I can tell where I am used well,
Such usage in Heaven will never do well.

But if at the Church they would give us some ale,
And a pleasant fire our souls to regale,
We'd sing and we'd pray all the livelong day,
Nor ever once wish from the Church to stray.

Then the Parson might preach, and drink, and sing,
And we'd be as happy as birds in the spring;
And modest Dame Lurch, who is always at church,
Would not have bandy children, nor fasting, nor birch.

And God, like a father, rejoicing to see
His children as pleasant and happy as He,
Would have no more quarrel with the Devil or the barrel,
But kiss him, and give him both drink and apparel.

Blake, of course, was neither the only nor the first visionary with an eye for irony. Jesus himself spoke pithily and often about religious absurdity. He surely elicited some laughs when he portrayed religious leaders as straining at gnats and swallowing camels, whitewashing tombs, scrubbing only the outside of a filthy bowl, and so on. His whole ministry was a kind of guerrilla theatre, playing—can we say devilishly?—on irony, overturning figuratively as well as literally the money-laden tables of the religious elite.

If the Temple has been turned into a den of robbers—a joke, in other words—where then can the Spirit be found? Jesus dramatizes the answer. The Spirit, driven from the Temple, shows up in one surprising place after another...in the treetops like the wind, on the sandy banks of the muddy Jordan River, on a hillside in the presence of the birds of the air and the flowers of the field, among wine bibbers and sinners, by a crime scene on the Jericho road, among rowdy children and a boisterous crowd, in a stranger on the road to Emmaus, in the last, the least, and the lost.[12]

Given the bizarre and hostile state of our religious communities too often these days, isn't a roadside or a bar the perfect place for the Spirit to convene a scandalous parliament of the world's religious leaders? Don't we need some "secular" social space where diverse people of faith can encounter one another with some level of privacy and anonymity? Isn't the real scandal not that our religious leaders might be imagined walking across a road or talking as friends together in a bar, but rather that their followers are found speaking against one another as enemies, day after day in situation after situation?

Questions like these have always mattered. But in the years since 9/11/01, more and more of us are realizing just how much they matter. So to imagine Jesus, Moses, the Buddha, and Mohammed taking a walk across a road or even getting together as friends for a meal and conversation doesn't have to introduce a joke: it could introduce one of the most important conversations possible in today's world.

And all over the world, this is the conversation Christians want and need to have. In Capetown and Bujumbura, in Bethlehem and Amsterdam, in Mombassa and Santo Domingo, in Santiago and Kuala Lumpur, in San Francisco and Phnom Penh, I've heard deeply earnest and highly committed Christians raise questions about what it means to be Christian in a multi-faith world. They convinced me that I should write on the subject, but what approach should I take? I could take an educational approach—informing Christians about other religions, overturning misconceptions, and showing what Christians do and don't have in common with people of other faiths. I could take an apologetic or evangelistic approach—showing what is special and

---

12. And, we might add, in a crucified man and among a ragtag band of his followers.

Theme #4

unique about Christianity, encouraging people to become or remain Christians—without insulting or misrepresenting other religions. I could take an approach of moral outrage, venting righteous fury about religious violence and bigotry. I could follow a deconstructive approach, grappling with the problematic philosophical assumptions that commonly lead to violence and bigotry. But in the end I felt I should take a different tack—a practical, pastoral, and constructive one, focusing on how to develop a healthy, sane, and faithful Christian identity in a multi-faith world like ours.[13]

Simply put, we Christians already know how to do two things very well. First, some of us know how to have a strong Christian identity that responds negatively toward other religions. The stronger our Christian commitment, the stronger our aversion or opposition to other religions. The stronger our Christian commitment, the more we emphasize our differences with other faiths and the more we frame those differences in terms of good/evil, right/wrong, and better/worse. We may be friendly to individuals of other religions, but our friendship always has a pretext: we want them to switch sides and be won over to our better way. We love them (or say that we do) *in spite of* their religious identity, hoping that they

---

13. The best single book I'm aware of on the subject of Christian identity is Kwame Bediako's masterpiece, *Theology and Identity* (Oxford: Regnum, 1992). In addition, Diana Butler Bass helpfully summarizes and applies the work of Anthony Wallace and William McLoughlan in the first chapter of *Christianity After Religion* (New York: HarperOne, 2012). But much more scholarly work is needed on the subject of Christian identity—its desired characteristics, its formation, its decline, its health, its dysfunctions, its relation to solidarity, and so on. On the subject of religious pluralism from a Christian perspective, Catholic (and formerly Catholic) writers have been most helpful to me—among them Peter Phan, Paul Knitter, Raimon Pannikkar, Anthony de Mello, Leonardo Boff, and Jacques Dupuis. Samir Selmanovic, quoted in this chapter's epigram, has been a leader and example for many of us in the emergent conversation, as have Native American Christians like Richard Twiss, Randy Woodley, Ray Aldred, and Terry LeBlanc.

will see the light and abandon who they have been to find shelter under the tent of who we are.[14]

Alternatively, others of us know how to have a more positive, accepting response to other religions. We never proselytize. We always show respect for other religions and their adherents. We always minimize differences and maximize commonalities. But we typically achieve coexistence by weakening our Christian identity. We make it matter less that *they* are Muslim or Hindu by making it matter less that *we* are Christian. We might even say that we love them in spite of *our own* religious identity.

For reasons that will become clear in the pages ahead, I'm convinced that neither of these responses is good enough for today's world. So I will explore the possibility of a third option, a Christian identity that is both strong and kind. By *strong* I mean vigorous, vital, durable, motivating, faithful, attractive, and defining—an authentic Christian identity that matters.[15] By *kind* I mean something far more robust than mere tolerance, political correctness, or coexis-

---

14. This kind of pseudofriendship expresses the "love the sinner, hate the sin" mind-set: love the Hindu but hate his Hinduism. We Christians can understand how this would make a Hindu feel if we imagine him saying, "I love you as a person, I really do, but I hate Christianity." To accept friendship of this sort would feel like a betrayal of our faith, as if to say, "That's okay. My religion isn't that important to my identity anyway. No big deal if you hate it, as long as you like me." My friend and mentor Tony Campolo frequently points out that "Love the sinner, hate the sin" is not what Jesus taught in Matthew 7:1–5. Instead, Jesus taught, "Love the sinner, and hate your own sin." In *New Seeds of Contemplation* (New York: New Directions, 2007), Thomas Merton made the same point: "So instead of loving what you think is peace, love other [people] and love God above all. And instead of hating the people you think are warmakers, hate the appetites and the disorder in your own soul, which are the causes of war. If you love peace, then hate injustice, hate tyranny, hate greed—but hate these things in yourself, not in another."

15. In contrast, by *weak* I mean a faith that is nominal and of little practical significance to one's way of life. Weak or nominal faith tends to grow weaker, less fertile, more brittle, and more disposable from one generation to the next, while robust faith inspires future generations to keep it alive so that it can continue to grow, adapt, and produce more and better fruit in the future.

tence. I mean benevolent, hospitable, accepting, interested, and loving, so that the stronger our Christian faith, the more goodwill we will feel and show toward those of other faiths, seeking to understand and appreciate their religion from their point of view.[16] My pursuit, not just in this book but in my life, is a Christian identity that moves me toward people of other faiths in wholehearted love, not in spite of their non-Christian identity and not in spite of my own Christian identity, but *because of* my identity as a follower of God in the way of Jesus.

As in all of my books, I'm writing for a general audience of thoughtful Christians, especially Christian leaders, rather than a specialized audience of scholars.[17] Even though I've been somewhat restrained in quoting and footnoting scholarship in these pages, I hope it will be clear that I myself am an avid reader of relevant scholarship.[18] With over two decades of my life invested as a pastor in a local congregation, and another decade invested in writing for and speaking with Christian leaders, I love to bring good scholarship to bear on the grassroots struggles faced by pastors and laypeople day to day in our multi-faith world.

I'm especially mindful of two other audiences as I write. First, I'm conscious of a new generation of young Christians—high school and college students, young adults coming of age, and emerging leaders grappling with the formation of their identities. I hope they will find in these pages a way of being and staying wholeheartedly Christian

---

16. In contrast, by *hostile* I mean a faith identity that does not bear goodwill toward other religions, ultimately wishing that other religions would decline and disappear, or at least be marginalized and minimized.

17. Also, as in all my books, I've changed names and details in many of the stories to protect personal and organizational anonymity.

18. It will also be clear that there are important scholars I haven't yet discovered, an inevitability in a field this important, wide-ranging, and fast-growing.

without hostility, and I hope they will pioneer ways of raising future generations of children and youth in that path as well. And I also think of the young nonreligious or postreligious adults I meet almost every week—not practicing any religion, but deeply interested in finding a way to be human that is informed by the best of our religious traditions—including the hard lessons to be learned from the failures of those religious traditions.

Although I find the integrated vision presented in these pages to be persuasive, coherent, and beautiful, I expect some readers to find the book baffling because it proposes not minor changes within the existing paradigm of Christian identity, and not even major changes, but rather a different paradigm altogether. (It is terribly difficult to understand a different paradigm from the outside.) I expect some readers to say, "I'm with you in certain chapters, not so much in others." Rather than being disappointed in less than complete agreement or understanding, I'll be grateful for even small steps we can take together in challenging dangerous features of the status quo and opening up better possibilities for the future. Where you can't follow some of my proposals, I plead only that you pursue—in your own way, according to the lines of reasoning and imagination that seem best to you—the benevolence, the kindness, and the love without which all our words are noise and we ourselves are nothing. We are increasingly faced with a choice, I believe, not between kindness and hostility, but between kindness and nonexistence.[19]

That is the choice we must make, the road we must cross.

---

19. This urgent choice suggests another possible answer to the title's question: *Why did Jesus, Moses, the Buddha, and Mohammed cross the road? Because they hoped we would follow them.*

Chapter 2

Conflicted Religious Identity Syndrome

Give people a common enemy, and you will give them a common identity. Deprive them of an enemy and you will deprive them of the crutch by which they know who they are.

—*James Alison*[1]

What does it mean to be a Christian in a multi-faith world?[2] Does Christian fidelity require us to stand against Islam, Hinduism, Buddhism, Sikhism, Judaism, and other religions as rivals,

---

1. From James Alison, *Broken Hearts and New Creations* (London: Continuum, 2010), p. 165, quoted online in Suzanne Ross, "Left Behind: Now What?" *Copy That!* (blog), http://www .ravenfoundation.org/blogs/copy-that/left-behind-now-what/. HarperOne Executive Editor Mickey Maudlin made a similar point in an article about Rob Bell's book, *Love Wins*: "As a young evangelical, I was socialized to see the biggest threat to the church as theological liberalism. But now I think the biggest threat is Christian tribalism, where God's interests are reduced to and measured by those sharing your history, tradition, and beliefs, and where one needs an 'enemy' in order for you to feel 'right with God'" (http://www.newsandpews .com/2011/07/rob-bells-hell-by-mickey-maudlin-harperone-senior-v-p-executive-editor/).

2. Christians, it should be noted, have always lived in a multifaith world. But for many, living in a mono-religious neighborhood or nation (whether in Europe, the US, or else-where) became so familiar that having Hindu or Muslim neighbors move in next door now comes as a shock, even more so when they challenge the notions of Christian privilege to which many Christians have become accustomed.

imposters, or enemies? Does Christian charity require us to believe that all religions are the same, that religious affiliation is an accident of birth or matter of taste, or that it doesn't really matter what you believe, as long as you're sincere? Is it okay to create a kind of religious salad, tossing together elements from many different faiths and adding some ideological dressing for flavor? Is it possible to be both faithful to Christian faith and charitable to other faiths?

I've struggled with these questions since I was a teenager.[3] Even at this moment, I feel two opposing realities churning within me. On the one hand, I feel the pull of Jesus' words "Blessed are the peacemakers," or Paul's words about the gospel being a message of reconciliation, or James's assertion that God's wisdom is first pure and then peaceable.[4] But on the other hand, I keep noticing how my religion has, over its first two thousand years of existence, spent too little energy making peace and too much erecting and perfecting walls of separation, suspicion, and hostility. In the Bible I read about love, love, love, but in various Christian subcultures in which I've participated, I keep encountering fear, superiority, and hostility. In a wild array of forms, the message comes to me from the centers of religious power: I can't belong to our *us* unless I am against our *them.*

I've found that a lot of old-fashioned nastiness can lurk within that old-time religion. And new-fangled religion is sometimes worse.

Over the decades, I suppose I have in some ways grown more realistic and perhaps resigned, more willing to accept the Christian tradition for what it is, hostilities, hypocrisies, and all. I've tempered my youthful idealism, you might say. At the same time, I've tried to avoid the bitter, cynical, sullen, or whiny reactivity that one often encoun-

---

3. Graduate students have a saying that explains how dissertation topics are chosen: *All research is me-search.* "All" may be an overstatement. But the saying reminds us that beneath the shades-of-gray paint of scholarly objectivity, intensely colorful, personal motivations inspire most if not all our important work.

4. Matt. 5:9, 2 Cor. 5:16–21, James 3:13–18.

ters in the religiously disillusioned. I've resisted, sometimes not very successfully, the urge to accuse or vilify the easy target of a corrupt majority and I've fought the related urge to idealize a superior, elite minority. But even so, I haven't been able to reconcile myself to the status quo in the Christian community to which I belong—a status quo that too often pits Christian faith against every other faith in a cosmic death-match.

There is something real and good in my faith—a call to love God and neighbors—that I can't abandon without feeling a pang of betrayal. There is also something wrong in my faith—a vague hostility toward the cherished religions of my non-Christian neighbors—that I can't tacitly support without feeling an equal and opposite pang of betrayal.[5] To accept and love God, must I betray my neighbor of another religion? To accept and love my neighbor, must I betray the God of my religion? The stronger this internal conflict grows, the more certain is my sense of calling to imagine and strive for something better. Hence this book.

You may share this conflicted identity to some degree. An internal unrest about your Christian identity may have factored in your decision to open this book. You are seeking a way of being Christian that makes you more hospitable, not more hostile...more loving, not more judgmental...more like Christ and less (I'm sad to have to say this) like many churchgoers you have met. More and more of us are seeking treatment for what we might call Conflicted Religious Identity Syndrome (CRIS).

Novelist Anne Rice went public about her case of CRIS a few years ago when she officially "quit Christianity." I blogged about Anne's struggle a few days after her announcement:

---

5. I've explored this tension between something real and something wrong in several of my books, most notably *A New Kind of Christian* (San Francisco: Jossey-Bass, 2001) and *A New Kind of Christianity* (New York: HarperOne, 2010).

Anne was raised Catholic, left the faith at 18, described herself as an atheist for most of her adult life, returned to Catholicism in her fifties, and then last week announced—via Facebook—that she is no longer a Christian.

She has concluded that she will never truly belong to the "quarrelsome, hostile, disputatious, and deservedly infamous group" known as Christians unless she becomes "anti-gay...anti-feminist... anti–artificial birth control...anti-Democrat...anti–secular humanism...anti-science...anti-life."

That cost of membership simply isn't worth it. So she's opting out.

Tell that much of the story, and you have the sort of thing the news media love to report—another celebrity break-up, if you will. But this time, the celebrity is divorcing God.

But that's not the whole story. Really, it's not the story at all. Anne explains that, "My faith in Christ is central to my life." She is still "an optimistic believer in a universe created and sustained by a loving God." "But," she says, "following Christ does not mean following His followers. Christ is infinitely more important than Christianity and always will be, no matter what Christianity is, has been or might become."

And so, she concludes, "In the name of Christ...I quit Christianity and being Christian."

Her brief announcement raises lots of fascinating questions. For example, when a person quits Christianity in the name of Christ, what do you call that person? If Christianity means "following Christ's followers," what do you call someone who wants to skip the middlemen?[6]

You can sense some of my own identity struggle in my reflections on Anne's.

---

6. You can read "My Take: Why I Support Anne Rice But Am Still a Christian" on my blog at http://www.brianmclaren.net/archives/blog/my-take-why-i-support-anne-rice.html.

Many of us haven't gone as far as quitting Christianity, but we too show signs of CRIS when we compulsively add adjectives in front of the noun *Christian*, as in, "I'm a/an _____ Christian." We might fill the blank with a single, simple adjective like "progressive" or "emergent" or (I like this one for its ironic boldness) "bad."[7] Or we might fill it with a string of highly nuanced adjectives: "non-religious-right-mainstream Evangelical" or "missional post-institutional post-colonial mainline Protestant" or "Red-letter Social-Justice" or "Big-Tent Barthian-Reformed" or "Vatican II Progressive Catholic" or "generously orthodox Quaker-Anabaptist Contemplative-Activist" or whatever. Proof positive of my CRIS diagnosis came when I subtitled my book *Generous Orthodoxy* (Zondervan, 2004) in this memory-defying way:

> Why I am a missional, evangelical, post/protestant, liberal/conservative, mystical/poetic, biblical, charismatic/contemplative, fundamentalist/calvinist, anabaptist/anglican, methodist, catholic, green, incarnational, depressed-yet-hopeful, emergent, unfinished Christian.

The noun *Christian* alone either says too much for us or not enough, so it must be either dropped (as Anne Rice did) or modified (as many of us do). Bring in the adjectives.[8]

So what happens when an Evangelical/Pentecostal pastor in Florida burns a Quran? Or when a famous Christian televangelist

---

7. Simon Barnes uses *bad* in just this sense in *How to Be a (Bad) Birdwatcher* (New York: Pantheon, 2005), and Dave Tomlinson similarly employs *bad* in *How to be a Bad Christian* (London: Hodder & Stoughton, 2012).

8. "I'm a Christian, but…" is another symptom of CRIS, as explained by Bill Dahl: "I became tired of answering their questions with, 'I'm a Christian, but…'…They had crammed me in a readily available mental box right along with *everybody else*. I instantaneously become 'one of those.' I placed myself at an immediate and distinct disadvantage by using the *Christian* label." (From *The Questians*, an e-book available here: http://www.theporpoisedivinglife.com/porpoise-diving-life.asp?pageID=622.)

describes the tragic Haitian earthquake as God's punishment for Haitian sins? Or when a bizarre Baptist sect sends still more protesters to yet another military funeral holding up the same old "God hates fags" signs? Or when a hyper-Calvinist radio preacher predicts the world will end on May 21, 2011, and then on May 22 offers a fallback date in October, which passes uneventfully as well? Or when some officials in the Catholic church secretly protect pedophile priests while refusing to consider ordaining married men or even celibate women?[9]

You feel symptoms of CRIS twitching on your face, rumbling in your gut, and aching in your lower back. You think, *Give me some adjectives, quick, so I won't be identified with "that kind" of Christian.* Or maybe you think, like Anne Rice, *I'll keep loving and following Christ, but if being identified as a Christian requires me to be hostile toward others, it's about time for me to turn in my ID card as a member of the Christian religion.*

Of course, CRIS isn't just a Christian problem. Islamic terrorists shout "God is great!" as they blow up soldiers and civilians without distinction. As they maim, torture, and murder their fellow human beings, their shouts reveal an absolute certainty, without a shred of Dylan-esque irony, that God is on their side. Their confident violence sends the majority of Muslims to their verbal medicine cabinets, seeking their own palliative adjectives to modify their affiliation— *moderate, progressive, peace-loving,* and so on—so they can distinguish themselves from "that kind" of Muslim. And the same could

---

9. Or when the son of a beloved iconic evangelist insults Mohammed and Muslims? Or when self-identifying Evangelical Christians in the USA rank statistically highest in support of the use of torture, and lowest in support for foreign aid? Or when Bible-quoting Christian Zionists defend Israeli colonists in their expanding violations of Palestinian human rights? Or when their equal-and-opposite counterparts defend Palestinians without speaking against violence used against innocent Israeli citizens? Or when American Christian radio personalities accuse the environmental movement of being a Satanic conspiracy they call "the Green Dragon"? Or when prosperity-gospel preachers create a kind of religious mafia through which they ensnare and exploit sincere and gullible member/donors? And so on.

be said for Jews, Hindus, Buddhists, and atheists, too. For example, if you're simultaneously Jewish and deeply committed to human rights for Palestinians, how do you deal with CRIS?[10] If you're an atheist, yet you respect the valid role of religion in society, how do you self-differentiate from more militant atheists? What is it about our faith (and even nonfaith) traditions that we are so uneasy about?

Whether we realize it or not, most of us who suffer from CRIS are trying to distance ourselves from religious hostility. By *hostility* I mean opposition, the sense that the other is the enemy.[11] Hostility makes one unwilling to be a host (the two words are historically related). The other must be turned away, kept at a distance as an unwanted outsider, not welcomed in hospitality as a guest or friend.[12] Hostility is an attitude of exclusion, not embrace; of repugnance, not respect; of suspicion, not extending the benefit of the doubt; of conflict, not conviviality.[13]

---

10. If you're Mark Braverman or Marc Ellis or Michael Lerner, you write courageous books like *Fatal Embrace* (New York: Beaufort, 2012) or *Judaism Does Not Equal Israel* (New York: New Press, 2009), or *Embracing Israel/Palestine* (Berkeley: Tikkun Books and North Atlantic Books, 2012).

11. By "the other," I mean anyone who is considered to be an outsider, not "one of us," belonging to a differing group, gender, orientation, party, community, religion, race, culture, or creed. This definition suggests one of the best punch lines for the title's question: *Why did Jesus, Moses, the Buddha, and Mohammed cross the road? To get to the other.*

12. For more on "the other," see Kester Brewin, *Other* (London: Hodder and Stoughton, 2010). John Franke, in his important book *Manifold Witness: The Plurality of Truth* (Nashville: Abingdon, 2009), writes of "the Other in its eschatological sense": "It is the Other that bursts through and shatters all the pretensions of our God talk and leaves our words and ourselves undone. As theologian William Stacy Johnson maintains, the Other...enters into our lives and shatters the protective totalities that we construct around ourselves for our security and protection. It is an infinity that claims us and will not let go in its call to move us beyond the constraints of our selfhood, beyond the limitations of our versions of reality and truth and toward the Other, the God in whom we live and move and have our being" (112).

13. The word *host* comes from the Middle English of the thirteenth century. The *host* welcomed the *hostis*—which meant "stranger." One can see how the stranger, if trusted, would become the welcome guest, but if feared, would become the enemy—

host = stranger welcomed

Those of us with CRIS don't want to be held hostage (another related word) to a religion that is hostile toward science and learning, hostile toward honest questions and new ways of thinking, and above all, hostile toward other human beings—especially those of other religions (or other versions of our own religion). Something deep in our conscience tells us that hostility is part of the problem to be overcome in the world, not the means by which problems will be overcome. Hostility is a symptom of the disease, not part of the cure.

Consider the wise words of Catholic theologian James Alison with which this chapter began. When religions develop an oppositional identity—*we oppose, therefore we are*, or *we know who we are because we know whom we oppose*—their strong identity comes at a high cost, first to others and eventually to themselves. No wonder so many of us are running to the adjective cabinet seeking relief, while others of us are taking out a pair of scissors to cut up our religious ID cards.

Yes, something good still shines from the heart of our religions—a saving drive toward peace, goodness, self-control, integrity, charity, beauty, duty. And something shadowy struggles to overcome that luminosity—a hostile drive, dangerous, resilient, and deeply ingrained, a black hole in our identity that needs an enemy to help us know who we are and how good we are.[14] How do we disassociate from the hostility without abandoning the identity? How do we remain loyal to what is good and real in our faith without giving tacit support to what is wrong and dangerous? How do we, as Christians, faithfully affirm the uniqueness and universality of Christ without turning that belief into an insult or a weapon?

---

engendering hostility. For more on the relationship between stranger and guest, see Miroslav Volf's *Exclusion and Embrace: A Theological Exploration of Identity, Otherness, and Reconciliation* (Nashville: Abingdon, 1996). See also Volf's *Allah: A Christian Response* (New York: HarperOne, 2011). Both are extremely important contributions to the subject of Christian identity in a multi-faith world.

14. The allusion to John 1:5 is intentional.

There lies our—my—conflicted identity in a nutshell.

As soon as you crack open this nut, additional questions begin spilling out: How do you oppose hostility without becoming hostile against its promoters? How do you oppose division without dividing from dividers? How do you oppose exclusion without excluding excluders? How do you oppose rage without raging against the ragers? How do you distinguish yourself from those who need enemies to know who they are—without rendering them the enemy by whom you know who you are?

Looking back, much of my writing has been literary self-therapy for my own chronic case of CRIS. Even in my blog post about Anne Rice's decision to disaffiliate from Christian identity once and for all, I made my own confession:

> I reached a conclusion very close to Anne's in my book *A New Kind of Christianity*: "I do not believe in Christianity the way I believe in Jesus. I am a Christian who does not believe in Christianity as I used to, but who believes in Christ with all my heart, more than ever."[15]
>
> So I do not condemn or criticize Anne in any way. I'm glad she has followed her conscience and articulated the reasons for doing so. That's good for her, and it may be good for the church, too. Sometimes, powerful people only listen when they see enough people voting with their feet.
>
> I haven't taken that step myself, though I think about it quite often. (As recently as last week when I heard about the pastor planning to burn Qurans on September 11. Sheesh.)
>
> I hang in there for several reasons. First, if I want to be affiliated with any group of human beings, sooner or later I will be associated with bigotry, intolerance, violence, stupidity, and pride. In fact, even if I stand alone, distancing myself from every other group, I know that within me there are the seeds of all these things. So there's no escaping the human condition.

---

15. *A New Kind of Christianity* (New York: HarperCollins, 2010), pages 293-294 (note 10).

Second, if I were to leave to join some new religion that claims to have—at last!—perfected the way of being pristine and genuine through and through, we all know where that's going to lead. There's one thing worse than a failed old religion: a naïve and arrogant new one. In that light, maybe only religions that have acknowledged and learned from their failures have much to offer.

Third, I've decided that if I'm going to have solidarity with one failed religion, I might as well have solidarity with them all. So rather than surrendering my identity as a Christian, I've redefined it so it doesn't mean that I feel superior to anybody. Instead, it means that as a failed member of a failed religion, I'm in solidarity with all other failed members of failed religions... and with people who have dropped out of failed religions as well.

Perhaps it's this truly catholic (small-c) solidarity in failure that really counts most, for Catholics, Protestants, and everybody else. Those who leave religion and those who stay can work to expand that gracious space of solidarity, which, I think, is what Jesus called "the kingdom of God."

This is a book about finding and inhabiting that gracious space and welcoming others into it. Writing it has been part of my ongoing therapy for CRIS, and reading it will, I hope, be part of yours. I have real hope that a great turning is underway, a profound emergence and reformulation, a worldwide spiritual awakening, a healing of our conflicted identities.[16] This healing won't come easy. It will require some profound rethinking—repentance, in the sturdiest and best sense of the word. It will, as every important breakthrough does, engender push-back and critique, which will call for humble, thoughtful, and

16. For perspectives on this shift, see David Korten, *The Great Turning* (Bloomfield, Conn.: Kumarian; San Francisco: Berrett-Koehler, 2006), and Diana Butler Bass, *Christianity after Religion* (New York: HarperOne, 2012), along with the many equally valuable contributions by Phyllis Tickle, Tony Jones, Doug Pagitt, Dominic Crossan, Marcus Borg, Michael Hardin, Ton Bartlett, James Alison, Philip Clayton, John Franke, and others.

patient response. (Ironically, there are few actions better guaranteed to engender conflict than proposing love and understanding for those identified as outsiders and enemies.) And along with repentance and humble, thoughtful patience, it will demand an appropriate urgency.

At a party recently, I was introduced to a fellow who asked what I do for a living. I replied, "Well, I used to be a college English teacher, and then I spent twenty-four years as a pastor. Now I'm an author and speaker, and I guess a sort of activist too."

"What do you write and speak and activate about?" he asked.

"Among other things, these days I try to convince religious people to stop hating and killing each other and to work for the common good instead," I replied.

He nodded, paused for a moment, and replied, "I'm not religious myself. On most days I'm an atheist. But I've always wondered why more religious people don't get off their [hindquarters] and work harder for peace than their counterparts do for violence. So...good luck with your work. It's about time. Even though I'm pretty much agnostic, I just have to say, 'God bless you.'"

"Thanks," I said. "I take that to heart." After we both moved on to other conversations, I kept thinking about his impromptu blessing. Doesn't God seem more plausible, more real, more present, in the presence of peacemakers? And in the presence of hostile religious people, doesn't God seem less and less credible?[17]

---

17. Evangelicals and Pentecostals, specialists in evangelism, face a special challenge and opportunity in this light. Strong-hostile identity is common among them. (Citizen-journalists Rachel Tabachnick and Greg Metzger have undertaken the difficult task of monitoring hostile rhetoric and behavior in these circles. See http://www.talk2action.org/user/Rachel%20Tabachnick and http://debatingobama.blogspot.com/.) Yet anyone involved with evangelism among postmodern people soon realizes that to them, a gospel characterized by hostility toward the other (religiously other, sexually other, etc.) is no gospel at all. It may be, then, that some courageous Evangelicals and Pentecostals will make a break from hostility while retaining their evangelistic passion. If so, they could well be among the pioneers and promoters of the strong-benevolent Christian identity advocated in this book.

I've written this book primarily for my fellow Christians, but I'm sure that peaceable Muslims, Jews, Hindus, Buddhists, and others will find much to stimulate their own creative engagement with their own epidemics of CRIS. If my proposals about Christian identity are in any way legitimate, they will be easy to translate into other contexts.

PART I

THE CRISIS OF CHRISTIAN IDENTITY

I can't know if God exists, but I do know the word *God* is operating in the world, running around doing all kinds of work, good and bad, and I think, as a theologian, I have a responsibility to think critically about the kinds of gods we make and worship and to try to come up with versions of god that might make the world a more just and life-giving place for everyone.

—*Sarah Sentilles*[1]

1. Sarah Sentilles, *"Breaking Up with God*: I Didn't Lose My Faith, I Left It," *Religion Dispatches*, June 2, 2011, http://www.religiondispatches.org/books/rd10q/4650/breaking_up_with_god%3A_i_didn't_lose_my_faith,_i_left_it.

Claim of superiority
Community of communities learning
for each other.

Chapter 3

How a Muslim Boy Converted Me

Given the geo-political state of our world today, given the role that religions are playing in that world and the role that they are called to play, given the looming necessity of turning the impending clash of civilizations into a dialogue of civilizations, the religious communities that populate our planet have reached a point in their history in which they must lay aside or radically reinterpret their traditional and various ways of claiming that "My God is bigger than your God." The religions can no longer continue to make the kinds of claims of superiority that most of them have made in the past.... The religious communities of the world can and must form a "community of communities"—a community in which each tradition will preserve its identity and at the same time deepen and broaden that identity through learning from, appealing to, and working with other communities.

—*Paul Knitter*[1]

J ust before our wedding day, Grace and I signed a rental agreement on an apartment. It was going to be cleaned and painted while we were away on our honeymoon. My brother Peter kindly

---

1. Paul Knitter, "My God Is Bigger Than Your God! Time for Another Axial Shift in the History of Religions," *Studies in Interreligious Dialogue* 17, no. 1 (2007): 100–118.

offered to move in some furniture for us while we were gone so we could go directly from the airport to our new apartment when we returned.

As brothers often do at times like this, Peter decided a practical joke was in order. After hauling in the furniture, he blew up what seemed like a few million balloons and filled the apartment's only bathroom with them. When I say filled, I mean that the room was jammed with balloons floor to almost-ceiling. (It must have been a challenge to squeeze the last few dozen in there.)

Imagine us returning to the airport about midnight, catching a taxi to an apartment we had never been inside before, and finding the key under a welcome mat—right where Peter had left it for us. Bleary-eyed and excited about spending our first night in our own place, we wandered around with a mix of excitement and exhaustion, seeing what our shabby-chic assemblage of hand-me-down furniture looked like in our new residence. But when we tried to open the bathroom door, it...wouldn't...open!

Once we diagnosed the problem, the question became how to treat it. We felt a predictable sense of urgency in doing so, having just completed a long plane ride. Popping several hundred balloons after midnight would surely elicit 911 calls from our new neighbors, and not make the ideal first impression: "They're setting off fireworks down there in Apartment 101!" Or "Wow, that new marriage doesn't seem to be going too well. Gunshots already!"

So we gingerly reached in and began pulling out balloons, one at a time, careful not to pop any but driven by our intensifying biological need to use the toilet. After fifteen or twenty minutes, the bathroom was more or less empty, but an ankle-deep flood of balloons had spread through our apartment, covering the floor of our living room, dining room, and kitchen like a motley tide. "I'll deal with it in the morning," I told Grace, trying to sound like a competent, problem-solving husband.

The next morning, as Grace slept in, I stepped out on our front stoop to survey our new neighborhood. There I bumped into a boy of about eight, rushing into the apartment building like a bat into a cave. He struck me as friendly and energetic, maybe precocious, maybe even brash. "You're the new guy," he said, eyeing me for a moment. "Gotta go!" I heard his sneakers slapping the stairs up to the second floor.

I sat down on the stoop to ponder what I was going to do with a couple million—more or less—balloons. A few minutes later, the boy returned and plopped down on the step next to me, still breathless but talkative. He was Aatif, eight years old, from Iran, living in the apartment directly above ours.

If life were a cartoon, about three minutes into our conversation, one of those little light bulbs would have appeared above my head with a little *ta-ting!* sound. "Hey Aatif, do you like balloons?" "Sure. You got some?" "Come with me," I replied.

We went inside and I opened our door and he peered in. His eyes widened and he flashed me a huge smile. "I can help you, Brian. I can help you with these." But instead of grabbing even one, he raced out the door. As I listened to the sound of his sneakers slapping down the sidewalk outside, I was a little puzzled, but Aatif seemed like a young man who knew what he was doing.

A few minutes later, the door opened—no knock: I learned that Aatif never knocked. In came a stream of kids, seven, eight, nine, ten, eleven. Each of them took as many balloons as he or she could hold, the little ones two, the bigger ones three or four. A few minutes later, they came back for a second load, and after a few loads, all the balloons were gone.

That day earned us a heroic reputation with the neighborhood kids and a slightly less stellar reputation with their parents who had to endure the random bangs of balloons popping for days to come. My friendship with Aatif also began that day. I'd have to say that Aatif was my first Muslim friend.

Soon we got to know his mom, Liza (Anglicized from a Farsi name). We never succeeded in getting Aatif to knock. I think we became his second family, which meant a lot to both him and his mom, for reasons that gradually became clear.

Aatif's dad was a graduate student at the university where I was also studying and teaching. He had come to the United States a year before his family to get things ready for their arrival and to get acclimated to his studies in a foreign language. A few months after their arrival, Liza realized that her husband had grown close—very close—with an American student. Soon he moved in with her, leaving Liza and Aatif stuck in America with no husband, no father, no work, and no English.

We and our balloons moved in about a year after the break-up. In that time, Aatif had gone to school and mastered English as only kids can. Liza got a job at a McDonald's, and her English had improved from nonexistent to broken but functional. Over the next few years, our friendship deepened, and Liza expressed that friendship in a most delicious way: Iranian dishes delivered to our door. We once hosted a party for her Iranian friends. It turned out Americans, back in those days after the Iranian Revolution and the hostage situation, weren't very welcoming to Iranians, so word spread that Liza knew some Americans who liked Iranians.

My brain was filled with the same ignorant stereotypes about Islam and Muslims that many Americans share today. Liza and Aatif reeducated me. They helped me know Muslims as my neighbors, my friends, human beings who struggled with the same mice and cockroaches that Grace and I did in that grimy little apartment building.

———

Since then, I've been blessed with many more Muslim friends in my life. Each has brought a gift to me, but none greater than Aatif. By becoming my first Muslim friend, he forever shattered my preconcep-

LOCKED DOORS

tions and false assumptions. Through him, "the other" became my neighbor.[2]

The standard approach to Muslims from my conservative Evangelical upbringing was clear: be nice to them when necessary in order to convert them to Christianity; otherwise, see them as spiritual competitors and potential enemies. In effect, this approach tended to dehumanize the other, turning others into "evangelistic targets" (an ugly phrase if ever there was one), rivals, and threats. Aatif had no interest in being converted, and as a child he was neither rival nor threat. His jubilant, exuberant, invincible humanity overwhelmed any move to dehumanize him, and so he began converting me—not from my Christianity to his Islam, but from an old kind of Christian identity to a new kind. As a naturally bold and precocious child who never learned to knock before entering, he was determined to be part of my life—in all his charming, irreducible humanity—unless I locked the door.

I'm glad I didn't.

I lost touch with Aatif and Liza. But their friendship left its mark on me. Since they became friends in my neighborhood, guests at my table, and part of my life, *Muslim* could never again be a faceless label for me. And my own Christian identity could no longer be a locked door that kept them at a distance.

As a committed Christian, I have always struggled with locked doors—doors by which we on the inside lock out "the others"—Jews, Muslims, Mormons, liberals, doubters, agnostics, gay folks, whomever. The more we insiders succeed in shutting others out, the more I tend to feel locked in, caged, trapped.

So over the years, like many of my fellow Christians, I have increasingly found myself trapped between a strong Christian identity that is

---

2. A version of this story also appears in *My Neighbor's Faith: Stories of Interreligious Encounter, Growth, and Transformation*, ed. Jennifer Howe Peace, Rabbi Or Rose, and Gregory Mobley (Maryknoll, N.Y.: Orbis, 2012).

hostile toward outsiders and a weak Christian identity that is benign (or harmless) toward outsiders. The stronger my Christian identity grows, the stronger my opposition grows toward non-Christian religions, and the more hostile I appear to their faithful adherents. But if I try to reduce that hostility by weakening my Christian identity, I have less and less reason for staying Christian. Meanwhile, if my friends of other faiths have a strong religious identity, my suppressed Christian identity may pressure them to similarly inhibit their own, leaving both of us feeling less than wholehearted or faithful.

Why can't there be a third option? Couldn't the kind of friendship I enjoyed with Aatif and Liza be—not unusual and exceptional, but normal and normative? Shouldn't it be possible to have a strong Christian identity that is strongly benevolent toward people of other faiths, accepting them not *in spite of* the religion they love, but *with* the religion they love? Could my love and respect for them as human beings lead me to a loving and respectful encounter with their religion as well?

In order to explore that kind of identity, we'll have to deal with a host of questions. Why has the Christian faith been so irreconcilable to other faiths? Why is deep commitment to Christian faith so deeply linked with aversion to all other faiths? When Christians claim that Jesus is the only way, what do they mean, and does that mean that other religions must be opposed as frauds, mistakes, delusions, or distractions? Can one wholeheartedly love and trust Jesus as Lord and Savior without hating—or at least opposing—the Buddha, Mohammed, Lao Tzu, or Confucius? Must sincere commitment to the Bible make Christians antagonistic toward the Quran, the Baghavad Gita, the Analects of Confucius, the coyote myths of the Plains Indians, or the Tao Te Ching? Does sincere faith in the uniqueness and universality of Jesus Christ require one to see other faiths as false, dangerous, or even demonic?

We'll address these questions in due time. But we can't answer them without seeking to understand what lies behind them, what they assume, and why these questions remain so provocative in many circles. I hope you'll find the journey from questions to answers to be as fascinating, rewarding, and enlightening as I have.

Bible: Unless a man is born of the Spirit he cannot enter the Kdg of Heaven.
(not a quote per se)

Chapter 4

How a Book in the 1970s Anticipated the Story Line of the Early 21st Century

Why is it that the choice among churches always seems to be the choice between intelligence on ice and ignorance on fire?
                                                        —*as quoted by Diana Butler Bass*[1]

M any of us have felt unable to accept either of the two typical responses of Christian faith to other faiths. On the one
hand, we can't in good conscience maintain a position of hostility
toward or superiority over the religious commitments of our Jewish,
Muslim, Hindu, Buddhist, and other friends. On the other hand, we
don't feel right or faithful in watering down or suppressing our own
deep commitment to Christ, the Bible, and the rich inheritance we
have received in the Christian community. We hope, we dream, we
pray that another option will come into view—one that doesn't pit
us against others in hostility, and one that allows us to remain true
to our own deepest Christian convictions.

---

1. Diana Butler Bass, *Christianity after Religion* (New York: HarperOne, 2012), p. 121.
Diana is quoting a Facebook correspondent.

We aren't the first people to seek this third option. Back in 1972, Dean Kelley rocked the religious world with *Why Conservative Churches Are Growing*.[2] He spoke the then-shocking truth that "Mainline" Protestantism, which had historically been the main form of Christianity in the United States, was fast becoming "old line" as it declined in numbers.[3] It was losing ground to a "new line" of conservative churches characterized by *seriousness* and *strictness*. These churches were *serious* about the meaning they offered and *strict* in regards to wholehearted conformity to their norms of belief and behavior. This seriousness and strictness, Kelley asserted, made them *socially strong*, and this social strength made them grow—as their adherents enthusiastically recruited others.

In contrast, old-line churches were increasingly ecumenical—respectful of and open to dialogue with other faith communities and the meaning they offered. They were about making friends, not converts. Old-line churches valued individual freedom over group conformity when it came to issues of purpose, belief, and behavior.[4]

To old-liners, ecumenism, respect, dialogue, individualism, nonconformity, and freedom were precious qualities. But in terms of

2. Dean Kelley, *Why Conservative Churches are Growing*, Rose edition (Macon, Ga.: Mercer University Press, 1986), xxiv–xxv. Hereinafter, page references will be given in the text.

3. The term *mainline* derives from a train line in Philadelphia that led to the affluent suburban neighborhoods where upwardly mobile European immigrants and their descendants lived. These established immigrants—many of them Presbyterians, Lutherans, Episcopalians, and Methodists—brought their Protestant affiliations with them from Northern Europe (in contrast to more recent Southern European and Irish immigrants, most of whom were Roman Catholic, and at that time, less affluent).

4. The reasons that old-line and new-line churches developed these differing characteristics are many and complex. Among them—many mainline churches derived their identity from state churches in Europe. State churches had to hold diverse groups together and couldn't so easily divide when differences arose. In contrast, the more "sectarian" churches came into being by dividing from other groups; their minority identity from the start was a choice (*choice*, by the way, is at the root of the word *heresy*) of resistance. The former had to learn the skills of containing, managing, and resolving diversity and conflict, while the latter mastered the skills of fomenting, mobilizing, and maintaining difference and separateness.

creating growth or even sustainability for the future, Kelley claimed they were counterproductive at least, and potentially even suicidal.[5] Because these qualities discouraged energetic proselytizing and might even tempt adherents to stop adhering so strongly, Kelley described old-line churches with unflattering terms like *lukewarmness* and *leniency*. Kelley portrayed the contrast between old-line lukewarmness/leniency and new-line strictness/seriousness as a paradox:

> Though the paradox can be reduced, it cannot be eliminated without being unfair to one pole or the other. There is about any serious meaning venture a certain irreducible fierceness, asperity, insistence, exclusiveness, rigor—a fanaticism that brushes everything else aside. Yet that very single-mindedness renders it objectionable to those who value balance, brotherhood, respect for individual diversity, mutual forbearance and self-restraint, civic peace, pluralism—and dialogue—as much as, or more than, they value any single formulation of meaning or any one meaning-system (including their own). (164)

Those who haven't actually read the book might conclude that Kelley was himself a conservative apologist. But he made it clear that his sympathies lay with the declining "liberal" churches. Kelley saw, as many of us have since, that the same intensity that produced strength and growth in strict and serious churches also produced problems, and those problems were real. Strict, serious, and growing groups are characterized by dogmatism, judgmental moralism,

---

5. In a critical response to Kelley, Laurence Iannacone argued that rational choice theory offers a better explanation for contrasting growth rates in different kinds of churches: it is not strictness per se, but rather the exclusion of undependable, uncommitted fellow members ("free riders") that makes membership in some churches more rewarding than others. High-demand groups produce high-commitment members who provide greater benefits to fellow members. I don't see their explanations as mutually exclusive.

obsession with cultic purity, fanaticism, and unwillingness to listen (except to find weaknesses to exploit in rebuttal). They

> are not "reasonable," they are not "tolerant," they are not ecumenical, they are not "relevant."[6] Quite the contrary! They often refuse to recognize the validity of other churches' teachings, ordinations, sacraments. They observe unusual rituals…they [persist] in irrational behavior…. They try to impose uniformity of belief and practice among members by censorship, heresy trials, and the like. (25–26)

So for Kelley, however attractive the dynamism of growing groups may be, "living in close proximity to such movements, trying to get along with their members, can be strenuous, if not intensely irritating" (78). One can almost guess what his next-door neighbors were like.

In light of this paradox—that irritating and obnoxious faith communities tend to grow, and that compassionate and neighborly faith communities tend to decline—it's no wonder Kelley entitles Chapter 6 of his book, "Why Not a Strong Ecumenical Religion?" Interestingly, no clear answer comes in that chapter. Almost a hundred pages later, he describes the pain of Christian church leaders who are committed "to the ultimate meaning embodied in the Christian faith" on the one hand, and yet are equally committed on the other hand to "freedom, justice, beauty, (empirical) truth, and respect for others—including those who are deeply devoted to non-Christian ultimate meanings, or to none at all." And at this point the question raised back in Chapter 6 resurfaces:

> But why must there be any conflict? Are not freedom, justice, respect for others essential parts of the Christian faith? Ideally they should

---

6. In a follow-up article, Kelley sought for a way to describe the stricter, more demanding churches. He offered this: "Perhaps the least pejorative label would be *non-ecumenical*." What Kelley labels "non-ecumenical" will, in these pages, be described as inhospitable or hostile to the other. See http://www.jstor.org/pss/1386160.

be, if rightly understood. One can conceive of a high-demand religious movement devoted to justice, freedom, beauty, respect for others, and so on, which could effectively explain life to [humankind] without fanaticism, absolutism, intolerance, or judgmental moralism. That is what—ideally—Christianity ought to be. (165)

Sadly, Kelley cannot see that kind of Christianity anywhere on the horizon, as his next sentence indicates: "Yet where is such a phenomenon to be found?" It's not that he says such a strong-and-benevolent faith is inconceivable or impossible; it's just that he has not yet found it actual or visible.

As the twenty-first century unfolds, the need for this ideal-but-as-yet-uncommon Christianity becomes more acute.[7] That's where people like you and me come in. It remains for us to explore and embody the possibility that Kelley opened in his book—the possibility of a Christian faith that combines certain key elements of conservative "new-line" Christianity (strength, commitment, intensity of meaning) with other elements of liberal "old-line" Christianity (ecumenism, reasonableness, a peaceable attitude). Perhaps such a strong-benevolent faith will never be "main line," but it can certainly be a lifeline in these conflicted and challenging times.

From his vantage point in the 1970s, Kelley couldn't have predicted 9/11/01 in the US or 7/7/05 in the UK. He couldn't have

---

7. If the Christian third of the world's population—in its Catholic, Pentecostal, Evangelical, Orthodox, Anglican, Mainline Protestant, and indigenous forms—can't or won't acknowledge and address its own hostility toward people of other faiths, the whole world will suffer. Conversely, if a third of the world's population becomes more robustly benevolent toward the other two-thirds, the whole world will benefit. Together, Christianity and Islam account for about 57 percent of the world's population, and that percentage is expected to climb to two-thirds by the century's end. Christians and Muslims possess the vast majority of the world's financial and energy wealth, and the lion's share of the world's weapons, including nuclear weapons. Clearly, the development of more benevolent faith-identities among Christians and Muslims in particular has become an urgent matter of planetary survival.

anticipated the ways that Christian, Muslim, and Jewish fundamentalism would move from the religion pages to the front pages of our newspapers. He couldn't foresee that a generation later, the new-line groups of his day would have lost their luster so that their statistics would show similar patterns of plateau and decline.[8]

But by naming a trend that was emerging in his day, he sensitized a generation of Christian leaders to an issue they and their children would not be able to avoid: what it means to have a strong Christian identity in a world torn by religious hostility.

---

8. Many new-line Christians in the US still think that they are growing while "the liberals" are declining. But in the new century, new-line trend lines have begun to mirror those of the old-line, just thirty or forty years later. Diana Butler Bass describes this new reality as the "religious bear market" in Chapter 3 of *Christianity after Religion*.

Chapter 5

How a Mentor Shocked Me—and Gently Nudged Me toward Higher Ground

Human beings never do evil so completely and so joyously as when they do it from a religious motivation.

—*Blaise Pascal*[1]

G ood mentors sometimes unsettle you. It's part of their job. One of mine got me squirming one Sunday morning when I was driving him from his hotel to a church service where he was about to speak. It was about four months after September 11, 2001, and I was sharing with him my discomfort with the anti-Muslim sentiment that was rising among our fellow Evangelicals. He commented, "*Remember, Brian: in a pluralistic world, a religion is judged by the benefits it brings to its nonmembers.*"

His words jolted me because I assumed, as most people probably do, that religions survive and thrive by promising benefits to their

---

1. The quote is usually translated from the French as "men" instead of "human beings," and "religious motivation" is sometimes rendered "conscience."

members—and conversely, by either withholding benefits from non-members or threatening them with punishment in this life or the next. The idea of a religion bringing benefits to nonmembers sounded crazy to me. I was too taken aback even to ask him to explain what he meant, much less argue. So after a few seconds of uncomfortable silence, I guess we moved on to another topic. But his seemingly offhand comment stuck with me like the hook of a popular song. I couldn't get it out of my head.

I now suspect he knew how unsettling and curious his statement would appear to me. He knew that I might not be ready for it yet. But rather than spare me the discomfort, he simply let the statement fall like a seed into disturbed soil, waiting to germinate in its own time.

I lived, as many people do, on a line between liberal and conservative forms of Christian faith. On the conservative side (B), there was a strong identity characterized by strong hostility toward non-Christians. On the liberal side (A), there was a benign attitude toward non-Christians—what we might call tolerance, with (to a conservative mind, anyway) a correspondingly weak identity. In between, there was a more moderate zone, (C), characterized by moderated tolerance, moderated hostility, and moderately strong identity:

A: Weak/Benign	C. Moderately Strong/Moderately Benign	B: Strong/Hostile

In my twenties and thirties, I had been moving slowly from the right side of the diagram toward the middle—in my terms at the time, from conservative Fundamentalist to Mainstream Evangelical.

But my mentor was talking about something that I couldn't locate in my frame of reference. He wasn't pointing farther to the left on the line, but rather toward a third alternative (D) I hadn't even imagined, a space above the line entirely, where a strong, generous, benevolent Christian identity was possible.

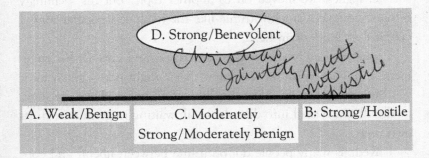

What Dean Kelley pointed toward back in 1974, my mentor was pointing toward over twenty-five years later: a new kind of Christian identity, common ground on higher ground "above the line," characterized by strong benevolence, generosity, and hospitality toward others, not hostility on the one hand and not mere "niceness" or "tolerance" on the other.[2]

This little diagram helps me be more understanding and less judgmental about my fellow Christians. It helps me remember that

---

2. Again, by *hostility* I mean animosity, ill will, antagonism, and opposition that can be removed only when the other stops being one of "them" and becomes one of "us." By *benignity*, I mean tolerance, harmlessness, a willingness to coexist. And by *benevolence*, I mean affection, good will, neighborliness, solidarity, and support...conviviality that doesn't require conversion or assimilation but that appreciates otherness. While those characterized by *hostility* would prefer other religions to remain in error until they are eliminated, and while those characterized by *benignity* would be more or less indifferent to the growth or regression of other religions, those characterized by *benevolence* would hope for other religions to grow into greater wholeness and truth, just as they would hope for their own religion. *Benevolence*, then, is a facet of loving one's neighbor as oneself.

Christians settle on the right side not because they want hostility but because they want a strong faith identity. Christians cluster on the left side not because they want weakness but because they don't want hostility. And Christians in the middle want to manifest not mediocrity, but as much strength and as much tolerance as possible, avoiding the extremes on both sides. That understanding is essential. If we judge, shame, and reject those on the line, whether on the left or right or somewhere in between, if we paint them as the enemy and develop an identity in opposition to or hostile toward them, we lock them in a defensive posture. And we lock ourselves into mirroring the very behavior we condemn.

I'm convinced that the only viable response to religious hostility is love, empathy, compassion, understanding—not more hostility. (What could be more pathetic than a hostile fight against hostility?) And so I must have the empathy to understand that some readers have already been deeply offended by the diagnosis I'm offering. *We are not hostile*, I can imagine them saying. *That term is inherently judgmental. We are faithful, and if you judge our faithfulness as hostility, that's your problem, not ours.*

I am sensitive to this response in large part because I can imagine that I might have made it myself twenty years ago. Few hostile people would ever see hostility lurking in their hearts: they would see love—love for God as they understand God, love for their religion, love for their community, their ancestors, their history, their future. And this is part of the power of religion—not that it inspires hate, but rather that it inspires loves so powerful that they can be expressed without conscious intention through hateful actions. Here's how Georgetown University's Ariel Glucklich has expressed it:

> The biggest myth about religion and violence, I believe, is that reli-
> gion teaches hatred. . . . I think the violence comes from a kind of

love or desire for love for one's own group and a willingness to do whatever it takes to obtain it.[3]

Glucklich's words can help us see why many faithful Christians see our plea for them to become less hostile as a temptation to love God, their religion, their community, their ancestors, their history, and their future less. Before they'll listen to our case for a new kind of strong-benevolent Christian identity, they must be convinced it is the path to more love and fidelity, more strength and meaning, not less. But even then, embracing a new Christian identity will not be easy for them. People from strong-hostile backgrounds like mine know how costly it will be to depart from their home turf on the conventional liberal-moderate-conservative line. They know they will face a sense of betrayal from their closest religious friends, even their own family members, those they most trust and love.

That's why identity formation—and reformation—takes time and can't be forced or pushed. It involves many dangers, toils, and snares—threats and setbacks, wrong turns and recoveries. Even under the best of conditions, there are limits to the speed by which a religious identity can come of age and face the challenges before it. Perhaps that's why a book like this can be important: it can provide privacy, time, and space for people to consider the unsettling

---

3. From David Gibson, "Does Religion Cause Terrorism? It's Complicated," *The Christian Century*, September 1, 2011, http://www.christiancentury.org/article/2011-09/does -religion-cause-terrorism-its-complicated/. The article surveys many of the key researchers studying religious violence today: Charles Kurzman, Mark Juergensmeyer, William Cavanaugh, James Jones, David Schanzer, Jessica Stern, Charles Kimball, and Ariel Glucklich. Gibson concludes, "In general, scholars have concluded that religion—be it Islam or any other faith—is neither the chicken nor the egg when it comes to creating terrorists. Rather, religion is one of many factors in the explosive brew of politics, culture and psychology that leads fanatics to target innocents—and take their own lives in the process." Glucklich is the author of *Dying for Heaven: Holy Pleasure and Suicide Bombers—Why the Best Qualities of Religion Are Also Its Most Dangerous* (New York: HarperOne, 2009). The book points out the powerful roles of joy and love in motivating religious violence.

and dangerous proposal of an identity change. Like my gentle mentor who casually dropped his comment about a religion providing benefits to its nonadherents and then left me to ponder what he had said on my own, a book makes no demands. It remains easy to put down and easy to ignore. That very gentleness can be its greatest power. It is hard to defend against something that is not aggressive.

Chapter 6

How Your Friends Can Be More Dangerous Than Your Enemies (And How You Can Be More Dangerous Than Both)

The causes of religious violence are like bad breath: you need other people to make you aware of it.

—*Paul Knitter*[1]

If you dare depart from traditional identity categories—whether in the strong/hostile zone, in the weak/benign zone, or in the moderate zone in between—you will be seen with suspicion by your former colleagues in that zone. They will see you as abandoning them personally, betraying your heritage and its ideals, violating the "us-ness" by which you once were identified with them. In response, they may threaten you, hoping that fear will make you stay, not realizing that it will more likely drive you farther away.

I recently saw this dynamic playing out in a fascinating online

---

1. From a presentation made at the United Nations' "2007 High-Level Dialogue of the General Assembly on Interreligious and Intercultural Understanding and Cooperation for Peace," Informal Interactive Hearing with Civil Society (October 4–5, 2007), p. 1; http://www.un.org/ga/president/62/issues/interreligiousintercultural/remarks.pdf.

conversation of which I was part—a conversation that included Christians, Muslims, and Jews. The conversation was launched by an Evangelical Christian friend who has devoted his life to building bridges between people of different faiths. He would post an observation or question that would get us talking, first with him, and then with each other. When conversation died down, he would post another prompt. In one of these interchanges, a Christian participant told how he had recently been harshly criticized by a friend for asserting that Christians and Muslims pray to the same God. I posted this in response:

us   *the other*

All of us are poised between two dangers. The obvious one is "The Other." The subtle one is "Us." If we defend ourselves against the Other, if we attack the Other, we gain credibility with "Us." We show that we are loyal, supportive, believers, members of Us, and we are generously rewarded and affirmed. We gain a lot by attacking the Other—in religious circles as well as political ones.

Ironically, Us can be as great a threat to each of us as the other is, probably greater. Us might withdraw its approval of me. It might label me disloyal, unsupportive, unbeliever, unorthodox, liberal, anathema, etc. To be rebuked, marginalized, or excluded by Us is an even greater threat than to be attacked by the Other.

I don't think we Christians often realize the great degree to which we live in fear of Us. This is true whether we're Evangelical, Catholic, Mainline Protestant, Orthodox, Pentecostal, or whatever. (Each religion has its various Us groups, and then there are the Us groups of academia, politics, ethnicity, etc.)

Our fear becomes all the more acute when we venture to do what many of us in this dialogue are doing: we are daring to defend and humanize the Other. We are showing—however feebly and adolescently—a grain of neighborliness and solidarity with the Other. At that moment, we become vulnerable as never before to attacks by Us, i.e. our fellow Christians. In my experience, it takes much more courage to stand up to or apart from Us than it does to stand either against or with the Other. . . .

Sometimes, when I've tried to insert myself between Us and Other, I managed to get shot at by both sides. It's hazardous work. As they say, being a bridge means you'll get walked on from both sides. . . . I offer this simply because I think we in this discussion need to face the great power that Us holds over each of us. In attempting to avoid the punishment or suspicion of Us, even as we try to communicate to our fellow Christians on behalf of our Muslim friends, we can unintentionally play to dangerous, powerful Christian prejudices and unintentionally reinforce them.

This is the perilous situation, I think we would agree, into which Jesus went, as did Paul and Peter and St. Francis and Dr. King and Desmond Tutu and many others in our tradition and outside of it. Crucifixion happens, not at the hands of the Other, but Us. It is not easy risking that, even when we are trying to build solidarity with the Other.

So, even as I seek to build relationships with my Muslim friends (or whomever), I confess that I am held hostage to fear of what Us will say. To give myself to the Other without reserve or concern for what Us will say . . . that is a level of love I do not think I often attain. But it is something to which I aspire because of the example and teaching of Jesus, and because my heart/the Spirit tells me it is right or at least my calling.

By the way, I wouldn't be surprised if this tension with Us helps explain why [famous novelist] Anne Rice famously quit Christianity recently. . . . Perhaps Anne felt that remaining a member in good standing of the Us of Christianity made it impossible for her to show Christ-like solidarity with the Other, whether the other is gay, liberal, Muslim, etc.

One last tangent—I suspect this is what Paul was trying to say in 2 Corinthians (and elsewhere, i.e. 1 Cor 9 or Gal 3). To be "in Christ" is to be in solidarity with all people—and all creation. That solidarity contrasts starkly with the realities of being "in

Christianity" or any other "Us" religion. I think that's what your [critic] was getting at when he said "as if man were outside of God." To be in God or in Christ would mean—or should mean—to be in a one-anotherness that transcends and in some way includes all the smaller "us" and "other" groups. Again, forgive me for all the ways in which I have misspoken, and feel free to disagree.

Several participants—Christians, Muslim, Jewish—contacted me in private, apart from the group, and responded positively, saying that yes, their greatest opposition came not from "Them" but "Us." For example, a Muslim man who lives in the Middle East responded with great passion:

> We don't know each other, yet I want to tell you how courageous and admirable your approach is and I can understand how difficult one's life can become just because of "Us's" intolerance. But believe me, how much intolerant and extremist your "Us" could be, ours are ten times more extremist and more intolerant with the difference that you can survive the intolerance from your "Us" while we cannot survive the ones coming from our "Us-es."

He went on to explain how a famous Saudi anthropologist had recently called for the sword to be removed from the Saudi flag, where it sits below the words *La-Ilah-Illa-Allah* (There is no God but God). The sword, the anthropologist suggested, presents an unflattering view of Islam, seeming to combine the essential creed of Islam with a threat of violence, as if God needs a sword to enforce God's will. In response, the anthropologist was threatened with death. "I am not talking about stuff that happened centuries ago. This was months ago," he said:

> Islam is an Identity Religion and you probably know that there are several Islamic particular identities all in conflict one with each

other. When I speak with a Muslim, telling him that I too am a Muslim means nothing to him. I could have been Atheist or Christian or Jew, it would have made more sense. But if I add that I am a Sunni Muslim then it starts to make sense—a good sense if he too is a Sunni and a bad one if he is a Shiite and of course vice-versa.

Another Muslim participant wrote that he tried to distinguish between hostile religious institutions and the spirit of faith:

I know many people started to consider themselves outsiders to their religious institutions while they stay committed to the spirit and the faith. They see themselves as victims of the very institutions supposedly meant to help them become better followers and ambassadors of their faith. This is true for every religious establishment without any exception. That was the real cause behind the establishment of Sufi orders as rejection to the heavily politicized Islamic establishment at that time. Sufi orders were themselves later rejected by many when they started to see them falling into the same trap of heavy politicization. Hope this will help a little bit in drawing a clear differentiating line between Christ and the Christian institutions in the same way we, Muslims, are trying desperately to differentiate between the spirit of Islam and its establishment.... There is nothing that hurts any religion today more than its own establishment. Established and well funded religious institutions are becoming their own enemies. There is no better way to say it than: "We find the enemy and it is us."[2] Salaam.

A Jewish participant spoke up as well, reflecting on his own experience as an advocate for human rights for Palestinians who suffer under the Israeli occupation:

---

2. The original saying, "We have met the enemy and he is us," came from the comic-strip character Pogo of the Okefenokee Swamp, created by Walt Kelly. It originally appeared in a 1970 poster and a 1971 comic strip.

"Us" is the biggest threat to the Jewish community today as we try to deal with the horror of what our national homeland project has brought us to. There is a civil war going on within the Jewish community—brother/sister against brother/sister. There are very clear rules on what you cannot feel and say about Israel. They are based on a profound denial of the pain of our history (yes—denial, although that may seem strange to say, given the focus, even preoccupation with the Nazi Holocaust, and indeed all of Jewish history for the past 2,000 years.) But here's the evidence for that fundamental denial: the projection of our fear and pain onto the Palestinians. The behavior that says: we are only safe if we take what is yours. The behavior that says: the violence is in you, not us. That says: the danger is out there, not in here. And in order to maintain the denial, avoid the fear, disown the violence, the rules are enforced. The rules are two: (1) Jewish "sensitivities" trump all other values: "don't say that, it makes us feel insecure." "Don't say that, it could be perceived as anti-Semitism." (2) Don't touch the Zionist ideology. Nibble around the edges, talk about Palestinian rights, but don't touch the thing itself: the Land is ours. Those of us who break the rules pay that price.

I was especially fascinated when he added this:

[This] is why the story of the gospels is so critically relevant for us now. The critical conversation happening in the first century when the church was being born was among Jews, not between Jews and Gentiles. Jesus, as a Jew, came as a reformer, as one challenging who "Us" had become. So that's why we need Jesus today. I mean we Jews need Jesus. Not to become Christians, but to become better Jews.[3]

---

3. What my Jewish friend meant by Jews needing Jesus will, I hope, become more clear in Part III, where I will argue that Christians also need Jesus—a fresh vision of him—to become better Christians.

My Muslim and Jewish friends, like many of my Christian friends, are converging on a similar conclusion: all our religious identities need reform. We need to become better Muslims, better Jews, and better Christians. (And we all agree that Jesus has a lot to offer to all of us in this predicament.) But doing so will demand a high cost from us. It will subject us to criticism and maybe even threats and worse—from our religious fellows.

Even so, the single greatest obstacle to rethinking Christian identity won't be imposed from the outside by other people, whether "us" or "them." The single greatest obstacle will arise inside each of us. Your greatest obstacle will be in you and mine will be in me. In the end, it's not the threats of others that cause me to shrink back, but rather my own fear. It's not the difficulty of rethinking long-held beliefs that will discourage me, but my stubborn refusal to accept that difficulty. It's not the danger of being criticized or rejected that will cause me to abandon identity reform, but my self-protective reflex to avoid the danger. If enough of us count these internal costs and accept them—beginning with the fear, refusal, and self-protective reflexes within each of us, a strong-benevolent Christian identity can and will emerge.

But there's always an easy way out, an escape clause—the temptation to stop thinking, to suppress our questions and concerns, to submit to intimidation, to "go along" and "get along," to resign ourselves to hostility—maybe a nice, respectable, moderate hostility. And of course, there's a cost to that escape route, too.

So there are costs either way, costs we all must count, some of them agonizing.

Many parents of gay children feel this agony (these days, anyway—it may be different in the future). I think of a friend of mine who came from the same background of Christian fundamentalism I hail from. When his son came out, he had no support to help him accept the possibility that his son could be both gay and good.

With deep ambivalence, he stood with his tradition and condemned his son. The cost—alienation from his son—was high, but it grew unspeakably higher when his son internalized the rejection and condemnation of his community and took his own life. Or I think of another friend, the mother of a gay son, also from my heritage. She came to me in secret to talk, knowing that one of my sons had come out around the same time as hers. Through tears she said, "I feel like I'm being forced to choose between my father and my son. If I affirm my son, I'm rejecting everything my father stood for. If I stand with my father, I'm rejecting my son."

In religion as in parenthood, uncritical loyalty to our ancestors may implicate us in an injustice against our descendants: imprisoning them in the errors of our ancestors. Yes, there are costs either way.

Chapter 7

How an Atheist Made—and Missed—an Essential Point about Religion

In fact, it may well be that, for all our talk of a postenlightenment new world order, most wars in our time are still, at root, fueled by (pathological religious passions) however vehemently denied at the official levels.... Despotic theology ... leads directly to despotic theocracy. Tyrannical Gods breed tyrannical humans. And vice versa.

—*Richard Kearney*[1]

D o you hear statements like these as often as I do?

"Religions, especially monotheistic ones, are inherently violent."

"Most wars are caused by religion."

"Imagine a world with no religions. Wouldn't it be a more peaceable place?"

Whether you consider them to be clichés, truisms, exaggerations, myths, or blasphemies depends on your assumptions and experience. Many people agree with outspoken atheist Sam Harris who, before

---

1. Richard Kearney, *Anatheism: Returning to God after God* (New York: Columbia University Press, 2011), pp. 138, 147.

specifying about a dozen centers of conflict in today's world, makes this generalization:

> Incompatible religious doctrines have balkanized our world into separate moral communities, and these divisions have become a continuous source of bloodshed. Indeed, religion is as much a living spring of violence today as it has been at any time in the past.... Religion has been the explicit cause of literally millions of deaths in recent decades.[2]

Then he asks why religion has been so fruitful in terms of violence rather than peace, and answers his question simply and confidently:

> There is no other sphere of discourse in which human beings so fully articulate their differences from one another, or cast these differences in terms of everlasting rewards and punishments. Religion is the one endeavor in which us–them thinking achieves a transcendent significance. If you really believe that calling God by the right name can spell the difference between eternal happiness and eternal suffering, then it becomes quite reasonable to treat heretics and unbelievers rather badly. The stakes of our religious differences are immeasurably higher than those born of mere tribalism, racism, or politics.

Obviously, I agree with Sam Harris that religion plays a big and ugly role in creating and sustaining hostility in our world.[3] But I think

---

2. Sam Harris, "Killing the Buddha," http://www.samharris.org/site/full_text/killing-the-buddha/.

3. According to R. Scott Appleby in *Ambivalence of the Sacred* (New York: Rowman and Littlefield, 2000, p. 17), "about two thirds of contemporary wars turn on issues of religious, ethnic, or national identity. Less than 10 percent begin as interstate conflicts." Appleby acknowledges that religion is simultaneously a source of "intolerance, human rights violations, and extremist violence" and a resource for "non-violent conflict transformation, the defense of human rights, integrity in government, and

he's only partially right when he locates the tensions between religions only in their differences.[4] Yes, religious differences can indeed lead to division, and division to hostility, and hostility to violence, and so there is indeed a danger to religious differences.[5] But achieving and sustaining sameness can lead us into other cycles of violence no less vicious. Secular totalitarian regimes, for example, typically attempt to produce their version of peace through the suppression of difference and the promotion of sameness. The results have been horrifying.[6]

---

reconciliation and stability in divided societies." Quoted in Saira Yamin, "Understanding Religious Identity and the Causes of Religious Violence," *Peace Prints: South Asian Journal of Peacebuilding* 1, no. 1 (Spring 2008): pp. 1, 5; available at http://www.wis comp.org/pp-v1/Saira_Yamin.pdf.

4. Jack Nelson-Pallmeyer (*Is Religion Killing Us? Violence in the Bible and the Quran* [Harrisburg, Pa.: Trinity Press International, 2003], p. xi) qualifies Sam Harris's blame of religion as the "explicit cause of literally millions of deaths" when he says, "People rarely kill each other for reasons of religious difference alone. They do frequently use God and religion, however, to justify killing when conflicts escalate between individuals, groups, or nations. In the midst of problems rooted in land, oppression, discrimination, or any number of other historical grievances, religion is often called on to justify human violence with subtle or not so subtle references to 'sacred' texts, divine mission, or moral purpose."

5. Miroslav Volf explained the danger in these terms: "If you are someone who has determined to resort to animosity and violence, then I think it's very hard not to exaggerate differences in our fundamental values. In a sense, hatred needs to emphasize difference so it can appropriately latch itself onto the object of our hatred. Violence needs difference so it can unleash itself. That's why Jews were called vermin in the Holocaust. That's why Tutsis were called cockroaches in Rwanda. Emphasizing difference precedes violence. We need to see each other as alien in order to unleash our hatred in violence" (http://www.readthespirit.com/explore/2011/2/16/meet-miroslav-volf-whose -allah-is-a-path-to-peace.html). This danger deriving from difference helps explain why many people say that "All religions are the same," not realizing that the blurring or erasure of differences can create other dangers as well.

6. The atheism of the former Soviet Union, for example, demonstrated that a strong economic and political identity could create no less hostility than a religious identity, as did the Maoist revolution in China and the Khmer Rouge regime in Cambodia. It turns out that the famous dictum, associated with Dostoevsky's Ivan Karamazov, can run both ways: yes, without God everything is theoretically permissible . . . but believers can find ways to use God to justify just about anything as well.

Treating difference-based religious violence with peace through secular sameness may be like treating stage-four pancreatic cancer with stage-four colon cancer. When secularists see no hope for peace apart from the eradication of religion from the earth, they open up possible atheistic scenarios that could easily become as scary as the theocratic scenarios of their counterparts.[7]

That's why, as someone who agrees with Sam Harris about the danger of religious violence, I propose a diagnosis quite different from his. *The tensions between our conflicted religions arise not from our differences, but from one thing we all hold in common: an oppositional religious identity that derives strength from hostility.*

When religions—including Christianity—grow strong by incorporating hostility to otherness into their identity, they become more like one another. In light of that similarity, their differences seem increasingly trivial. Like rival twins, they are joined in the conflicted unity of a hostile identity, differing in content but mirroring one another in attitude and behavior.[8] As a result, they begin to appear as different manifestations of the same religion—the religion of us-them hostility—rather than as different religions. As Jack Nelson-

---

7. Imagine if a movement of skeptics decided that religious people were such a threat worldwide that they must be "cleansed," leaving only the "pure"—namely, members of their movement of pure rationalists or skeptics—to inherit the earth.

8. Rene Girard calls these mirror-imaging hostile pairs "doubles," and he describes their mutually reinforcing imitation with the term *mimesis* (see *Things Hidden Since the Foundation of the World* [New York: Continuum Books, 2003]). Psychoanalyst Vamik Volkan sees this "similarity between enemies" as a facet of regression and observes, "I do not think that humans (as large groups) have ever developed the idea or ability to refrain from being like their enemies once they feel threatened or hurt" ("Large Group Identity, Large Group Regression and Massive Violence," p. 22, available online here: http://www.austenriggs.org/education-research-the-erikson-institute/erikson -scholar-applications/senior-erikson-scholar/dr-volkans-sample-papers/). Skye Jethani offers a similar diagnosis—saying that all religions have a danger-avoidance component that renders them, ironically, dangerous to one another. See "Do All Paths Lead to God?" at: http://us2.campaign-archive2.com/?u=87188c8737bc50c1a2fb8e2c9&id =fe94144554.

Pallmeyer says: "If religion and faith are about ultimate allegiance, then it can be said that violence is the world's principal religion."[9]

Now by *identity* I mean an array of characteristics that make an individual recognizable as a member or an affiliate of a group, or that make one group recognizable and distinct from others. Those characteristics might include matters of dress, hairstyle, bodily marking or mutilation, or skin color.[10] They might include matters of diet, schedule, ritual, or language. They might include matters of belief, attitude, affection, or opposition. Whatever the markers, these indicators help us transcend personal selfishness in what Jonathan Haidt calls *groupishness,* and groupishness has survival value that grows from a group's ability to circle around a sacred center:

Despite what you might have learned in Economics 101, people aren't always selfish. In politics, they're more often groupish. When

___

9. *Is Religion Killing Us?* p. xv.

10. Skin color and race deserve special attention. In an important *Christian Century* article, Jonathan Tran quotes James Cone: "American theology is racist.... It identifies theology as dispassionate analysis of 'the tradition,' unrelated to the suffering of the oppressed." See Jonathan Tran, "The New Black Theology, *Christian Century,* http://christiancentury.org/article/2012-01/new-black-theology/. Tran explains how the racial construction of whiteness in theology plays a critical role, not only in ignoring the suffering of the oppressed, but also in increasing it:

"In European Christianity, the general question about difference settled on the specific question of Jewish difference—what came to be called *der Judenfrage* (the Jewish question). Attempting to espouse a universal conception of humanness independent of and over against the Jewish covenant of promise, European Christians crafted a rival discourse to help explain the Jews (and the non-European others whom the Jews exemplified): race. Speech about 'race' helped construe the Jews as a people inordinately attached to their peculiar practices and outdated laws. The Jews become 'the other' by which European Christianity defined itself. European Christians, in this view, are the universal race because they, unlike the Jews, are able to shed their religious particularity just the way Jesus superseded the particularity of Jewish law. Or so the story went.... 'Whiteness' is not so much something as nothing—a mythic conception of nonparticularity, the achievement of genuine transcendence, true reason. It is purity, existence free of the blemishes that colored all other races. Thus race became the way Westerners came to understand people's differences and where people belong in the hierarchy of existence."

people feel that a group they value—be it racial, religious, regional or ideological—is under attack, they rally to its defense, even at some cost to themselves. We evolved to be tribal, and politics is a competition among coalitions of tribes.

The key to understanding tribal behavior is not money, it's sacredness. The great trick that humans developed at some point in the last few hundred thousand years is the ability to circle around a tree, rock, ancestor, flag, book or god, and then treat that thing as sacred. People who worship the same idol can trust one another, work as a team and prevail over less cohesive groups. So if you want to understand politics, and especially our divisive culture wars, you must follow the sacredness.[11]

us/them

Social psychoanalyst Vamik Volkan theorizes that groupishness produces a potentially dangerous side effect: an attitude of superiority about "us" and a corresponding tendency to dehumanize "them":

> ...at the outset of human history, each human group developed a distinct sense of identity, wearing skins and feathers like armor to protect it from other groups who wore different kinds of skins and feathers. [Erik] Erikson hypothesized that each group became convinced that it was the sole possessor of the true human identity. Thus each group became a pseudospecies, adopting an attitude of superiority over other groups.[12]

With Erikson, Volkan describes how children enter the world as "generalists," devoid of the concepts or categories of nationality, ethnicity, and religion. Gradually, influential adults induct children

---

11. From http://campaignstops.blogs.nytimes.com/2012/03/17/forget-the-money-follow-the-sacredness/. Haidt explores these ideas in more depth in *The Righteous Mind: Why Good People are Divided by Politics and Religion* (New York: Pantheon Books, 2012).

12. From Vamik Volkan, *Killing in the Name of Identity* (Charlottesville, Va.: Pitchstone Publishing, 2006), p. 14, quoted in Yamin, p. 8.

into the various large-group identities that frame adult lives: they are male or female, Americans or Australians, Hutu or Twa, Republicans or Democrats, Christians or agnostics, rich or poor, high-caste or low-caste, and so on. In imagery parallel to Haidt's description of a tribe circling around a sacred center, Volkan adapts Peter Berger's image of a "sacred canopy," comparing large-group identities to big tents under which children grow.[13] In the shelter of these big tents of ethnic, national, tribal, and religious identity, children develop their individual identities, expressed for example in their chosen styles of dress or hair or speech. They normally take the larger identity for granted until it is threatened or becomes a problem for them in some way.[14] A problematized group identity may then plunge them into a crisis of personal identity—because *who I am* is bound up in the struggle of *who we are*. Volkan explains:

> In our routine lives we are more concerned with subgroups under the tent: families or professional organizations, for example. Our relationship with our large-group identity, in ordinary times, is like breathing. While we breathe constantly, we do not usually notice it unless our ability to breathe is threatened, such as if we are caught in a smoke-filled house on fire. When the large-group identity is threatened, people under the metaphorical tent become like the people who are caught in a smoke-filled room. They become constantly aware of their large-group identities and become preoccupied

---

13. See Volkan, "Large Group Identity, Large Group Regression and Massive Violence."

14. For example, their group may have been shamed or traumatized in some way that complicates their individual lives. Or they may fall in love with someone their group forbids. Or they may feel the ongoing development of their individual identity is limited or harmed by the restrictions of the large-group identity. Or they may be attracted to affiliate with a rival group, which will require them to leave the shelter of their ancestral tent. By the way, Volkan's use of the term "big tent" should not be confused with Philip Clayton and Tripp Fuller's more hospitable use of the term, as in *Transforming Christian Theology* (Minneapolis: Fortress Press, 2010).

who I am is bound up in the struggle of who we are.

with its [*sic*] protection and maintenance, even if this preoccupation leads to destructive acts.[15]

So my evolving personal sense of *who I am* is normally strengthened and supported by a stable groupish sense of *who we are*. But when *who we are* is threatened or destabilized in some way, my *who I am* is also threatened, and not just mine, but also the *who I am* of all my neighbors. Unified and energized by a perceived threat, and driven by survival instincts from our unconscious, evolutionary past, our fight/flight mechanisms activate, preparing us—if we cannot flee—for hostility.

The individual body prepares for a fight by pumping adrenaline into the system. The heart beats faster, respiration accelerates, muscles tense and warm, pain centers prepare for an onslaught, reactions are heightened. The religious, social, or political body similarly prepares by pumping a kind of social adrenaline into society. This social adrenaline must prepare us for conflict, conflict that each society must normally inhibit in order to keep the peace. The group must, in other words, prepare to break the rules by which it normally functions. We in the group must, to a degree, suspend our normal pursuits—business, agriculture, art, sport, and recreation in civil society, and worship, teaching, fellowship, and prayer in religious communities. We must divert a portion of our attention and energy to hostility, and we must focus that hostility on a target—real or imagined, legitimate or manufactured, among *them* (as a classic enemy) or among *us* (as an internal scapegoat).

———

Once the target of hostility is identified, our threatened group identity begins to energize itself by emphasizing our goodness and the

15. Vamik Volkan, "Religious Fundamentalism and Violence," p. 21, available online here: http://www.austenriggs.org/education-research-the-erikson-institute/erikson-scholar-applications/senior-erikson-scholar-dr-volkans-sample-papers/.

target's evil, our innocence and the target's guilt, our uniqueness or chosen-ness and the target's banality, our desire for peace and the target's desire for violence, and so on. Thus we are given permission to see ourselves as good, as innocent victims, as lovers of peace who are authorized to use violence in order to restore peace. And we are given permission to see the enemy as irrational, evil, demonic, even subhuman. Recalling the words of James Alison we considered earlier, we are simultaneously defining ourselves and uniting ourselves through our shared hostility.[16]

The identified enemy may pose an actual threat. For example, the Al Queda network may actually plot the murder of Christians (perhaps more as Westerners than as Christians per se, a worthwhile distinction to keep in mind). And some Christian extremists really do believe that Muslims must be either converted, contained and marginalized, or eradicated.

But the identified enemy may also simply be an innocent bystander, chosen to fill the role of a scapegoat upon whom the group's anxieties may be focused and around whose removal (by expulsion or killing) the group may be unified. One thinks, for example, of women identified as witches during the outbreaks of witch-hunting in Christian history, or the peculiar obsession among some Christians in America and Africa with "the gay agenda." Sometimes, the enemy may not even exist except in the imaginations of the anxious, as is often the case with conspiracy theories.

When we increasingly understand who we are in relation to an enemy—whether that enemy is legitimate, innocent, or imaginary—we develop an increasingly hostile identity. Such an identity teaches

---

16. Alison continues, "Having an enemy is not about the truth; it's about knowing we are good." See the Raven Foundation website (especially Suzanne Ross, "Left Behind: Now What?" *Copy That!* [blog], at http://www.ravenfoundation.org/blogs/copy-that/left-behind-now-what) for more information on the development of hostility. Also, see Ted Schwartz's powerful play, *I'd Like to Buy An Enemy*, here: http://tedandcompany.com/id-like-to-buy-an-enemy/.

us to see *sameness as safety* and *otherness as danger*. It is characterized by duality: us and them, right and wrong, good and evil, light and darkness. It promotes a mentality of us *versus* them, us *apart from* them, us *instead of* them, us *without* them, us *over* them, us *using* them, us *in spite of* them, us *oppressed by* them, or us *occupying* them, but never us *for* them or us *with* them.

It teaches us to see the long-term existence and well-being of *them* or *the other* as unacceptable, perhaps as an offense or threat to us and our religion, and perhaps even as an offense to God. It requires us to believe that the world would be a better place without *them* in it as *them*, and it only allows us to accept the other by converting them to be part of *us*, so they are no longer *other*. Ultimately, a hostile or oppositional identity values *us* as inherently more human, more holy, more acceptable, more pure, or more worthy than *them*. After all, if *they* were good, they would ask to be admitted under *our* sacred canopy and they would join us in circling around *our* sacred center.

So I'm convinced, with Sam Harris and many others, that religion does indeed play a critical role in human conflict. But I'm certain the problem is less simple and more interesting than our typical discussions of the subject might suggest. Our root problem is neither religious *difference* nor religious *identity* nor even *strong* religious identity. Our root problem is the *hostility* that we often employ to make and keep our identities strong—whether those identities are political, economic, philosophical, scientific, or religious.

———

It is not merely our differences that divide us, then, but a profound similarity—the oppositional way in which we build strong identities. It's an easy shortcut that takes us places we never intended to go.

Chapter 8

How (Not) to Create a Strong-Benevolent Christian Identity

It's difficult to get a man to understand something when his salary
depends upon his not understanding it.

—*Upton Sinclair*

Let's imagine we are so brokenhearted by the fruits of hostility
in our Christian history that we decide to water down, dilute,
de-emphasize, and otherwise weaken Christian identity altogether
so there will be less hostility in the future. What might happen?

With a loss of strong Christian identity, we could for a while draw
on the bank account of Christian legacy, the accumulated personal and
social capital created when Christian identity was strong. But over time,
if we make more withdrawals than deposits, the benefits of that legacy
will shrink. If no strong-and-benevolent religious identity replaces our
strong-and-hostile Christian identity, the majority of us would in all
likelihood be left with consumerism as our dominant cultural ethos.[1]

---

1. It would be interesting to analyze a typical "secular" day in terms of the religious rituals of consumerism. For example, people willingly watch hours of corporate
propaganda daily in the form of advertisements. They submit themselves to daily

We would then embark on a massive cultural experiment: can humanity live by bread (and circuses, and gadgets) alone? Can a healthy, sustainable identity—personal and social—be built under the big tent of corporate media and corporate politics by whose godlike provision we enjoy our daily bread? Can our lives consist in the abundance of products we buy, the standard of living we seek, the economic policies we consider orthodox, and the debt load we carry?

If we in the so-called *developed world* embark on this experiment (might we have done so already without realizing it?), we will find consumerism to be the strongest but most subtle identity of all. We will discover that consumerism comes equipped with its own set of hostilities and consequences, many of which will prove every bit as catastrophic as those of the old Christian hostility.[2] And here's the kicker: in such a consumerist system, a weak and benign form of Christianity or any other religion would be cherished and rewarded. It would provide the perfect chaplaincy or priesthood to support and enhance the established consumerist enterprise, giving it an air of legitimacy and even sacredness, and never playing the role of prophet to confront the status quo and challenge its legitimacy.[3]

---

indoctrination by the corporate media. They sing the songs of their religion in the form of corporate jingles or popular songs that praise the ecstasy of commodified romantic love. I explore this theme under Thomas M. Beaudoin's term *theocapitalism* in *Everything Must Change* (Nashville: Thomas Nelson, 2007).

2. I explored some of these consequences in *Everything Must Change* (Nashville: Thomas Nelson, 2007). For example, consumerism promotes greed that creates hostility between nations and classes; it rewards rapid resource extraction that impoverishes and degrades the environment for future generations; it seeks the quickest return on investment without taking into account long-range social consequences; it empowers corporations that privatize profits for shareholders and externalize costs especially upon the poor and powerless; it turns governments into puppets that serve the interests of those corporations without regard for justice and the common good; and it even co-opts and corrupts authentic spirituality by commodifying it for a religious-industrial complex.

3. In this scenario, where most of us abandon strong-hostile Christian identity for a weaker one, what might happen back in the dwindling Christian community where hostility is accepted as a necessary accompaniment to strength? The continuing departure

Let's play out the scenario a little bit further. A consumerist society, without a higher framing story or sacred vision to resource it, would likely produce decreasing levels of personal responsibility, self-restraint, community-mindedness, reconciliation, or concern for equity, fidelity, loyalty, and personal morality. Losses in those areas would probably lead to corresponding losses in personal and social well-being that may in turn lead to rising levels of addiction, competition, divorce, crime, social conflict, violence, accelerated exploitation of others and of the environment, and so on.

What will be left to hold individuals, families, communities, and nations together when our legacy of Christian virtues breaks down like decaying, unmaintained social infrastructure, and when consumerism runs its bitter course?

Many of us would probably feel a poignant nostalgia for the good old days when Christian identity was strong. A whole range of new strong identities would then form to fill the vacuum. Some of us might affiliate with a reinvigorated ideology like capitalism, communism, libertarianism, or Ayn Randian objectivism. Some might gravitate toward a revived ethnic or class identity—white supremacy, black power, or the proletariat. Some might join strong secular political parties or nativist movements, and others would choose (or be chosen by) a strong nonreligious power structure like a gang or mafia. Some of us might move toward strong and violent revolutionary movements—whether religious (like Al Queda) or nonreligious (like Pol Pot's Khmer Rouge). And many of us, no doubt, would seek to revive old forms of oppositional, hostile Christianity, seeking a neo-Christendom complete with neo-Crusades, neo–witch hunts, and so on.

---

of Christians with an aversion to hostility intensifies the corporate ethos of those who remain. As the Christian community's hostility quotient rises, members of other groups accurately assess Christianity as more and more of a threat to them. From there, any number of unpleasant scenarios might play out, all of them arguing for the pursuit of a strong and benevolent Christian identity.

When we engage in this kind of imaginative exercise, a sobering realization begins to set in. In our attempts to exorcise the strong and hostile religious identities that are so familiar to us, we may be possessed by the demons of other identities that are equally strong and perhaps even more hostile.[4] The old truism echoes back to us once again: the only good antidote to bad religion is not no religion, but good religion, or, slightly altered, the antidote to strong-hostile religion is not weak-benign religion, but strong-benevolent religion.

So, if both strong-hostile and weak-benign Christian identities produce undesirable unintended consequences, we have to imagine ways both can be redeemed and transformed into what we need. This thought experiment involving a ten-item test might help us in that re-imagination process:

Respond to each item using this 0–5 scale:

0 = absolutely untrue

1 = strongly disagree

2 = disagree

3 = somewhat agree

4 = agree

5 = strongly agree

_5_ 1. *Validity*: My Christian faith is highly significant to me because it adds true meaning and value to my life.

---

4. Actually, Jesus suggested that repossession is seven times worse than the original possession (Matthew 12:43ff.). Time will tell if that formula holds in our case. The relationship between possession by demons and possession by identities deserves further consideration. Walter Wink's work is an ideal starting point, including *The Powers That Be* (New York: Three Rivers Press, 1999).

Solidarity

2. *Intentionality:* For me, Christian faith is not merely an unchosen inheritance, a social custom, a matter of convenience, or the path of least resistance; it is an intentional commitment that I uphold and practice by conscious choice.

3. *Durability:* I plan to remain at least as committed to my Christian faith as I am now, over the course of my lifetime, through both hard times and easy times, and I hope to pass vital Christian faith on to my children and grandchildren.

4. *Intensity:* My Christian faith is so central to my life that it requires of me sacrifices and commitments that are sometimes costly and even painful.

5. *Purity/Consistency:* I conform to the beliefs, behaviors, habits, examples, prohibitions, ideas, and values that are consistent with my Christian faith, and I resist or reject their opposites as inconsistent with my Christian faith.

6. *History:* I consider myself to be part of the history and traditions of my faith community; Christian history is in some real sense my history.

7. *Responsibility:* I feel responsible for the health and well-being of the Christian community, now and in the future.

8. *Missionality:* I invest my time, energy, money, and abilities to participate in the Christian mission as I understand it.

9. *Loyalty:* I feel a special sense of loyalty to my fellow Christians because we are connected to one another through our shared faith and mission.

—6

NO 10. *Hostility*: I see other faiths as wrong, false, or evil, and I maintain a posture of opposition to all faiths but the Christian faith.

Now imagine that a score of zero to twenty-five would indicate a weak Christian identity, a score of twenty-six to thirty-nine would indicate a moderate Christian identity, and a score of forty to fifty would indicate a strong Christian identity. How would you score on this test? Would you consider these results an accurate assessment of the strength of your Christian identity?

If your score was low or moderate, would you say that an aversion to hostility (Item 10) has led to an overall weakening of your Christian identity? If your score was high, how do you feel about the tenth item? Is it essential to the list? Must you as a Christian maintain hostility to other faiths if you are going to hold a strong Christian identity? Could you imagine the tenth item being replaced with this alternative indicator?

✓ 10. *Solidarity*: My understanding of Jesus and his message leads me to see each faith tradition, including my own, as having its own history, value, strengths, and weaknesses. I seek to affirm and celebrate all that is good in each faith tradition, and I build intentional relationships of mutual sharing and respectful collaboration with people of all faith traditions, so all our faiths can keep growing and contributing to God's will being done on earth as in heaven.

If hostility could be replaced by solidarity, would any of the previous nine items need to be changed?[5] How might the substitution

---

5. I rely on the word *solidarity* heavily in this book, and it deserves further definition. David Hollinger, in "From Identity to Solidarity," defines it as "an experience of willed affiliation" (*Daedalus*, Fall 2006, pp. 23–31). He contrasts it with "mere membership" in a "community of fate," explaining that "[f]eminism is a solidarity, but womanhood is not. Judaism is a solidarity, but having a Jewish ancestor ... is not" (24–25). Solidarity,

strengthen them? What obstacles stand in the way of this kind of substitution? What kind of reengineering of the first nine items would a substitution of the tenth require? For example, if we replaced hostility with solidarity, how would we need to rethink the validity or history of our faith, or how would our understanding of mission and loyalty change? Do these kinds of changes seem sensible and modest to you, or radical and revolutionary?

Clearly, if the Christian faith of 2117 or 2517 is going to be less hostile and more peaceable than the Christian faith of 1517 or 2017, profound change at all levels will be required of us.

We might wish for our paid clergy to provide bold leadership in this change process. But we must be realistic about the ways in which "the religious-industrial complex" profits by maintaining the status quo of strong-oppositional identity on the one hand and weak-benign identity on the other. Every religious professional can imagine a scenario of fear playing out like this: *If we boldly step out and*

---

he says, "implies a special claim, even if modest in dimensions, that individuals have on each other's energies, compassion, and resources" (24). He explains that "we all have multiple identities (national, ethnoracial, religious, sexual, geographical, ideological, professional, generational, etc.) and are capable of several solidarities," and we struggle to negotiate the competing claims and entitlements they entail (27). All this is complicated when identities and solidarities are contested, under threat, and in flux, and especially when they are internally torn between "the impulse for concentration (hold your familiar ground; stick with your own kind; consolidate the richness of your heritage) and the impulse for incorporation (expand your horizons; take on as much of the world as you can; try to locate the source of your dilemmas, however remote)" (27). What I call "Conflicted Religious Identity Syndrome" is a matter of solidarity that grapples with these three questions: 1. By choosing to affiliate with a group, am I obligated to endorse the hostilities it holds against other groups? 2. Is it possible for me to will affiliation with all people and all creation—especially if I understand Jesus and his gospel as a call to universal solidarity? 3. What do I do when my answer to the second question is in conflict with my answer to the first? As upcoming chapters will make clear, in core Christian doctrines and practices like the incarnation and the eucharist, Christians affirm that God shows solidarity with all humanity and with all creation. And in Jesus' life and teaching, we see him demonstrating extraordinary, boundary-crossing solidarity with the poor, the oppressed, the outcast, the outsider, the other, even the enemy. It's no wonder that many of us believe *solidarity* will become a critical category for Christian theology and practice in this century and beyond.

preach against Christian hostility, we will be seen as betrayers of strong identity. Religious gatekeepers on websites and in magazines will single us out as liberal, relativist, and weak.[6] *As a result, our vital statistics will plummet—meaning losses of butts in seats and dollars in budgets. Our churches, denominations, agencies, seminaries, mission agencies, and pensions will suffer. And shortly thereafter, we will be unemployed.*[7]

Just as we might wish that more clergy were willing to take that risk, our clergy might wish that more of the rest of us were willing to step forward in a grassroots movement of RSR (religious social responsibility) to complement CSR (corporate social responsibility). Just as we need corporations to convert from dirty fossil fuels to clean, sustainable energy, we need the religion industry to be converted from its reliance on the toxic energy of oppositional identity and hostility. We need to research, develop, and deploy the renewable and renewing fuel source of divine-human kindness and benevolence. Through advocacy, education, and conversation—and perhaps the religious equivalents of boycotts, carrot mobs, and buycotts—we will need to gently but firmly pressure our religious institutions to stop polluting our environment with toxic beliefs and rhetoric that raise our global social temperature and push us ever closer to conflict and collapse.[8] We need our religious institutions to do what we need all our institutions to do: put long-term benefit (or *the common good*) over short-term profit (for *us* and not *them*). We need to imagine

---

6. Or: *If we boldly step out and preach against Christian nominality or lukewarmness, people will assume we are hostile extremists and troublemakers. Religious gatekeepers on websites and in magazines will single us out as conservative and hostile.*

7. In all likelihood, those who seek to "save their lives" by siding with hostility will, in the long run, be losers, too, because eventually people will be no more willing to stay in religious institutions that support interfaith hostility than they were in the past to stay in religious institutions that supported slavery and racism.

8. *Buycotts* are the opposite of *boycotts*: instead of mobilizing people to avoid businesses and organizations that do harm, they mobilize people to patronize those that do good. The mobilized patrons who intentionally patronize socially beneficial organizations are called *carrot mobs*. See www.carrotmob.org/.

Jesus' own voice asking, "What shall it profit you to have a big, fat, rich, powerful religion when the bullets are flying and the nuclear bombs are falling and the world is being destroyed because of your religious hostility?"

As this kind of grassroots movement gains momentum, more and more courageous and creative Christian leaders will emerge to communicate and embed this new strong-benevolent identity in sermons, books, liturgies, prayers, hymns, curricula for adults and kids, and mission plans. Over time, as others "taste and see" how good this new identity is in practice, it will spread and become increasingly normative. The ultimate result won't simply be a change in Christian identity: it will be a new direction in human history.

But before we consider that new direction in the future, we need to look back at our past, because the past walks with us in the present in more ways than we know.

Chapter 9

How a Liberal Arts Education Ruined My Opinion of Christopher Columbus

There is a word, an Igbo word, that I think about whenever I think about the power structures of the world, and it is *nkali*. It's a noun that loosely translates to "to be greater than another." Like our economic and political worlds, stories too are defined by the principle of nkali. How they are told, who tells them, when they're told, how many stories are told, are really dependent on power.

Power is the ability not just to tell the story of another person, but to make it the definitive story of that person. The Palestinian poet Mourid Barghouti writes that if you want to dispossess a people, the simplest way to do it is to tell their story, and to start with, "secondly." Start the story with the arrows of the Native Americans, and not with the arrival of the British, and you have an entirely different story. Start the story with the failure of the African state, and not with the colonial creation of the African state, and you have an entirely different story.

—*Chimamanda Adichie*[1]

1. From a brilliant TED talk called "Chimamanda Adichie: The Danger of a Single Story," available as a video here: http://www.ted.com/talks/chimamanda_adichie_the_danger_of_a_single_story.html.

Why do we Christians have an oppositional or hostile identity today? In large part, the answer lies in our history. And our history hides more complexity than many of us realize. Yes, we are rooted in Jesus and the apostles, as we'd expect, and yes, Jesus and the apostles were rooted in Judaism. But Christians today also have deep historical roots in the Roman empire, and so to understand our hostility, we must come to terms with our Roman imperial history.

Now by *history*, I don't simply mean the objective record of *what we did and what happened to us*. Rather, our history is *how we understand and interpret what we did and how we understand and interpret what happened to us*. The differences and tensions between *what happened* and *how we interpret and understand what happened* are highly nuanced and highly interesting.

I began to grapple with these differences and tensions, as many people do, in my teenage years, especially when I went to university. The "liberal" in "liberal arts education," I came to understand, had to do with being liberated or freed from one unchallenged viewpoint, one single, unquestioned story, one authorized and conventional interpretation of our past. When I was exposed to the insights of people from across many centuries in my own culture, and even more, when I was exposed to the insights from varied historical contexts from many diverse cultures, I began to experience that liberation. But it wasn't all pleasant. Liberation of this sort can be rather disillusioning and depressing, at least in the short run. Take my view of the man who "discovered" America, Christopher Columbus.

I had grown up in one of the most highly rated public school systems in the United States. There I learned the standard, state-of-the-art 1960s version of American history. I knew without any doubt, as did my classmates, that my history classes taught me objective fact, not propaganda. Of course in other countries, especially Communist countries, teachers taught their children distorted, sanitized, and false histories. But here in the United States, I knew we were free and we learned the truth, the whole truth, and nothing but the truth. So in my primary and secondary education, like most kids, I read my history textbooks, watched a few films (older readers will remember *filmstrips*, the archaic precursor to the slideshow and video), listened to lectures, took notes, and usually passed my tests with flying colors, thinking I "knew American history," which included knowing about Christopher Columbus.

Early on I learned, as all American schoolkids do, that Columbus sailed the ocean blue in 1492. Because of his courageous voyage into the unknown, he was a hero, a brave explorer, a model worthy of a public holiday every October. Yes, I learned that he mistakenly thought he had arrived in India when he had actually made landfall in what we call the Dominican Republic, part of the island of Hispaniola. (My Native American friends like to say that their ancestors discovered Columbus in 1492.) But apart from that one small and highly forgivable error, Columbus remained for us a heroic figure.

It wasn't until my college years that I learned the darker sides of the Christopher Columbus story, starting with his brutal treatment of the native people of Hispaniola, the Taino. As Thom Hartmann explains in *The Last Hours of Ancient Sunlight*, part of the "booty" of Columbus's second voyage in 1495 were sixteen hundred male and female Taino slaves to be exported to Spain.[2] He wrote to the Spanish king and queen, "It is possible, with the name of the Holy Trinity, to sell all the slaves which it is possible to sell...Here there are so many of these slaves...although they are living things they are as good as gold."[3]

The Spaniards who remained in Hispaniola were encouraged to take Taino slaves "in the amount desired." Columbus himself gave

---

2. Thom Hartmann, *The Last Hours of Ancient Sunlight* (New York: Broadway Books, 2004), pp. 50ff.

3. The semantic and theological functions of "the name of the Holy Trinity" in that sentence deserve reflection.

a teenage girl to one of his crew, Miguel Cuneo, for his personal "use." Cuneo wrote that she "resisted with all her strength" when he attempted to have sex with her, so he "thrashed her mercilessly and raped her." Being given a Taino woman to rape was, in fact, a popular "company perk" for Columbus's men. Columbus himself wrote to a friend, "There are plenty of dealers who go about looking for girls; those from nine to ten [years old] are now in demand."

If the Taino people resisted Spanish exploitation (and if they survived smallpox and other diseases the Spanish brought with them), they would be maimed, attacked with dogs, "skewered on poles from anus to mouth," or shot. No wonder many committed suicide, as a more sympathetic Spaniard wrote in 1517. It is hard to read his account without tears:

> As a result of the sufferings and hard labor they endured, the Indians choose and have chosen suicide. Occasionally a hundred have committed mass suicide. The women, exhausted by labor, have shunned conception and childbirth....Many, when pregnant, have taken something to abort and have aborted. Others after delivery have killed their children with their own hands, so as not to leave them in such oppressive slavery.[4]

Of the estimated 300,000 Taino alive when Columbus "discovered" them in 1492, about 12,000 remained in 1516, fewer than 200 in 1546, and zero in 1555. What our history calls "the discovery of America," Taino history might call "the arrival of the Christian genociders," if, that is, any Taino survived to tell an alternate history. None did.

I never learned the story of the Taino in my K–12 education. But

---

4. Hartmann, *The Last Hours of Ancient Sunlight*, p. 57. See also "A Serpent in the Garden: An Unholy Worldview on Sacred Land," by Waziyatawin, PhD, in an as-yet untitled collection to be published by the Mennonite Church in Canada.

I did learn a cute (and misleading) tale about the pilgrims inviting Squanto over for a hospitable Thanksgiving dinner. I never learned about the early colonists' common practice of comparing the Native Peoples of New England to the Canaanites in the Bible, thus rendering them a legitimate target for displacement and genocide.[5] But I did learn an inspiring (and distorted) story of a romance between John Smith and Pocahontas.[6] I never learned about the US government's staggering record of slaughter, land theft, and broken treaties with the Native Americans from the Atlantic to the Pacific, nor did I learn about the boarding schools and their abuse of Native American children. But I did learn about the Indian Wars, always told from the perspective of the good white people who, on their intrepid journey west, were constantly being harassed and attacked by those brutal, ignorant, rebellious, and duplicitous savages.

I imagine that Canadian, Mexican, and Filipino children (and more recently, no doubt, Panamanian, Haitian, Iraqi, and Afghan children) learn in their history classes about US invasions of their countries. But according to my K–12 education in the 1960s, the United States never invaded anybody.[7] We may have come in to

5. Consider these words from John Winthrop, governor of the Massachusetts Bay Colony, in 1634: "But for the natives in these parts, God hath so pursued them, as for 300 miles space the greatest part of them are swept away by the smallpox which still continues among them. So...God hath thereby cleared our title to this place" (in Hartmann, p. 219). Puritan preacher Increase Mather shared Winthrop's theology of displacement: "God ended the controversy by sending the smallpox among the Indians. Whole towns of them were swept away, in some of them not so much as one Soul escaping the Destruction."

6. For a withering critique of Disney's Pocahontas story, see *Islam, Postmodernism and Other Futures: A Ziauddin Sardar Reader*, ed. Sohail Inayatullah and Gail Boxwell (London: Pluto Press, 2003).

7. Thankfully, I think kids in the United States today learn a slightly more balanced and honest view of American history. Meanwhile, some from my generation regularly complain of a "liberal" bias in textbooks and seek to have them rewritten to reflect the sensibilities of their own childhood education. They apparently believe that their "conservative" K–12 education from the 1970s and before was objective, thorough, balanced, and accurate. Whether this is innocent naivete or willful ignorance, I cannot

help when needed, but our intentions were always purely humanitarian. After all, we were and are "one nation, under God, indivisible, with liberty and justice for all."

If these were simply isolated incidents, a few gaps or slips in an otherwise excellent history education, they would be serious enough. But during and after my university years, I came to see that there was a pattern to the errors and omissions in my education. An agenda was in play. Far from being objective, my textbooks and teachers and therefore my exams and term paper assignments all expressed a consistent point of view, a single story, a *vested interest*. They embedded certain unconscious assumptions in all our minds. They supported a predetermined set of values, a specific alignment of powers, and a coherent way of behavior. In other words, their single, unquestioned story helped form a useful American identity which I, as a good American boy, embraced and inhabited as my own.

Since college, under the ongoing influence of a good liberal arts education, I've continued to read, travel, meet people, and listen to their stories. My "American exceptionalism" has been repeatedly sideswiped and finally totaled. Now I must acknowledge that my nation's history is not so exceptional, but rather has much in common with the histories of Rwanda, Sierra Leone, Israel-Palestine, or South Africa.[8] Now I must acknowledge that my country's history is both heroic and tragic, glorious and shameful, beautiful and blemished. Now, as my sense of American history has been revolutionized, so has my American identity. You've probably had similar awakenings—more or less rude—that led you to similar conclusions

---

say. (Readers in Canada, the UK, Germany, France, the Netherlands, and elsewhere can, no doubt, find parallel tensions in their standard accounts of national-colonial history.)

8. For more on American exceptionalism, see my *Sojourners* article "America the Exceptional" and Randy Woodley's blog on the subject, both available here: http://brianmclaren.net/archives/blog/american-exceptionalism-continue.html.

and disorientations. (And if you haven't, may I recommend a liberal arts education?)[9]

Once we acknowledge that there's a big and complex difference between *what actually happened* and *how we interpret, understand, and recount what actually happened,* an obvious question presents itself: What effects might this kind of history education—or indoctrination—have on a whole nation of kids as they grow up and take the reins of power in America? How would this or that version of American history tend to shape American identity—who we invade, who we bomb, who we protect, who we welcome, who we shun, who we trust, who we fear?

What is true for Americans is also true for Christians—in the US, but also in Denmark and the UK, in Nigeria and Kenya, in India and Singapore, in Guatemala and Brazil. We Christians will not experience a reorientation of our identity until we are willing to go through a profound rethinking of our history. We will never truly deal with the worst parts of our past by denying or minimizing them, but only by facing them, honestly, humbly, and fully. That is what the Bible calls *repentance.*

In Kent Nerburn's *Wolf at Twilight,* a Lakota elder powerfully articulates to a Caucasian writer what historical repentance looks like: "When you look at black people, you see ghosts of all the slavery and the rapes and the hangings and the chains. When you look at Jews, you see ghosts of all those bodies piled up in the death camps. And those ghosts keep you trying to do the right thing." But the stories of the Native Peoples are still minimized and marginalized, he explains, so "when you look at us, you don't see the ghosts of the little babies with their heads smashed in by rifle butts at the Big Hole, or the old folks dying by the side of the trail on the way to Oklahoma while

---

9. For North Americans seeking to begin such a liberal arts education, I would recommend Dee Brown, *Bury My Heart at Wounded Knee* (New York: Henry Holt, 2007); Jared Diamond, *Guns, Germs, and Steel* (New York: Norton, 2005); Kent Nerburn, *Neither Wolf Nor Dog* (New York: New World Library, 2002); etc.

their families cried and tried to make them comfortable, or the dead mothers at Wounded Knee or the little kids at Sand Creek who were shot for target practice."

Until we hear those stories and feel their import, the Lakota elder suggests, others remain *the other*, not *us*; *their kind*, not *our kind*. If we sustain ourselves in an oppositional identity by the way we sanitize our history, if we hold ourselves at a distance from the other, we "can turn them into slaves or kill six million of them or shoot them into mass graves at Wounded Knee." If, to put a twist on an old saying, we only learn and tell one sanitized, privileged version of our history, we will repeat the worst parts of it. But if we bring our secrets into the light, according to the Good News we proclaim, we can be redeemed, re-identified, born again.

Chapter 10

How Constantine Prepared the Way for Columbus

Once one comes to possess an identity document, one is bound to the ground of that identity document, whether it be about national or religious affiliation, or a particular advocacy cause, and so on. One begins then to be "attached" to the very ground of such "identity." Here a passport symbolizes classification, categorization, homogenization, totalization, genderization, sexualization, racialization, ethnicization, and so forth. The passport fundamentally limits the endless dimension of one's "neighbors," one's "friends," to a certain "category," especially when there is, in our reality, a "strong" passport and a "weak" one. Theologians-without-passports intentionally dissociate themselves from the dominant power, practice, or discourse that totalizes, categorizes, classifies an individual person into a stereotypical box, numbers and data. Theologians-without-passports commit themselves to "make a contribution to the universal community," to the Reign of God, where every individual human being is equal to everyone else, treated justly, accepted fully as who one is.

—*Namsoon Kang*[1]

---

1. Namsoon Kang, "Toward a Cosmopolitan Theology: Constructing Public Theology From the Future," in *Planetary Loves: Spivak, Postcoloniality, and Theology*, ed. Stephen D. Moore and Mayra Riviera (New York: Fordham University Press, 2011), p. 280. The

If we Christians are taught much Christian history at all, we learn versions that are no less sanitized than my introduction to Christopher Columbus in public school. Take, for example, the historical episode often called "the conversion of Emperor Constantine."

Whether it's in Sunday School, youth group, summer camp, a sermon, a confirmation class, or a Christian college or seminary classroom, we typically learn that in AD 312, the Emperor had a vision of a cross in the sky, and we're told that the cross had an inscription of three words: "Conquer by this."[2] So far, so accurate.

But are we ever encouraged to ponder what these three fateful words meant—perhaps, "Terrorize by this," or "Force conversions by

---

section begins, "Empire-building is all about power-building by creating a devalued other...."

2. Here is an excerpt from Eusebius' original telling of the story:

"[Constantine] said that about noon, when the day was already beginning to decline, he saw with his own eyes the trophy of a cross of light in the heavens, above the sun, and bearing the inscription, CONQUER BY THIS. At this sight he himself was struck with amazement, and his whole army also, which followed him on this expedition, and witnessed the miracle...[That night] in his sleep the Christ of God appeared to him with the same sign which he had seen in the heavens, and commanded him to make a likeness of that sign which he had seen in the heavens, and to use it as a safeguard in all engagements with his enemies.

"At dawn of day he arose, and communicated the marvel to his friends: and then, calling together the workers in gold and precious stones, he sat in the midst of them, and described to them the figure of the sign he had seen, bidding them represent it in gold and precious stones. And this representation I myself have had an opportunity of seeing.

"Now it was made in the following manner. A long spear, overlaid with gold, formed the figure of the cross by means of a transverse bar laid over it. On the top of the whole was fixed a wreath of gold and precious stones; and within this, the symbol of the Saviour's name..."

This spear-cross was further adorned with an embroidered banner that featured the emperor and his family. The finished product, Eusebius said, "presented an indescribable degree of beauty to the beholder." He added, "The emperor constantly made use of this sign of salvation as a safeguard against every adverse and hostile power, and commanded that others similar to it should be carried at the head of all his armies." Eusebius, it should be noted, would be considered more of a propagandist than a historian in the modern sense. For more on Constantine's life and work, see James Carroll, *Constantine's Sword: The Church and the Jews—A History* (New York: Mariner Books, 2001).

this," or "Kill by this," or "Expand your violent theocracy by this"? Do these words trouble us?

Are we told that the upright beam of the cross in Constantine's vision was a spear? Is any suggestion ever made that this reappropriation of the cross by Constantine signals its de-Christianization and re-Romanization? Is there any mention, in this context, of Jesus' words about the future of those who live by the sword (or, we might add, spear)? Do we ever see even a shred of irony when the instrument of Roman torture and execution on which Jesus had been brutally killed is once again employed to instill fear and terror, but now, not merely in the name of Rome and its emperor who nailed others to it, but in the name of…one who was once nailed to it?

All this becomes even clearer if we imagine a different conversion, one that never happened but could have. Instead of a gold-plated, bejeweled spear-cross with the words "Threaten and kill by this," imagine that Constantine had seen a vision of a basin and a towel with the words, "Serve by this," or a vision of a simple table of bread and wine with "Reconcile around this," or a vision of Christ's outstretched arms with "Embrace like this," or a vision of the birds of the air and flowers of the field with "Trust like this," or a vision of a mother hen gathering her chicks with "Love like this," or a vision of a dove descending from heaven with the words, "Be as kind as this."[3] But it was not so.

As with Columbus in 1492, so with Constantine in 312: the ways we retell our history form our identity. Our Christian histories, like our political ones, shield us from the full truth about how we became who we are, and in so doing, they keep us from seeing ourselves as others see us. Our standard histories support an oppositional identity where "we" are the virtuous ones, the victims, the defenders of truth,

---

3. Or imagine, as James Carroll suggests, that Constantine converted to Judaism rather than Christianity. How different history would have been.

the peacemakers, and "they" are the aggressors, the invaders, the heretics, the evil ones. Some no doubt overreact to this self-defensive history by exaggerating "our" evil and minimizing theirs. But this mirror image of historical distortion doesn't buffer its opposite as intended; in fact, it only serves to strengthen the defensiveness of those who tell the single dominant story with its more familiar distortions.

In seeking to strike a healthy and honest balance in telling our history (a never-ending task, by the way), I'm convinced that we Christians—Western Christians in particular—must acknowledge the degree to which our faith has become a syncretized faith, a compromised faith, we might even say a corrupted faith. From Constantine to Columbus to the other Conquistadors to the Colonizers to the present, we have mixed authentically Christian elements of love, joy, peace, and reconciliation with strictly imperial elements of superiority, conquest, domination, and hostility. We have created a new religion with an identity far different from the one proclaimed and embodied by Jesus in Galilee, or by James and Peter in Jerusalem, or by Paul around the Mediterranean, or by the Christian scholars of the second and third centuries. In other words, what we call Christianity today has a history, and this history reveals it as a Roman, imperial version of Christianity.[4]

The word *imperial*, of course, requires definition. By it I mean a system of thought and behavior based on empire, which is an integrated system of domination, subordination, expansion, and assimilation.[5] In particular, recalling the pivotal story of Constantine's

---

4. In this sense, we could refer to Roman Catholic and Roman Protestant Christianity—two wings of a project shaped in part by Jesus and the apostles and in part by Rome and its emperors.

5. In *An Introduction to Political Geography* by Martin Jones, Rhys Jones, and Michael Voods (Vancouver, B.C.: Routledge, 2004, p. 40), *imperialism* is defined as "the creation and/or maintenance of an unequal economic, cultural, and territorial relationship, usually between states and often in the form of an empire, based on domination

Christian conversion (ambiguity intended), I mean a system of Christian thought and practice that functions within (and often as a fractal of) the Roman Empire's prime model of domination, subordination, expansion, and assimilation. Seen in this light, Columbus truly was a faithful Roman-Imperial Christian, however gravely his violent deeds betray the actual life and teachings of Jesus.

If we are to move forward wisely from this point, we can't simply seek to remove those imperial elements from our telling. It's not enough, in other words, to cover up the past and promise to do better going forward. To do so would be to deny and minimize the damage that has already been done to others and to ourselves.

So we must not soft-pedal the degree to which these hostile, imperial elements have become an inescapable feature of our Christian history. We must acknowledge that they have played a critical role in creating both Christianity as we show it and the world as we know it. And these imperial elements have also, we must realize, played a critical role in creating us. So many of us must confess that we are imperial Christian people, part of an imperial Christian faith, and our world has been infused with imperial Christian hostility.

If this imperial hostility is such a deeply embedded element of our Christian identity, we must do the hard work of recounting our whole history in light of it. Doing so will be humbling. It will have the character of a confession. It will force us to stop seeing ourselves as the good guys and others as the bad guys. It will require us to acknowledge, as I did in my blog post after novelist Anne Rice "quit

---

and subordination." Modern imperialism took two forms over the last three hundred years: capitalism and communism. Megacorporations may now be forming a more covert form of imperialism in which nation-states are subtly dominated and subordinated to protect and serve corporate hegemony. For more on imperialism, see Brian D. McLaren, *Everything Must Change* (Nashville: Thomas Nelson, 2007), and relevant works by Namsoon Kang, Joerg Rieger, Richard Horsley, Marcus Borg, David Korten, and John Dominic Crossan.

Christianity," that our religion, like every other religion, is in some real sense *a failed religion*.[6]

Contrary to expectations, these confessions will not prompt us to reject our heritage; they will rather make it possible for us to redeem our heritage and resurrect from it a new Christian identity, characterized by humility, strength, and benevolence.

Such confessions will also clear our vision, making it possible for us to see "the other" in a new light. Take, for example, the way we see adherents of the world's second-largest religion, Islam.

---

6. Southern novelist Walker Percy used this term in relation to Christianity's failures regarding race in the United States.

Chapter 11

How Constantine Prepared the Way for Today's Headlines

It is my ardent hope that Muslim and Christian religious leaders and teachers will present our two great religious communities as communities in respectful dialogue, never more as communities in conflict. It is crucial for the young to be taught the ways of respect and understanding, so that they will not be led to misuse religion itself to promote or justify hatred and violence. Violence destroys the image of the Creator in his creatures, and should never be considered as the fruit of religious conviction.

—*Pope John Paul II*[1]

Christians from conservative backgrounds like mine have a simple way of telling the story of Mohammed and his spiritual descendants. Our version of Muslim history, deeply embedded in the Roman Christian tradition of Constantine, goes like this:

---

1. From an address given in Damascus, Syria, on May 6, 2001, about four months before the 9/11 terrorist attacks and the resulting War on Terror. For more information, see Richard Boudreaux, "John Paul First Pope to Visit Mosque," *Los Angeles Times*, May 7, 2001, http://articles.latimes.com/2001/may/07/news/mn-60362.

Mohammed was a false prophet who received a demonic vision.[2] He denied key Christian doctrines and created a counterfeit religion that holds people in darkness and will lead them straight to hell unless Christians intervene so they can be converted. His religion spread by the sword, holding people as captives through tyranny and terror. It is (since the defeat of godless communism) the greatest existing threat to Christians and Christianity.[3]

Some might temper this rather harsh depiction, acknowledging that the "seeds of the Word" can even be sown into that dark and dangerous religion. They might acknowledge certain good elements in Islam. But they will generally follow those concessions with a statement of Christian superiority, suggesting, for example, that the Christian God is pure Reason while the Muslim God is pure Will.[4]

But there is another way to tell the story of Islam. This alternative telling emerges when we take seriously the historical impact of Constantine's vision in 312.

Whatever its source, inspiration, or legitimacy, Constantine's

---

2. It is interesting how seldom if ever anyone suggests that Constantine's vision was demonic in character, however one defines "demonic."

3. In *The Qur'an in the Light of Christ*, ed. Ron George (WIN Press, 2000), Fr. Giulio Basetti-Sani, a Franciscan missionary and scholar, describes his initial understandings of Islam in almost identical terms (pp. 20–26). He concludes, "These were the results I arrived at in 1941, when my sole purpose in studying Islam was to disprove it, to destroy an enemy. It was an enemy because I could not understand it and, hence, was unable to love it. . . . This incapacity to comprehend Islam is a heritage of most Christians. It goes back, in part, to their childhood study of history. It is not easy to free ourselves from the tangle of prejudices which envelops our minds and of which we are not even conscious" (pp. 24–25). Later, one of his mentors disturbed his assumptions (as I described my mentor doing for me in Chapter 5) by offering two quotes. One was from Augustine: *Amor dat novos oculos* (Love sees with new eyes). The other was from St. John of the Cross: *Where there is no love put love, and you will find Love Himself*. Thanks to Jeff Burns for giving me this remarkable book.

4. This is the claim Pope Benedict seemed to be making in his famous Regensburg speech, recounted by Miroslav Volf in *Allah: A Christian Response* (New York: HarperOne, 2011), pp. 24–25. Both sides of the equation would be disputed by scholars in each religion, no doubt.

vision worked. Constantine and his successors did indeed conquer under the sign of the cross. Constantine's cross image was carried at the head of armies going into battle, as if to say, "Resistance is futile. You will be assimilated...or eliminated." The Roman Empire became the Roman Christian Empire, and all who opposed the Empire—and its violent imperial ways—were understood to oppose Christianity and Christ.

Imagine yourself someone outside the Roman Empire, an inhabitant of what we now call Ireland, Germany, Central Asia, or Arabia. How would you feel about this Roman Christian Empire whose expansive ambitions include plans to assimilate you? Wouldn't you see Rome and its religion as a threat, ready to conquer you, perhaps kill or enslave you if you resisted, force you to convert if you submitted, and happy to tax and conscript you for its wars if you surrendered?[5] Wouldn't you fear or resent this threatening superpower and its religious chaplaincy?

Now imagine you have had a real spiritual experience, an authentic vision from the God of Adam, Noah, Abraham, Moses, and Jesus. You want to live your life as a loyal follower of God, submitting your life to God's will. What should you do? Obviously, you should find the religion that proclaims faith in the God of Adam, Noah, Abraham, Moses, and Jesus, and join it. In other words, you should become a Christian. Right?

But on second thought, why would you want to affiliate with the religion of an empire that threatens your security, history, culture, and economy...and does so in Christ's name? If you do join the religion of the empire, won't your neighbors consider you a traitor or a potential collaborator with the enemy? If Rome attacks, won't they

5. Thomas Cahill, in *How the Irish Saved Civilization* (New York: Knopf, 1996), recounts a different response to the Roman empire: a life-and-death drive to immigrate into it, since the food provided slaves in the empire was better than starvation outside its borders.

wonder whose side you'll be on? Won't becoming a Christian mean becoming a traitor to your people, your homeland? How will your neighbors ever accept your message from God if it is wrapped up with the military exploits of your most dangerous neighbor? How can you yourself accept a religion promoted and imposed by a violent empire, a regime driven by values and means that contradict the teachings of Christ himself?

In that light, consider the experience of a forty-year-old Arabian nearly three centuries after Constantine. He had a series of visions that convinced him there are not many gods as all his countrymen believed, but only one. He came to believe that this one true and living God was the same God who had been revealed to Adam, Noah, Abraham, Moses, and Jesus. He believed God had spoken to humanity through these great men and that each one's teaching and example should be trusted and followed. God was calling him to bring this revelation to all his fellow Arabs, and to the whole world.[6] What was he to do?

For many reasons, he couldn't become Jewish.[7] Nor could he affiliate with the Roman Christians; that would be tantamount to an act of treason against his countrymen and an act of surrender to a hostile alien force, as we have seen. He had only one option: to articulate his vision of monotheistic faith outside the confines of both Judaism and Christianity. In doing so, he could affirm his affinity with Jews and Christians as fellow believers in one God, and he could commit

---

6. Just as Christian texts and the narratives they teach are disputed by critical scholars, there are a number of critical theories within the Islamic world that challenge this standard version of the origins of Islam. For example, for an introduction to the quest for the historical Mohammed, see the work of Andreas Goerke (http://www.andreas -goerke.de/goerke_historical_muhammad.pdf) and F. E. Peters, *Muhammad and the Origins of Islam* (SUNY Press, 1994).

7. For example, Mohammed's message included deep love and respect for Jesus as a great prophet. But after centuries of Christian anti-Semitism and in the aftermath of Constantine, his Jewish neighbors couldn't be expected to warm to that proposal.

to nonhostile relationships with them unless they tried to harm or colonize his followers. He could form especially close ties with non-Roman Christians, and he may in fact have done so, especially with the Syrian Christian community then in exile in Arabia.[8]

Now in telling the story in this way, I am not making claims for or against Mohammed and Islam. I am simply suggesting that Constantine gave Roman-Imperial Christians a compelling reason to reject Mohammed (since Mohammed didn't submit to the theopolitical entity Constantine had created) and Constantine also gave Mohammed a compelling reason to reject so-called orthodox Roman Christianity (since Christianity required submission to the Roman theopolitical system). So, we might say, Constantine played a pivotal role in the development of Islam as a separate religion three centuries later. Because of Constantine and his bejeweled spear-cross, the face of Christianity toward Mohammed was a hostile one, and the face of Islam has often mirrored that hostility ever since, as today's newspaper headlines attest.

When we situate Mohammed in this way, just outside the borders of a powerful so-called Christian empire that claimed divine authority to conquer under the sign of the cross, I trust we can interpret Mohammed's choices and convictions in a more sympathetic light.[9]

---

8. Ron George suggests that 30 percent of the Quran comes from Syrian Christian hymnody and therefore gives evidence to pre-Islamic origins (in his prologue to *The Qu'ran in the Light of Christ*, p. 8).

9. By the way, Christians who seek to vilify Mohammed by pointing out his "polygamous lifestyle" should remember that biblical heroes from Abraham to David were polygamous, too, and even in the Christian Roman Empire polygamy was widely practiced for many centuries. And those who criticize Mohammed by pointing to his military exploits, including conversion by the sword, should be equally outraged by the similar exploits of the so-called Christian kings and emperors of Europe, a few episodes of which this chapter will briefly recount. And those who criticize Mohammed's denial of the Trinity should remember the role of the doctrine in solidifying Imperial control over minds as well as bodies. They should also remember that the understanding of the Trinity rejected by Mohammed was a misunderstanding, one that should be rejected by true Christians as well. So, we might say that Christians misunderstand the Muslim

And when we see later generations of Islamic leaders imitating the behavior of Roman Imperial Christian leaders, rivaling and in many cases outcompeting them, perhaps we can interpret their behavior in a more sympathetic light too. They aren't simply "them." They are also a reflection of "us."

A brief survey of the history of Christian hostility would include Theodosius, who, just several decades after Constantine's conversion, prohibited the practice of any religion other than Christianity even in the privacy of one's home. Around AD 800 came Charlemagne, who, with the support of Pope Leo III, aimed to renew the Roman Empire, which had disintegrated and fragmented in the aftermath of a series of brutal barbarian invasions.[10] Among his many exploits on behalf of the *Imperium Christianum*, he imposed the death penalty for all Saxons who would not convert to Christianity.

We might skip ahead to the middle of the sixteenth century, in the age of the Conquistadors, when King Charles V of Spain called together a conference to discuss whether the enslavement of Native

---

rejection of a misunderstood version of the doctrine of the Trinity. For more on the latter, see Volf, *Allah: A Christian Response*, especially Chapter 2. There Volf summarizes an important line of argument from Nicholas of Cusa (1401–64) like this (p. 54): "Nicholas argued that the Qur'an is not denying the authentic Christian doctrine of the Trinity, but is rightly rejecting a bastardized version of this doctrine. He stated tersely and categorically: 'In the manner in which Arabs and Jews deny the Trinity, assuredly it ought to be denied by all.'"

10. We should not minimize the brutality of the Goths, Visogoths, and Huns, and then, some centuries later, the Vikings. Nor should we assume a posture of moral superiority over the medieval Christian kings for doing what they believed was necessary to defend themselves. Nor should we discount the tragic losses that came with the fall of the Roman Empire. The Pax Romana may have been brutal, but few if any would claim the Huns or Vikings brought something better for those they conquered. The point that must be made, though, is that during these difficult times, the Christian faith became deeply complicit with behaviors that seem irreconcilable with the teachings of Jesus. One thinks of Churchill's words about World War I: "When all was over, torture and cannibalism were the only two expedients that the civilized, scientific, Christian States had been able to deny themselves: and these were of doubtful utility."

Americans was Christian or not. Defending the enslaved Native Peoples was Bartoleme de las Casas. Defending the enslaving Conquistadores was Juan Gines de Sepulveda. Pope Paul III had already declared the Native Peoples capable of receiving the gospel, giving the Spanish conquest an air of exploitation-evangelism. The current question was whether the kind of enslavement Columbus had pioneered would receive official church endorsement.

In the course of his argument, Sepulveda claimed that Christ's parable of the wedding feast (in Matthew 22) required Christians to kill those who resist evangelization, to which Las Casas replied, "There is tremendous rashness, then, in presuming to prove by any means of [the wedding feast] parable that Christ commanded his Church that... it should use physical compulsion on unbelievers before the faith is preached to them." Las Casas was echoing the sentiments of a fellow Dominican, Antonio de Montesinos, who had written from the Taino homeland of Hispaniola some forty years earlier: "I am the voice crying in the wilderness... the voice of Christ in the desert of this island... [saying that] you are all in mortal sin... on account of the cruelty and tyranny with which you use these innocent people. Are these not men? Have they not rational souls? Must not you love them as you love yourselves?"[11] Although the sentiments of Montesinos and Las Casas seem obvious to us now, theirs was clearly the minority report in the era of the Conquistadores.

---

11. See Bonar Ludwig Hernandez, "The Las Casas–Sepulveda Controversy," http://userwww.sfsu.edu/~epf/journal_archive/volume_X,_2001/hernandez_b.pdf. The article continues, "These phrases, spoken in 1511 by Antonio de Montesinos, one of the first Dominicans to arrive in the island of Hispaniola, reflect that the Spaniards were not a monolithic band of greedy *conquistadores* who merely sought to exploit and kill the American Indians. On the contrary, the Spanish discovery and subsequent conquest of the New World inspired a serious, if not heated, intellectual controversy regarding the rationality and Christianization of the Indians."

Both Montesinos and Las Casas were ignored. So Sepulveda's brutal protocols continued on, in the name of Christ.

We could go on to explore similar debates in North America among colonial Protestants, debates which continue today, by the way, under the rubric of "American Exceptionalism."[12] And we could quickly expand to consider British colonialism in Africa and India, or Dutch colonialism in Africa and Indonesia.[13] We could look at the tragic effects of Christian anti-Semitism through history, and then consider the contemporary impact of Christian Zionism on US foreign policy and its impact on Palestinians under Israeli occupation. Through all these episodes we can trace a common theme: a profound, almost unconscious union between Christian faith and an imperial or colonizing mind-set, a mind-set that asserts one group of people has been chosen by God to rule over others, which is closely related to the theological conviction that one group of people— Us—carries God's blessing and favor in a way others do not.[14] Taken further, the chosen become children of God and light; the unchosen,

---

12. See my article "America the Exceptional," *Sojourners*, January 2012, available at http://brianmclaren.net/archives/blog/american-exceptionalism-continue.html, and Randy Woodley, "Jesus and American Exceptionalism," *Emergent Village Voice*, http://www.patheos.com/blogs/emergentvillage/2012/02/jesus-and-american -exceptionalism-by-randy-woodley/.

13. See Richard Hughes, *Myths America Lives By* (Champaign: University of Illinois Press, 2004) and *Christian America and the Kingdom of God* (Champaign: University of Illinois Press, 2009).

14. Kwame Bediako strikes an important balance: "The revival of religion [in Europe] towards the end of the eighteenth century which produced the profound sense of missionary obligation, seems also to have intensified this European self-confidence. More radical spirits, it is true, were not unaware of the religious blemishes of the Christian nations of Europe. William Carey, foremost protagonist of the missionary enterprise, was one who held no belief in the religious superiority of Europeans or of 'those who bear the Christian name.' But this in no way undermined the general conviction that the civilised culture and institutions of Europe owed their enlightened status to Christianity, itself the most 'civilised' of all religions" (*Theology and Identity* [Oxford: Regnum Books, 1992], p. 229).

the children of the devil and darkness. In the stark shadows of that duality, how could hostility *not* grow?

For a long time already, voices from the margins—like Montesinos and Las Casas—have been advocating an alternative vision, a minority report. That minority report dares to whisper the dream of a postcolonial, postimperial Christian identity. Their voices have been systematically suppressed or studiously ignored. But they refuse to be silent. Perhaps the time has come for more of us to listen, learn, confess, change, and add our voices to theirs. And perhaps, having done so, we can turn to our neighbors—including the physical descendants of the colonized and enslaved, and the spiritual descendants of Mohammed, Moses, the Buddha, and others—and say, "We're beginning to see it now. We're sorry. We're learning from our history. And at long last, we're changing. We have a long way to go, but we're beginning the long, slow process of repentance."

Until we face this deep-running current of imperial hostility in our Christian history, we will not be able to forge a robustly benevolent Christian identity. Doing so will be painful. Many will shrink back from it.

But if we face and embrace this pain, new creative possibilities will open before us. We will be able to creatively rearticulate our *core Christian doctrines* in fresh, faithful, and profound ways, healing hostility and nourishing benevolence. We will then be able to creatively renew our *essential Christian liturgies* so they fulfill their potential for spiritual formation. And then we will be able to rediscover our *compelling Christian mission,* so we can be energized with a new conviction of who and what we are sent into the world to be and do. To these three creative challenges—doctrinal, liturgical, and missional—we now turn.

PART II
THE DOCTRINAL CHALLENGE

Indeed, the word *doctrine*, a word fallen on hard times in contemporary culture, actually means a "healing teaching," from the French word for *doctor*. The creeds, as doctrinal statements, were intended as healing instruments, life-giving words that would draw God's people into a deeper engagement with divine things. When creeds become fences to mark the borders of heresy, they lose their spiritual energy. Doctrine is to be the balm of a healing experience of God, not a theological scalpel to wound and exclude people.

—*Diana Butler Bass*[1]

---

1. Diana Butler Bass, *Christianity after Religion* (New York: HarperOne, 2012), pp. 134–135.

V.I.P

1. - not abandoning
2. finding central truth (heart)
3. JC came to show us how to live, Love

"Today"
"The Way" (1st 3 c)
→ Age of Belief
→ 4 - 20 c Orthodoxy came in
– 385 AD killed by other Christians for believing wrong
– after Constantine 25,000 killed for "errors"
→ "Age of Spirit" 50 yr ago started replacing formal Rel.

Strong but living in "the way" Credo in benevolent?

Chapter 12

How the Doctrine of Creation Can Create Humankind(ness)

Old Turtle spoke. "The world you describe is not the world that has always been, Little One.... It is because it is so close to a great, whole truth that it has such beauty, and thus the people love it so.... It is the lost portion of that broken truth that the people need, if the world is to be made whole again."

"But where is the missing piece?" asked the Little Girl. "Can we put the truth back together again?"

—*Douglas Wood*[1]

As we've seen, much of the strong/hostile/oppositional identity we find in the Christian faith today springs from the history of Western Roman-Imperial Christianity in the tradition of the Emperor Constantine.[2] This tradition contains incalculable riches and preserves unfathomed values, but it also serves as host

---

1. From a beautiful picture book for children of all ages, called *Old Turtle and the Broken Truth*, a sequel to the equally beautiful *Old Turtle* (New York: Scholastic Press, 2003, 1992).

2. The term *Christendom* could be a rough synonym for Roman-Imperial Christianity in its Catholic and Protestant forms. Eastern Orthodoxy certainly has areas of overlap with Western Christendom, along with many differences.

for dangerous social and spiritual viruses. What might happen if we were to run our contemporary versions of Christian faith through a debugging program where we scanned for and removed all imperial viruses?

Such a debugging process would no doubt be long, hard, complex, and highly contested. Some would mock the process as a futile, simplistic, reactionary, anti-Constantine "fall of the church" exercise. Some would argue that it was actually God's plan for Christian faith to experience this kind of synthesis, empowering the word of the Lord with Constantine's sword. To remove Roman-Imperial elements, they would argue, would be to reduce or plunder the faith and to oppose God's providence.[3] Others might argue that if we purge Christianity of its imperial viruses, there would be virtually nothing of value left; the religion has little to offer beyond a legitimization for Greco-Roman philosophy and politics.[4] But many others, and I am among them, would argue that we have no moral option but to run the program, whatever the consequences, in sincere faith and hope that a more healthy, robust, humble, honest, and benevolent faith will emerge.

But that wouldn't solve all of our problems. True, much of our hostility arises from destructive Roman-Imperial bugs that hide deep in our software, so to speak. But we must admit that some of our hostility flows from the Bible itself, or at least from our interpretations and applications of the Bible. If we are going to envision, articulate, and embody a strong-benevolent Christian identity, we must be willing to critically revisit even those central Christian doctrines we believe to be firmly rooted in the Bible. We must courageously and humbly uncover the ways our doctrines have been used to foster hostil-

---

3. Arguments like these were made in response to my book *A New Kind of Christianity* (New York: HarperOne, 2010).

4. Some of the new atheists make this argument.

ity and violence in the past, and then respond in faithful, ethical ways. This will be delicate work, not to be entered into unadvisedly or lightly, perhaps more akin to brain or heart surgery than computer debugging.

You'll notice I didn't say "we must be willing to *abandon* our central Christian doctrines." That kind of abandonment, history shows pretty convincingly, produces the weak-benign versions of Christian identity that I am firmly rejecting right along with the strong-hostile versions. Instead of rejecting these doctrines, we need to rediscover, reenvision, and reformulate them in a postimperial, postcolonial, post-Christendom way.

I am tempted to indulge in a major tangent here—that is, the question of whether "doctrine as we know it" is in itself an imperial product. Has the very concept of *doctrine* as popularly understood become so full of imperial bugs that it needs to be deconstructed—not just specific doctrines, but the very concept of doctrine itself? Is *doctrine* as popularly understood a tool of imperial control—restricting not only freedom of speech but also freedom of thought, thus promoting exactly the kind of political submission that totalitarian regimes depend upon? Can *doctrine* be rediscovered along the lines proposed by Diana Butler Bass—as a *healing teaching*, drawing from the same etymological root as *doctor*? In other words, can the idea of doctrine itself be reformulated not as an instrument of mind control and social pacification, but as an instrument of healing—including healing from the diseases of empire?

This kind of rediscovery/reformulation process—regarding both specific doctrines and the concept of doctrine itself—has, in fact, been underway for some time, often led, not surprisingly, by Christians who have experienced the downsides of imperial Christianity. From what postcolonial thinkers call "the subaltern position," from

---

5. *Christianity after Religion*, p. 134.

fresh understanding

the position of "others" living under domination, these Christian leaders saw things in the Bible and Christian tradition that others in more privileged positions could not or would not see.[6] These subaltern voices have been joined by growing numbers of people like myself, descendants of the colonizers who live with a range of unearned, inherited imperial privileges conferred by passport, gender, language, and skin color. Guided by our new mentors from among the formerly colonized, we discover that the gospel of Jesus Christ can liberate those who have been privileged by imperial systems just as it liberates the oppressed victims of those systems.

Together, we are seeking fresh understandings of our theological heritage. The pathway forward, we know, must be a path of partnership, not domination or isolation. On this path, many who were last in line in the colonial era move to the front as leaders, and many who were teachers and leaders in the colonial context become students again, learning from those they previously presumed to teach.

What happens when participants in this postcolonial partnership seek to rediscover the core doctrines in Christian theology? How can doctrinal sources of hostility be transformed into resources for solidarity? How can doctrinal instruments of thought and speech control become instruments of healing and liberation?

---

6. In Africa, this process has been led in recent years by Bolaji Idowu of Nigeria, John Mbiti of Kenya, Mulago gwa Cikala Musharhamina and Mabiala Kenzo of Congo, Alan Boesak of South Africa, Emmanuel Katangole of Uganda, Kwame Bediako of Ghana, Lamin Sanneh of Gambia, Claude Nikondeha of Burundi, *and many others.* In Latin America, the process has been led by Rene Padilla, Ruth Padilla DeBorst, Elisa Padilla, Samuel Escobar, Justo Gonzalez, Gustavo Gutierrez, Jon Sobrino, Leonardo Boff, *and many others.* Also essential have been minority voices in the United States and elsewhere, including African-Americans like Dr. Martin Luther King Jr. and James Cone; Native Americans like Randy Woodley, Ray Aldred, Terry LeBlanc, and Richard Twiss; Asian-Americans like Rita Takashimi Brock, Namsoon Kang, and Soong-Chan Rah; and Latinos like Gabriel Salguero; *and many others.* Asian leaders (like Fr. Jojo Fung in Malaysia) and Middle Eastern leaders (like Jean Zaru, Naim Ateek, and Salim Munayer in Israel-Palestine) are also making major contributions. And the process has only begun.

Peaceful creation - divine image

one human family

The doctrine of creation is a logical place to start. Many of us in the West have grown accustomed to hearing the words "versus evolution" whenever the word *creation* is uttered, because for us the doctrine was important only in relation to centuries-long Euro-American hostilities between faith and science. But when we resituate the doctrine of creation in the context of interreligious hostility, it becomes incandescent with possibilities for enlightenment and healing.

For example, in stark contrast to many ancient creation myths, Genesis tells us that the universe does not begin in conflict and rivalry among the gods. It begins peacefully, in the creative words, "Let there be."[7] Through these words of permission, space and time open up to make room for the new and the other to exist...since all creation is, in this sense, "other than God." All human beings, together with all created things, have their origin in the same unfolding story of making space for the other. We wouldn't be here if it weren't for the creative hospitality of the God who is host, not hostile, to the other.

Within that spacious story, all human beings share the same divine image. All human beings are, ultimately, sisters and brothers in one human family created in the image of God. As Douglas Wood's profound children's story *Old Turtle and the Broken Truth* makes clear, "God loves us" is only a fragment of the truth, a dangerous fragment, in fact; it must be reunited with "God loves others too."[8] We live within a relationship of diversity without division: *all equals*

---

7. The Mesopotamian source myths, grounded in conflict and violence, are creatively adapted in the Hebrew Scriptures, although their chaotic presence can be discerned in many places, just beneath the surface.

8. Wood's actual words for the first fragment are "You are loved," and for the second, "and so are they." The Lord's Prayer, it seems to me, creates this same healing of fractured truth when it asks for forgiveness for "our sins" and simultaneously forgives the sins of our oppressors, as does the Sermon on the Mount when it calls us to love our enemies, mirroring the compassionate perfection of God that loves both "the just and the unjust." In this world of ecological crisis and alienation from "nature," we must add that "and so are they" refers to nonhuman creatures and even to nonliving creations.

we are dif but related; distinct but united

we are made on the same creation day as the reptiles and cattle, for example, and we are formed from the same dust. All living things are different but related, distinct but united. Similarly, male and female are not two warring factions; one is not superior and the other inferior: we are different but related, distinct but united.

This creation, then, is a garden of harmony, not a war zone of hostility. It comes equipped, not with oppositional religions that divide, but rather with a naked spirituality that includes and unifies all things in one fabric of creation. Trees and rivers, sky and stars declare God's glory for everyone; exclusive temples and members-only cathedrals are unnecessary. And so, according to our doctrine of creation, we are created by God to live in harmony with God and with all creation in all its wild diversity. We are created for harmony with one another, meaning "one with the other," male with female, us with them, in dynamic unity without uniformity—different but not divided, distinct but related and unified. What doctrine could better orient us toward a strong and benevolent identity?

Sadly, though, when many Christians hear "doctrine of creation," they don't think of this stage set for otherliness, hospitality, harmony, and solidarity. They think of hostility—between religion and science, faith and reason, creation and evolution, and little more.[9]

The doctrine of creation has been broken into sharp and dangerous shards. It must be put back together again into a beautiful and harmonizing whole. In that way, it can become a healing teaching of unimagined power.

Sun dials

9. On the subject of evolution *and* faith (rather than *versus*), see the work of Michael Dowd (http://www.thankgodforevolution.com), especially *Thank God for Evolution* (New York: Plume, 2009). For a theology of evolution, see John Haught (http://web .mac.com/haughtj1/Site/Welcome.html), especially *God after Darwin* (Boulder: Westview Press, 2007).

CONFIRMATION, UNIVERSAL ALIENATION, AND THE ADULT POSTURE

Chapter 13

How the Doctrine of (Un)Original Sin Can Help Christians Be Less Sinful

The doctrine of original sin is a parting glance at the unnecessary nature of what we are ceasing to be.

—*James Alison*[1]

Imagine the doctrine of creation as a beautiful mountain range, visible from our picture window and front porch, a constant inspiration, a timeless reminder of our ancestry and our destiny as well.

Then imagine a fleet of trucks pulling up in front of our home, workers pouring out, chainsaws sawing and hammers hammering, scaffolding rising, clouds of dust and sawdust filling the air. A few hours later the workers clean up and the trucks depart, having constructed a huge billboard that now completely blocks our view of the mountain. On this side of the billboard, original harmony, original goodness, and original blessing are only a tragic memory. We can see only garish colors and huge, bold letters that declare UNIVERSAL

---

1. From "Being Saved and Being Wrong," http://www.jamesalison.co.uk/texts/eng18 .html.

CONDEMNATION, UNIVERSAL ALIENATION, AND UNIVERSAL HOSTILITY.

This billboard slogan, many knowledgeable theologians will argue, is not a proper understanding of the doctrine of original sin. And I agree. The proper understanding of the ancient doctrine intends to detour us away from several theological dead ends and washed-out roads that were encountered in the first several centuries of Christian history. We would be foolish to discard the doctrine and waste our time repeating those theological misadventures. Our problem isn't the *proper* understanding of the doctrine: our problem is the *popular* understanding of it. The two differ greatly, and sadly, holding the former doesn't automatically undo the damage caused by the latter.

The doctrine of original sin, as *popularly* understood, suggests that God views all humankind (and, for some, the whole created order) with hostility because it has lapsed from its original perfection. According to this popular understanding, God's particular form of perfection requires God to punish all imperfect beings with eternal conscious torment in hell. So in this popular view of original sin, God's response to anything that is less than absolutely perfect must be *absolute and infinite hostility*.

It might sound like good news, a sort of reprieve, to add that God forgives and saves a select few. For the select few, what could be better news than the promise that they will enjoy God's gracious gift of love and heaven forever, while their "unsaved" counterparts can only look forward to God's absolute hostility in an eternal hell? Good Christians by the millions believe exactly this (often under the threat that if they don't believe it, they will be consigned to an eternity among their counterparts). The gospel itself is thus a solution to the problem of original sin, understood in this way.

But how do we good Christians handle the heady belief that we are among the select few being saved from original sin? I've spent a lifetime both experiencing and observing the answer.

Baptism

First, we sing and speak with deep and sincere passion about how blessed and humbled we are to be chosen by God's sovereign grace alone, through no merit of our own. We rejoice with unspeakable joy to know ourselves as objects of God's mercy, and this grateful joy is heightened every time we contrast our bright destiny with the horrible doom of all those who remain objects of God's hostility.

Second, we learn to imitate the complex attitude that we understand God to have toward the fallen/unredeemed/sinners/infidels/unsaved/non-Christians around us. On the one hand, we know God loves them, and so we try to love them, too. But on the other hand, we know God finds them dirty, dangerous, depraved, and unacceptable, and so we imitate God's aversion, as we understand it. We try to love the sinners but hate the sin that permeates their lives. Some of us manage that dynamic tension more gracefully than others. Meanwhile, we show to our fellow Christians the same preferential option that we believe God shares: it's our fellow Christians who really matter, to God and so to us. And then we remind ourselves that the unsaved and unredeemed—they matter, too, in the sense that God wants them to join us. If they refuse, then . . . it's complicated.

Third, we translate these learned attitudes into actions and words. We welcome our fellow Christians (at least the ones we have been taught to see as members of our tribe) into our shared inner circle. We are good to each other. We try to conform all our interactions to a high and holy ideal. We fill our schedules with activities related to Christian fellowship. We love Us. And what about Them—Muslims, Hindus, atheists, Buddhists? For some of us, our aversion to "the other" carries the scent of fire and brimstone—a furious and fierce hostility that sends us into the world as culture warriors determined to vanquish the godless "other." Others of us are more defensive than aggressive in our reaction to those still imprisoned in original sin; they pose a constant threat against which we must protect ourselves with unflagging vigilance, which requires us to create

James Alison 5 key concepts

108 • Why Did Jesus, Moses, the Buddha, and Mohammed Cross the Road?

our own schools, radio and TV stations, political parties, and amusement parks. For others of us, our aversion has the more refined air of aloofness—we keep our polite distance, minimizing contact, holding "them" at arm's length, observing a kind of spiritual quarantine. For still others of us, our aversion is sweetened with pity, compassion, and duty—often motivating us to befriend them in order to evangelize them, in hopes they too can become one of us before it's too late.

Whichever path we take, though, we can be sure that to "the others" themselves, our doctrine of original sin, at least as popularly understood and translated into attitude and action, does not turn us into good neighbors.

But again, I do not propose we simply jettison the doctrine. Rather, I believe we need to get a fresh understanding of original sin—like the one offered by Catholic theologian James Alison. Drawing from the seminal theories of Rene Girard, Alison presents a doctrine of original sin that undermines a strong-hostile Christian identity, rejects a weak-benign Christian identity, and builds a strong-benevolent Christian identity. I summarize this fresh approach in terms of five key concepts.

1. Imitation: Human beings are by nature imitative (or mimetic) creatures. We aren't born with a large repertoire of instincts as most mammals are; we learn to survive by imitating others—from speaking to using spoons to driving. Even desire is imitative. A child learns what berries to desire as food and what berries to avoid as poison by imitating the desire and aversion of others, just as an adult learns what car to drive or what neighborhood to avoid by imitating the desire and aversion of others. Mimetic desire drives our survival and our economy as well.

2. Rivalry: When desire is mimetic, predictable problems arise. Whatever you desire, I desire. So if you want that cookie, that

bicycle, that girlfriend, that house in that neighborhood, that status in the community, or that fertile farmland, so do I. You start as my model for imitation, but when I compete with you to achieve the object of our now-shared desire, I become your rival (or vice versa).

3. Anxiety: Since I am most likely to imitate those closest at hand, then my parents, my siblings, my spouse, or my friends and I can most easily become rivals. And since rivalry often leads to violence, I face a unique threat: not the expected violence of a stranger or an enemy, but the unexpected violence of an envious companion. Not only that, but I may become the perpetrator of violence against those I envy. And since human beings are mimetic by nature, we imitate one another in violence, with disastrous consequences that easily spiral out of control. This threat of spiraling violence produces growing anxiety in any social system.

4. Scapegoating: When social anxiety reaches a critical point, it seeks an outlet. That outlet may be in an explosion of social disintegration—every person turning on his neighbor. But human societies have repeatedly discovered a less costly, less destructive option. One member (or one subgroup) of the group is identified as different in some way, and that difference provides the reason to exclude, banish, harm, or ultimately kill the victim. All imitate one another in shared aversion toward and violence against the victim—or scapegoat—and in so doing, all experience a catharsis of anxiety and a euphoria of unity. Potential disintegration has been replaced with unity, a unity that seems supernatural or magical in its power.[2]

---

2. Girardians use the term *sacred* to describe this supernatural, magical power of scapegoating. In Girardian conversation, *sacred* always carries with it the vestigial scent of violence.

5. Ritualization: Since a focused release of violence on an innocent victim produces such a useful result, societies find ways to
repeat this kind of unifying, cathartic violence preemptively,
so to speak. In primitive societies, human sacrifice becomes
a regular event presided over by a special class of priests. In
more ordered societies, animals are substituted for humans,
or human victims may be banished, defeated, enslaved, or
ghettoized rather than killed, and so on. Religious and political systems (and sports leagues) become the curators of our
rivalry-management mechanisms. They seek to keep the peace
by (a) providing mechanisms for the focused release of cathartic, unifying violence against a scapegoat of some kind, and
(b) pronouncing prohibitions on behaviors that would lead to
outbreaks of unmanageable, disintegrating rivalry.

How might a fresh understanding of original sin be articulated in
these terms? It would say that all human beings are caught in these
subtle webs of destructive imitation, rivalry, anxiety, scapegoating,
and ritualization. No sphere of life is untouched by these mechanisms; even our systems of religion and government are implicated.
No individual is pristine; all are complicit to some degree. As a result,
our very identity as human beings and as individuals has been distorted from the image envisioned in the doctrine of creation.

In this fresh light, the rich imagery of Genesis shimmers and spar-
kles as never before.[3] Adam and Eve were made to bear the image
of God—loving, generous, harmonious, beautiful, hospitable, creative, good. As God's image bearers, they were called to a constructive imitation ... exercising the benevolent stewardship over creation
modeled by the Creator who is host, not hostile, to otherness. But to

---

3. For more on Girardian readings of Scripture, arranged according to the Common
Lectionary, see Paul Nuechterlein's monumental contribution at http://girardianlec
tionary.net/.

bear God's image is not enough for them: they want to "be like God." They cease imitating God as model and become God's rivals, imitating the serpent's desire for the forbidden fruit.

This descent quickly renders them rivals to one another, too. They are no longer "naked but not ashamed" in front of one another; they have something to fear. That fear materializes as blame as well as shame as they become one another's accusers.

Their sons play out these destructive mechanisms. Soon sibling rivalry leads to fratricide. Cain is a settled farmer; Abel is a nomadic herder. But East of Eden, difference can no longer exist without division and hostility. So Cain must identify himself over against his brother, who has forged a different way of life and a different form of religion. After murdering the rival other, Cain naturally fears that others will imitate him and do the same to him. Not insignificantly, Cain then builds a city, suggesting that civilization itself is built on the dirty work of rivalry-driven murderers. Even God seems overwhelmed by the violence of civilization, wishing the whole creative project had never been started, and seeking to wash it all away.[4]

At Babel, humans seek to overcome difference with sameness (a classic imperial move, by the way), but God intervenes on the side of diversity. The story continues with more rivalry (Sarah and Hagar, Isaac and Ishmael, Jacob and Esau, Joseph and his brothers) and more violence. Slavery enters the story—the dramatic reduction of my brother or sister, made in the image of God, into a tool made in the image of my desire.

And so the beauty of creation—difference without division,

---

4. Because this is a brief overview, I can't pause to address all the moral ambivalence in the text—surrounding, for example, the flood narrative. I addressed some dimensions of this ambivalence in *A New Kind of Christianity* (New York: HarperOne, 2010), and we will return to the question of hostility and violence in the Bible in Chapter 22. For all its brevity and simplicity, I hope this overview of Genesis models a way of taking the text seriously without taking it literally, and of celebrating its actuality without arguing about its factuality.

Joseph forgives

112 • Why Did Jesus, Moses, the Buddha, and Mohammed Cross the Road?

diversity with harmony—recedes further and further from human grasp. It might help to think in terms of copying a document or file: all sin today is a copy, an imitation, a replication of this original departure from the aboriginal goodness. In this sense, there is nothing less original than sin because sin is utterly derivative, utterly imitative. We are all implicated in this brutal, devolving unoriginality, and there is no escape from dismal, degrading cycles of mimicry apart from a return to the creative goodness that is even more original than sin.

The book of Genesis would be a tragic epic of despair if it did not hold out exactly this hope in its final chapters. Joseph's brothers play out the script of original sin with vigor—imitative desire producing rivalry leading to violent plots of murder and enslavement. Joseph in the end survives all plots against him, and he forgives and rescues the very violent brothers who at first wanted to kill him. Joseph refuses to imitate the hatred of his rival brothers. Instead, he returns to the imitation of God whose will, Joseph knows, is always benevolent.[5] He steps out of the flow of original sin, so to speak, holding out the hope that with God's help, we can get back to the garden, so to speak, to live in solidarity, not hostility.

So what is a proper understanding of original sin? It is the crisis of identity that emerges as we reject our original God-given name…our original identity as soil creatively organized into "the image of God," within the original harmony and hospitality of creation. Whenever we try to climb above that identity, we fall below it. In grasping at superhumanity, we become subhuman. We become slaveholders who dehumanize others and so also dehumanize ourselves. We become plunderers of the earth who impoverish ourselves permanently in our foolish pursuit of short-term gain. We spin webs of violence in which we ourselves become stuck. We lose our identities as recipients and

---

5. Joseph realizes in the end that although human intentions are evil, God's intentions are good (Gen. 50:20), and so he imitates God's goodness, grace, and generosity.

imitators of the original divine benevolence. We lose our identities as apprentices of God. We lose our identities as fellow creatures in a beautiful creation. Instead, we each forge a distorted, hostile, oppositional identity—rivals with God, rivals with our spouses, rivals with our siblings, rivals with our fellow creatures, positioning ourselves over against creation instead of in and with it.

In this light, the choice between the two trees in the Garden of Eden takes on fresh significance. The tree of the knowledge of good and evil represents a godlike knowing that infects the consumers of its fruit with the tendency to accuse, to judge, and to condemn *the other* as evil and to crown *us* as good. The tree of life, in contrast, nourishes in us the ability to live in benevolent relationship—not accusing the other for being different, not judging or shaming the other for being naked, not condemning the other for being what it is, but rather living with the other in the divine and hospitable harmony of kindness.[6]

I hope it's becoming clear: the popular understanding of original sin too often aids and abets in the expansion of sin. It promotes a dualistic, judgmental, accusatory mind-set that embeds in us an oppositional identity that in turn breeds hostility and rivalry, thus fomenting the very sin it intended to expose and oppose. In contrast, however, a proper understanding of original sin exposes hostility and rivalry as the origins of sin, and so prepares the way for us to rediscover a strong-benevolent Christian identity. Instead of a billboard that obscures creation's original harmony, we might think of this understanding as a set of binoculars that helps us peer across the distance to see how good that original goodness was—and to feel it beckoning us, no matter how far we are from it now. This understanding of original sin resurrects rather than obscures the doctrine of

---

6. Thanks to Lutheran preacher Nadia Bolz-Weber for this insight from Dietrich Bonhoeffer; see "Joyless Christians and the Lord of the Rings" at: http://blog.sojo .net/2011/07/13/joyless-christians-and-the-lord-of-the-rings/.

creation, and it makes way for a resurrection of every other Christian doctrine, too—resurrecting each doctrine as a healing teaching that reveals our truest identity.

If, in our ancient narratives, a serpent once tempted us to eat from the tree that would allow us to pronounce *us* good and *them* evil, perhaps we need a new narrative today in which a beautiful songbird sings from the tree of life, inviting us to eat again of its original fruit: love, joy, peace, patience, kindness, goodness, gentleness, faithfulness, and self-control.

Chapter 14

How the Doctrine of Election (or Chosen-ness) Can Help Christians Choose Benevolence

We have just enough religion to make us hate but not enough to make us love one another.

—*Jonathan Swift*[1]

In May 2008, I participated in a gathering in Kigali, Rwanda, in East Africa, a setting of Edenic natural beauty. Scattered among the green hills and fertile farms all around us were museums and memorial sites recalling the hellish genocide that had erupted there fourteen years earlier—an orgy of rivalry, hostility, and violence. If there is a baptism into original sin, the Rwandese had experienced it. The Burundians and Ugandans present also knew the depths of human depravity firsthand through recent tragic decades of hostility and violence. Several dozen Kenyans were also present, all of them still traumatized by a recent outbreak of intertribal, post-election violence. Their psychological scars were still fresh, with

---

1. From the *Miscellanies* (1711–1726).

many of them still living in Internally Displaced Persons camps, their homes having been burned by their neighbors of different tribes.

I had lunch one day with a middle-aged widow who had been the co-pastor of a Pentecostal church in a small Kenyan village. Through tears she told me of the night five months earlier when there was a knock on her door. A crowd of people holding gasoline cans had gathered in her front yard. They told her it was time for all people of her tribe to leave their town. As she escaped through the crowd with nothing but the clothes on her back, she noticed many of her parishioners and, most heartbreaking of all, she saw the co-pastor among them as well. Fires were lit. The house was destroyed. She had been in an IDP camp ever since.

I asked her what her plans were. "I am going back," she said softly. "I have nowhere else to go. That is my village. That is my congregation. That man, even though he is from another tribe, and in spite of what he did, is still my colleague in ministry and my brother in Christ. I will return and rebuild my home. And somehow we must try to be reconciled to one another. With human beings this is impossible, but with God all things are possible." She paused, then added, "It may be difficult, yes, and there will be much heartbreak, but reconciliation must be possible."

The next day I was supposed to address the group.[2] What could I say to people in this kind of pain? Prayerfully and in fear and trembling, I drew stories from the Bible to illustrate seven possible relationships between Us and Them.[3]

---

2. For more on this network of emerging African Christian leaders, see http://www.amahoro-africa.org.

3. I have adapted and summarized this material in a short chapter called "Finding the Seventh Story," in *2010Boston: The Changing Contours of World Mission and Christianity* (Eugene, Ore.: Wipf and Stock, 2012).

Possibilities

Domination: Us over Them—This is the classic imperial/colonial narrative, based on the assumption that *we* can be safe and well only if we are in control.[4]

Revolution: Us overthrowing Them—This is the counterpart to the domination narrative, asserting that we can be safe and well only if *they* are no longer in control. If the revolution is successful, We often adopt the Domination Narrative that formerly animated our oppressors, and They adopt the Revolution Narrative that formerly animated us.[5]

Assimilation: Us absorbing Them—This narrative is based on the assumption that sometimes the best way to eliminate Them is by converting them to Us.[6]

Purification: Us eliminating Them—This is the narrative of ethnic cleansing and genocide that issues this ultimatum: you will either convert (Assimilation) or leave (as refugees) or be killed (via genocide).[7] It often focuses on a small minority and functions as a scapegoating narrative.

---

4. In the Bible, the Israelites experienced domination by the Egyptians, the Babylonians, the Assyrians, the Medo-Persians, and the Romans.

5. In the Gospels, the Zealots represented a group living by the Revolution Narrative, seeking a violent overthrow and expulsion of the Romans. The Pharisees were their close allies.

6. In the Book of Daniel, when the Babylonians required Shadrach, Meshach, and Abednego to eat a Babylonian diet, or when they required the Jewish deportees to worship Babylonian gods, they were attempting assimilation.

7. The Book of Ezra ends with a purification narrative, as Hebrew men are told to divorce their "foreign wives." The Pharisees exemplify this narrative as well in their condemnation of Jesus for eating with "the unclean." "Tax collectors and sinners" were their scapegoats. (It's worth noting how the Pharisees themselves—a complex group with an oft-misunderstood history—are frequently scapegoated by Christians due to their consistently negative portrayal in the gospels. This negative stereotyping has then been used across Christian history to vilify all Jewish people and Judaism in general. It remains for Christian scholars and communicators to revisit the Pharisees and recount their history in a more balanced and fair way.)

Competition: Us competing with Them—In this narrative, we coexist but see one another as rivals. We don't aspire to dominate, overthrow, eliminate, assimilate, or expel—just to outcompete and stay in a superior position of competitive advantage.[8]

Victimization/self-preservation: Us oppressed by Them—This is the narrative of those who have been defeated (by Domination), expelled (by Purification), survived pressures to abandon their identity (by Assimilation), or been weakened and marginalized (by Competition).[9] Survival is the primary focus upon which everything depends.

Isolation: Us apart from Them—Whether by migrating to another geographical location or by creating a distinct and insular subculture, this narrative argues for separation and avoidance of the other.[10]

After briefly explaining these common framing stories, I stepped back and invited participants to respond, and the discussion was electric. Members of various tribes in various countries seized upon this new language. It helped them, they said, to understand the tragic hostilities that plagued them. They could immediately sense

---

8. As we've already seen, sibling rivalry is a key theme in Genesis. More broadly speaking, the Book of Acts (Chapter 6) tells the story of foreign widows being marginalized in favor of "native" widows in the early church. And James preached against another expression of competition (James 2, 5)—condemning favoritism for the rich and the marginalization of the poor, using language that would probably earn him the label *socialist* or *communist* today.

9. Many of Jesus' countrymen saw themselves as victims, especially in Galilee, where they were victimized by both the Romans and the Judean elite who collaborated with the Romans. See Richard Horsley, *Jesus and Empire* (Minneapolis: Fortress Press, 2002).

10. Cultural separateness was maintained among the ancient Israelites through purity codes and strict adherence to the Torah, buttressed by their understanding of themselves as "clean" and of Gentiles as "unclean." Baptism originated (as we will see later) as a ritual of maintaining this isolation. Various separatist communities (like the Essenes, with whom John the Baptist shared certain similarities) pursued physical isolation by relocating to the wilderness region near the Dead Sea.

how these narratives formed strong identities in their tribes and how these strong identities in turn fomented the volatile social and political chemistry in which they lived.

"But is there an alternative?" they asked. "Is there any other identity that is open to us?" In reply, I directed them to a fresh view of another key Christian doctrine: the doctrine of election or choosing or vocation. This is the doctrine by which we define "us" as "the people of God." In its many popular forms, of course, the doctrine is causing all kinds of mischief and hostility. It serves as a theological justification for the seven hostile narratives we've just considered.

For example, a distorted doctrine of chosen-ness tells many sincere but misguided Christian Zionists that the Jews have been chosen by God to own certain land without concern for the well-being of their non-Jewish neighbors.[11] As a result, these Christians fervently support Israel in a Domination Narrative, justifying the continued military occupation of the West Bank and Gaza. They may even support the Purification Narrative that inspires some Israeli settlers and political parties to drive Palestinian Muslims and Christians from their homes, whether through sudden expulsion or gradual colonization and appropriation. These well-meaning Christians, often seeking to redress the horrible legacy of Christian Anti-Semitism, seem to have forgotten that the Domination script is not the way of Jesus. They forget how sincere Christians in South Africa abused the same doctrine of chosen-ness to justify apartheid, or how Christians in the United States used the same doctrine of chosen-ness to justify unnumbered crimes against Native Americans and African-Americans, or how Christian anti-Semites through the centuries used this doctrine to justify their unconscionable treatment of their Jewish neighbors in the first place.

---

11. The term *Zionism* is fraught with complexity. Here I am only critiquing the popular, superficial form of it that is common in American religious broadcasting and politics.

dynamic evolving story

120 • Why Did Jesus, Moses, the Buddha, and Mohammed Cross the Road?

Can the doctrine of chosen-ness be reformulated, and if so, how? If we return to the Bible, we see that the original calling of creation is a call to diversity, a call to blessedness, to fruitfulness, and to multiplication "after their kind." "Let there be," then, makes room for an evolving community of perpetual diversity. Each "kind" has a right to exist—and it has no right to deprive other kinds of their God-given right to exist. We might say that God's original calling to each species was not to domination, revolution, purification, assimilation, competition, victimization, or isolation—but to creative participation in a dynamic and evolving story whose source, unfolding, and destiny was in God.

But in the aftermath of original sin (properly understood) in Genesis 3–11, that original vocation to creative participation has been compromised and distorted by rivalry and scapegoating. So in Genesis 12, we find a new paradigm: God calls and commissions Abraham to a new and unique role—to a strong-distinct but nonhostile identity. God calls Abraham to leave his father's house (the source of his identity to date) in Ur (a center of the Domination Narrative for the Chaldean empire) and to venture into unknown territory— *other* suggestive of the forging of a new identity. In other words, God calls Abraham to become "other"—other than his father's house, other than the ethnic, political, and religious identity into which he had been born. In that otherness, God promises to make of Abraham's descendants "a great nation" with a great name—the word *great* suggesting, among other things, the strength of identity we have been grappling with in these pages.

But that great or strong identity isn't cast in hostility to other nations. Abraham's identity is not greatness exploiting others (domination), greatness overthrowing others (revolution), greatness absorbing others (assimilation), greatness excluding others (purification), greatness resenting others (victimization), greatness separated from others (isolation), or greatness at the expense of others (compe-

Abraham moves — different, resisting normal

Result = overthrowing, controlling

tition). Abraham's greatness is *for the sake of* others: *And all nations on earth will be blessed through you.*

This calling might sound noble, but it won't be easy. Yes, some will bless Abraham's tribe. But others will curse them—curse them for being different, curse them for resisting empire, curse them for not imitating the typical scripts of "normal" societal narratives. And so, God says, as others treat Abraham, so they will be treated: *I will bless those who bless you, and whoever curses you I will curse.* But even so, blessing will have the last word: *all nations on earth will be blessed through you.*

Sadly, Christians, Muslims, and Jews, for all their differences, have imitated one another again and again in misunderstanding and misapplying this doctrine of chosen-ness. Rather than receiving God's call as a vocation *to be the other for the sake of others*, they have received the call to be *us* controlling, *us* overthrowing, *us* absorbing, *us* distancing, *us* expelling, *us* outcompeting, *us* resenting . . . rather than *us being a blessing to others.*

But doesn't being a blessing imply a kind of superiority? Isn't there a kind of exclusivism, elitism, or at least paternalism inherent in being chosen by God? Interestingly, the unfolding narrative of the Book of Genesis conspires against this common misunderstanding. After receiving this promise of and vocation to a new kind of identity, Abraham sets out on his journey. After a brief (and nonviolent) stay in Canaan, he is forced by famine to Egypt, where he survives through the gracious hospitality of the Egyptians—the one who will be a blessing to others is not above being blessed by others. He refuses to enter into rivalry with his relative Lot and takes the "leftover" land, giving his potential competitor the advantage of first choice.

When a domination-revolution conflict breaks out and Lot's family is captured in the hostilities, Abraham goes into battle to rescue them and then refuses to be drawn further into the hostile us-them politics of the region. He soon encounters a strange character *mutuality abraham*

identified as Melchizedek, the King-Priest of Salem—of Shalom or Peace. Melchizedek shows hospitality to Abraham and blesses him, and Abraham reciprocates with a generous gift. This is an encounter of mutuality, not hostility; of neighborliness, not us-versus-otherness. Abraham's unique calling doesn't send him into the world with an exclusive, elitist, or paternalistic attitude: it sends him out with a strong, *benevolent* identity.

So in just a few chapters, we see Abraham journeying out of hostile identities and moving into the alternative identity to which God has called him. In the chapters to come, the story gets even more interesting with a second visitation-vocation (15:1–21) and then a third (18:1–15). The story of Hagar and Ishmael is a painful study in otherness, driven by rivalry between Sarah and her Egyptian slave Hagar. (It's not insignificant that the Egyptian people who will forever be known as the enslavers of the Israelites were, in Hagar, first introduced through one who was the enslaved.) When Hagar is treated as a despised "other" by Sarah, the Lord intervenes on Hagar's behalf and makes a promise to Hagar that shows she is of concern to the Lord as well: *I will so increase your descendants that they will be too numerous to count.* The Lord names him Ishmael, meaning *God hears*—and Hagar responds by naming God *The One Who Sees Me.*[12] So it must never be forgotten that God sees and hears the other.

Sarah vs Hagar

---

12. God pronounces a blessing on Hagar and Ishmael (Gen. 16:11ff.) that has become highly problematic in Jewish-Christian-Muslim relations. Not surprisingly, it is also notoriously problematic to translate. The blessing ostensibly calls Ishmael a "wild ass," although some say the translation should be "fruitful man" (which is more in keeping with verse 10). It continues (in the NRSV), "with his hand against everyone, and everyone's hand against him; and he shall live at odds with all his kin." But a reputable Jewish translation is far less dismissive: "And he will be a wild donkey of a man; his hand will be upon all, and everyone's hand upon him, and before all his brothers he will dwell" (http://www.chabad.org/library/bible.asp?aid=8211&showrashi=true). Some interpreters go even further, saying the Hebrew preposition translated by some as "against" and others as "upon" should actually be translated "with." The contested interpretations mirror the competing attitudes toward "the other" with which the text struggles.

Sarah's rivalry with Hagar resurges years later, after she has given
birth to Isaac. Abraham is father of both Ishmael and Isaac and is
distressed by the rivalry, but God assures Abraham that God will
bless Ishmael even if Sarah doesn't (21:13). Again Hagar is driven off,
this time with her boy, and again God comes to their rescue.

The whole book of Genesis—and indeed the whole Bible—
struggles with this issue of "us-ness" and "otherness." With Ishmael
and Isaac as with Cain and Abel, the other is brother, and both are
beloved by God. For Isaac to have a unique blessing does not mean
Ishmael can't also have a blessing of his own. For one to receive a
special vocation from God doesn't mean that others haven't also
received their own vocations. Centuries later, the prophet Amos will
remind his people of the same truth:

> "Are you not like the Ethiopians to me, O people of Israel?" says
> the Lord. "Did I not bring Israel up from the land of Egypt, and the
> Philistines from Caphtor, and the Arameans from Kir?" (Amos 9:7)

So to be blessed by the true and living God of all creation is not
an either-or thing; it is a both-and thing. God had a unique vocation
both for Israel *and* for the Ethiopians. God liberated *both* the Israelites *and* the Philistines and Arameans from their oppressors.[13] The
doctrine of calling, election, or chosen-ness has indeed been abused
as a vicious weapon of hostility. But we can rediscover it as an instrument of peace, an instrument of blessing. To do so will require us,

13. Jonathan Tran, reviewing important works by J. Kameron Carter and Willie J. Jen-
nings, writes: "Jewish flesh is most authentically itself when it welcomes the gentile.
This hospitality enacts what Carter calls 'the theodramatic constitution of existence.'
In the same way that God elects and receives Israel, elected Israel receives the gentiles
as an extension of God's reception history. 'Israel's meaning and significance,' writes
Carter, 'arise out of its being related to the nations before whom the drama of the Jews'
election unfolds. The drama of Israel thus is not insular, for it unfolds in such a way as
to enfold the nations into its drama'" ("The New Black Theology," *Christian Century*,
January 26, 2012, http://christiancentury.org/article/2012-01/new-black-theology).

like Abraham, to make a radical break with the hostile identities we inherited—identities of domination, revolution, assimilation, purification, competition, victimization, and isolation. It will require us to venture out—"not knowing where we are going"—learning to embody a new, strong identity, an identity of mission and reconciliation: blessed to be a blessing, others for the sake of others, giving and receiving blessings with other blessed people, and thus joining God in healing a world torn by human hostility.[14]

[handwritten annotations:]

Mission & recognition of reconciliation

— others for the sake of others
— giving & receiving blessings
— joining God in healing a world torn apart by human hostility

_____

14. In 2 Cor. 5 and 6, Paul depicts this unique identity in the image of peace ambassadors. We who are "in Christ" have a special identity—but that identity is not as a new "us" in rivalry with "them." We are sent as peace ambassadors seeking to bring everyone into reconciliation with God and one another. Our whole mission can thus be summed up as "the ministry of reconciliation."

Chapter 15

How the Doctrine of the Trinity Can Foment Harmony and Unity

Commonality

For it is in the depths, as Paul Ricouer insists, that we "touch on something unsaid...a mystical ground (*un fond mystique*) of what is most fundamental in each religion and which is not easily translatable into language but rather borders on a common profound silence." In other words, the best way to tackle the violent tendency within religious conviction is to go all the way down to the source that religion does not master and that refuses to be rendered into dogmatic formulae or ideological manifestos.... It is in this hearkening to a source beyond and beneath oneself, a superfluity one does not possess or manipulate, that we may find new resources for nonviolent resistance and peace.

—*Richard Kearney*[1]

I was sitting on the balcony of a high-rise hotel room in Southern California. The Pacific Ocean sparkled under a smog-free sky. A rabbi we'll call Sol was enjoying the view with me. I had originally met Sol a few years earlier through a phone call: "I represent a group of several dozen rabbis," he'd said, "who have read all of your books.

---

1. Richard Kearney, *Anatheism* (New York: Columbia University Press, 2010), p. 179.

wow!

We would like to meet with you sometime." I wasn't expecting that! Since that first phone call, we had met a couple times and a warm friendship had begun. I was in his neighborhood to speak at a local seminary, so he kindly came by to say hello.

"Sol, we've become good enough friends now that I can ask you something kind of personal, right?" I asked.

"Sure. Anything."

"What do you think of Jesus? I'm not asking that as a test question or as a prelude to an evangelistic presentation," I explained. "I'm just curious."

"Of course, he was one of ours," Sol said. "He was a Jew in the prophetic tradition. And many of my colleagues would agree with me when I say I think he spoke from God and the leaders of the priestly tradition were wrong to reject him."

There was a pause. We both surveyed the Pacific Ocean shimmering in the afternoon sun. Then Sol continued, "But look, after two thousand years of anti-Semitism, I hope you won't expect us to get excited about the doctrine of the Trinity anytime soon."

I hope you can feel the power of his words. Confessing the Trinity served as the litmus test of acceptability in much of European history, forcing Jews into the status of outsiders and outcasts, noncitizens in "Christian nations." This exclusion and marginalization led to ghettoes and pogroms, and eventually to gas chambers.[2] Muslims similarly experienced Trinitarian and related doctrines as a threat, as have Hindus, Buddhists, and members of indigenous religions. As a result, many sensitive Christians have concluded that Trinitarian doctrines are irredeemable, that they must be quietly minimized if not outright abandoned. Trinitarian controversies have been so

---

2. Again, for more on this dark side of Christian history, see James Carroll, *Constantine's Sword: The Church and the Jews—A History* (New York: Mariner Books, 2001).

Doc. of Trin = healing teachings - not as loyalty tests

much a part of the problem that Trinitarian thought cannot be part of the solution.

I agree that Trinitarian doctrines have indeed been part of the problem. But I also believe that Trinitarian doctrines—held as healing teachings, not as an imperial loyalty test—can, properly understood and practiced, contribute much to the solution.

Few doctrines can surpass the doctrine of the Trinity in either the fervency or the ambiguity with which it is held. The Councils of Nicaea and Chalcedon are seemingly convened all over again whenever the doctrine of the Trinity is seriously discussed, and seemingly orthodox Christians expose themselves—often to their own surprise—as closet adoptionists or Arians, unconscious Nestorians or Apollinarians, or implicit monophysitists or monothelitists. (I'll be interested to hear what fault doctrinal experts will find with something I say about the Trinity in this chapter.) The doctrine of the Trinity has been so central to the Christian faith that to deny it, and sometimes even to affirm it in a new way, has been an excommunicable offense.

As a result, many good Christians—perhaps most—avoid thinking about the doctrine of the Trinity as studiously as they avoid denying it. The less they think about it, the less they'll say about it, and the less trouble they'll get in for misspeaking about it. So, without venturing too far into the conceptual minefields of *homoousios* and *hypostases*, of being and persons, of nature and will, they try to uphold a few basic mysteries—that God is one and in some sense three; that Christ is man and in some sense God; that the Spirit is the Spirit of the Father and the Son but in some sense not reducible to the Father and the Son.

Most Christians understand that the doctrine of the Trinity is historically important, but they seldom understand why. As I've already noted, some suspect that the doctrine is little more than a

Breathed life into clay at creation of man. Wind. fire. = Spirit

3 independent persons (· monads)

128 • Why Did Jesus, Moses, the Buddha, and Mohammed Cross the Road?

being in relationship

sinister tool of mind and speech control, used from the time of Constantine to centralize the power of heresy hunters and to test Christian teachers on their submission to church authority. Others simply accept that Trinitarian doctrine is part of the gospel bargain: if you want to go to heaven, here's what God requires you to assent to.[3] Relatively few have grappled with the philosophical, biblical, and practical issues that energized Trinitarian controversies throughout Christian history. Fewer still have critically examined how the doctrine has been abused as a weapon against others through history, as my rabbi friend pointed out. And even fewer have imagined how the doctrine could become a bridge rather than a barrier in the future.

What might a strong-benevolent holding of Trinitarian theology look like? For starters we could explore an approach called Social Trinitarianism.

Social Trinitarianism is by no means a new approach: it has its origins in the thought of the Cappadocian Fathers of the fourth century, especially Gregory of Nazianzus. In the eighth century it was further explored by John of Damascus. It has been revitalized in recent decades by a range of theologians including Eastern Orthodox thinkers like John Zizoulas, historic Protestants like Jurgen Moltmann, and Evangelicals like Stanley Grenz, Miroslav Volf, and J. Baxter Krueger. At the heart of Social Trinitarianism is the concept of perichoresis, which images God as a dynamic unity-in-community of self-giving persons-in-relationship. The Father, Son, and Spirit in this view are not three independent units (or monads) eternally bound together in a larger unity. Nor is God one independent unit with three identical parts. Rather, each person of the Trinity exists in dynamic social relationship with the others, and God is the relational unity in which they relate.

---

3. The corollary professional bargain might be expressed like this: "If you want to have a job in a Christian institution, here's something you have to say you believe."

one in each other (personhood)

Of course, the term *person* in the previous sentence is a highly technical term. It doesn't simply mean *individual*. Some have employed the term *interdividual* (a neologism attributable to René Girard) to acknowledge how the being of one Trinitarian person is not independent of the others; one couldn't be subtracted, leaving the other two to stand as a Duality, for example. Nor does the identity of one Trinitarian person stand over against the identity of the others so the Father could be defined as "apart from the Son or the Spirit" or the Spirit as "apart from the Father or the Son," and so on. Rather, the Spirit is the Spirit *of the Son* and *of the Father*. The Father is the Father *of the Son* and vice versa. So the very idea of *person* is redefined in Social Trinitarianism as "being in relationship." A person's relationships with the others, in other words, aren't an accessory to the person who exists apart from them. Those relationships are what and who that person is, and that person cannot be said to exist apart from those relationships. *Being*, then, for God as for us, means "interbeing," being in relationship, so the three persons of the Holy Trinity are not merely one *with* each other: they are one *in* each other. We might say they are *interpersons*, or *interpersonalities*. And, as creatures made in the image of God, so are we.

However interesting this might sound to you (or not), it might also seem so esoteric and so highly nuanced that it can only lead to the rancorous theological quarrels and hostile excommunications that we're trying to escape. But a simple thought experiment can make clear how powerful and reconciling this Social Trinitarian vision of God, personhood, and ourselves can be.

First, imagine (recalling the previous paragraphs) God as this "being as communion," as this loving trinity of perichoresis, a sacred choreography of self-giving, other-receiving; honoring, being honored; fully seeing the other, fully revealing the self. Imagine (in stark contrast to the hostile narratives of the previous chapter) an eternal one-anotherness who is by nature nonassimilating, nonisolating, one otherness   triune God

130 • Why Did Jesus, Moses, the Buddha, and Mohammed Cross the Road?

nondominating, noneliminating, nonoverthrowing, noncompeting, and nonvictimized or nonvictimizing.

Now imagine this God self-expressing in a universe. What kind of universe would this kind of God create? It would not be a universe of independent, isolated individuals or monads (as in the isolation narrative from the preceding chapter) because God is not an independent, isolated monad. It would not be a universe of undifferentiated homogeneity (as in the domination, purification, and assimilation narratives) because God is not an undifferentiated homogeneity. Nor would it be a universe of unending rivalry leading to competition, revolution, and victimization, either, because God is not many-in-conflict but three-in-one, unity-in-community. It would not be a universe of duality, stuck in the conflict of one versus the other, because God is one: one one-another.

Clearly, then, this Trinitarian vision of God helps us imagine a relational universe of one-anotherness, community-in-unity, unity-in-community, being-in-interbeing, where benevolence toward the other is at home, and hostility toward the other is foreign, invasive, out of place. To draw from the world of music, this vision invites us to imagine the universe as a wild and wonderful symphony, full of polyphony and surprise, expansive in themes, each movement inspiring the possibility of more movements as yet unimagined, all woven together with coherent motifs and morphing rhythms, where even dissonance has a place within higher, more comprehensive patterns of harmony and wholeness.

Finally, imagine how people in this universe would manifest trust in this triune God. Imagine in particular how people who hold this trust would relate to others who don't understand or hold it. Would they do so by dominating their counterparts and requiring them to assent to their vision by threat of sword or banishment? By rejecting the other and isolating from the other unless and until they see

Benevolence and otherliness

God is us & them not required by them to believe

the light? By trying to overthrow or assimilate all their understandings into this one, robbing them of their individuality? Such actions would violate the very spirit or nature of the God these Trinitarians were supposedly being faithful to!

One could only manifest trust in "this new vision of God as deathless, creative relationality"[4] by manifesting undying, creative love toward those who didn't share the belief. This kind of Trinitarianism, then, compels those who hold it to encounter the other with a bias against hostility and clannishness and a bias toward benevolence and otherliness.[5]

Imagine that! Imagine that vision of the Holy Trinity and how it could convert its holders from their hostile old identities to a robust, energetic, harmonious new identity. God-with-God in community leads us to envision God-with-us in community. And that vision in turn dares us to imagine God-with-them in community. And that expansive vision invites us higher still: to envision God-with-us-and-with-them in community, which leads us further still to envision us-with-them in community. This approach to the Trinity need not be a litmus test used to legitimize us and delegitimize them. Instead, it can be a gift, offered to others like a poem, not an ultimatum—given not to require assent-leading-to-acceptance or dissent-leading-to-condemnation, but rather to inspire us to reverence

4. James Alison, *The Joy of Being Wrong* (New York: Crossroad, 1998), p. 237.

5. Jonathan Tran quotes J. Kameron Carter: "Difference theologically understood arises from the positivity of the hypostatic distinctions [in the Trinity] within which the possibility and, according to the will of God, the actuality or concreteness of creation is located. It is precisely this understanding of difference—difference as witness to and participation within the Trinitarian hypostatic distinctions—that modern logics of race foreclose." In other words, the politics of whiteness (or sameness, imperialism, or colorblindness) betray the doctrine of the Trinity by asserting that, for example, son-ness and spirit-ness should be abolished or marginalized because of the supremacy of father-ness. See "The New Black Theology," *Christian Century*, January 26, 2012, http://christiancentury.org/article/2012-01/new-black-theology/.

otherliness as a theological attribute.[6] At that moment, Trinitarianism becomes not only a healing doctrine but a healing practice.

As I try to take all this in, I go back in my memory to that balcony with my friend Sol. I see us sitting together, pondering and enjoying a sparkling sea that expands beyond all horizons. We are two men of two different religions, united in our awe at the unspeakable, expansive, profound beauty of it all. God is not a doctrine to be mastered but a mystery to be mastered by.

all a mystery

_____

6. Miroslav Volf, in *Allah: A Christian Response* (New York: HarperOne, 2011), helpfully quotes Augustine of Hippo—"the total transcendence of the godhead quite surpasses the capacity of ordinary speech" (pp. 139–140)—and offers Nicholas of Cusa as an example of a Christian who offered the Trinity as this kind of gift rather than wielding it like a weapon.

Iman—

Transcendent divine non-violent love revealed in Christ, loving + peaceful

Chapter 16

How a Deeper Christology Can Save Christians from Hostility

The New Testament contains what amounts to a genuine episte-mology of love, the principle of which is clearly formulated in the first Epistle of John:

> He who loves his brother abides in the light, and in it there is no cause for stumbling. But he who hates his brother is in the darkness and walks in the darkness, and does not know where he is going, because the darkness has blinded his eyes. (1 John 2:10–11)

> ...Only Christ's perfect love can achieve without violence the perfect revelation toward which we have been progressing....
>   —René Girard[1]

I had lunch a few years ago in an Afghan restaurant with my Muslim friend Ahmad, who is an imam. I asked him to tell me how he came to be an imam, and what he loves most about Islam. He shared from his heart and I was deeply moved. Then he asked,

---

1. René Girard, *Things Hidden Since the Foundation of the World* (New York: Continuum Books, 2003), p. 277. When Girard speaks of "only Christ's perfect love," it's safe to say he doesn't intend the word *only* as an exclusive claim for the Christian religion that implies an insult to other religions. Rather, he is contrasting the transcendent, divine, nonviolent love revealed in Christ with our typical human energies that are polluted by rivalry and sabotaged by violence.

"How would you respond to that same question? How did you become a pastor and what do you love about Christianity?" I followed his example and shared from my heart too, starting like this: "Well, could I begin by telling you what I love about Jesus?"

When I paused a few minutes later, our eyes met, and I could see my friend was uncomfortable. "What's wrong?" I asked. "Did I say something that offended you?"

"Oh, no, no, no, no," he said. "I suddenly realize that everything I have heard about Christianity until now I learned from my fellow Muslims, and they passed on to me the misunderstandings they learned from other Muslims. Until now I have never listened to a sincere Christian explain his faith as a love for Jesus, peace and blessings be upon him. I have been so terribly misinformed and I have likewise misinformed others. I feel so sorry, so sorry. From now on, I will more adequately share with my congregation what Christianity truly is, because now I have learned it from a Christian who knows firsthand, not a Muslim who only passes on what he has heard."[2]

He paused, and then added, "When you say that you love Jesus, it fills my heart with joy. We Muslims love Jesus, too. We believe Jesus is a great prophet and we love him dearly. So you and I—we have this in common. We both love Jesus."

At that moment, I could have said, "But Ahmad, you don't think of Jesus in the same way we do. So your love for Jesus doesn't count." Then I could have entered into an argument to set him right. Instead, I asked him what it meant for him as a Muslim to call Jesus

2. Among other things, my Muslim friend had heard that we Christians believe that God is anatomically a male, and that God had physical sex with Mary. When we say Jesus is the Son of God, he assumed we meant that Jesus was the love-child of this impossible sexual union. When he heard me speak about Jesus, he didn't hear this kind of obscenity. Rather, he heard sincerity and devotion and reverence, which made possible a new level of communication between us.

Jesus as a prophet speaks about god

a great prophet. His response surprised me. Believing that Jesus was a great prophet meant that God was speaking to all humanity through Jesus. It meant that Jesus' word and example must be followed and that God would evaluate us against the measure of Jesus' life and teaching.

As he explained this, I couldn't help but notice an irony. We Christians believe that Jesus was more than a prophet, but that means, all too often for all too many of us, that his life and teaching can be largely ignored. As long as we believe certain things about his divinity, death, and resurrection, maybe with some auxiliary beliefs about (depending on our denomination) Mary, Peter, or the Bible, we're Christians in good standing, no questions asked. Then I thought of Jesus' own words, "Why do you call me 'Lord, Lord,' but do not do the things I say?"

Sadly, too often in church history—and too often today—Jesus has not been a point of contact as he was that day for Ahmad and me. As my friend Rabbi Sol knew all too well from the history of Christian anti-Semitism, Jesus has often been presented as a weapon and a threat, more wolf of God than lamb of God, filled more with the spirit of a hawk than a dove, more avenger of heretics than friend of sinners. Our Christology, however "high" in theory, has produced in practice far too many Christians with an elevated sense of superiority. And that superiority can only lead to hostility: *My religion is better than your religion. My theology is better than your theology. My God is better than your God. My Jesus is better than your . . . what? Your Moses? Your Jehovah? Your Elohim? Your Mohammed? Your Allah? Your Buddha? Your Atman? Your Great Spirit? Your Gaia? Your Imani?*

The ridiculousness of pitting Jesus as a rival against other prophets or gods or saviors becomes evident when you try to imagine Jesus himself doing so. Imagine a group of Christians bringing Mohammed to Jesus, and then Jesus questioning Mohammed. When Mohammed's answers don't pass his orthodoxy tests, imagine Jesus washing his hands and turning Mohammed over to the Christians to execute him. *No, that's not Jesus—that's Pontius Pilate!* Or imagine Jesus dragging the Buddha before a crowd of Christians and commanding them to stone him as a false prophet. *No, that's not Jesus commanding the Buddha to be stoned—that's Jesus standing with the Buddha, defending him from those about to throw stones!* Or imagine Jesus bringing Mohammed, the Buddha, Moses, and a panel of leading atheists to the top of a mountain so they can see the whole earth spread out below them in all directions. Imagine Jesus saying, "I'll let you all share in the ownership of all of this—if only you'll bow down and worship me!" *No, wait a minute. That's not Jesus, that's . . .* You get the point.[3]

The absurdity of these scenarios becomes even more stark when you consider the message of our two earliest Christological hymns, both found in Paul's letters, ostensibly written sometime between AD 53 and 61.[4]

The Colossian hymn presents Jesus in stunning counterimperial language (not insignificant in light of our faith's tragic identification with the Roman empire, as we've seen repeatedly already).[5] The hymn celebrates him as the true king or emperor: he is the true image of God, the true firstborn destined to inherit the throne, the

3. I've written a short fictional tale in e-book form that explores a story like this. You can find more information about *The Girl with the Dove Tattoo* at my website, http://www.brianmclaren.net.

4. Even those who question the Pauline authorship of these texts acknowledge their importance as windows into the early Christian community.

5. See Brian Walsh and Sylvia Keesmaat's *Colossians Remixed* (Downers Grove, Ill.: InterVarsity Press, 2004) for a stunning reading of this text. See also Dominic Crossan, Richard Horsley, Marcus Borg, Joerg Rieger, and N. T. Wright for additional insights into counterimperial themes in the New Testament.

true source and purpose of creation, the true head of the body politic, the true embodiment of the fullness of God, the true source of peace and reconciliation. But then the hymn ends with this staggering conceptual coup d'état: while Caesar gains and holds power and enforces the Pax Romana by shedding the blood of all who resist him, Jesus exercises his sovereignty and brings the Pax Christi by shedding his own blood. The power of Christ (and what Jesus called the Kingdom of God) is manifest not in hostile conquest and killing, but in benevolent self-giving to the point of death. We must not define Jesus and his kingdom by fitting them within conventional understandings of kings and kingdoms. Rather, we must judge and deconstruct those conventional definitions in light of Jesus and his example.

The Philippian hymn makes a similar point.[6] Christ as a true image bearer of God does not climb to a place of prominence and glory through the normal means of rivalry and conquest. Rather, he descends—down into common humanity, down into servanthood, down into suffering, down into death—even death on a cross. This descending, openhanded humility rather than climbing, clutching pride, this self-giving rather than selfish ambition, this preference for others rather than competitive superiority...this is the attitude that honors God, and that God honors, and that in fact reveals the true nature of God. How could followers of this Christ and this God justify treating others with contempt, disdaining them as inferior, rejecting them as other and enemy? How could any of these all-too-common hostilities be done in the name of this Christ?

Where our Christology has been so strong, oppositional, and distorted, it's easy to understand why many have advocated weakening

---

6. Thanks to a personal communication from Dr. William Stacy Johnson for many of the insights on Philippians 2 conveyed here and later in the chapter.

Redefining strength gaining thru losing!

138 • Why Did Jesus, Moses, the Buddha, and Mohammed Cross the Road?

our Christology to weaken its hostile distortions. But my hope is that a deeper, more vigorous, more robust Christology will become as much a part of the solution to Christian hostility as the old approaches have been part of the problem. This new kind of strong Christology begins by redefining strength itself in light of Christ's strength-through-weakness, gaining-through-losing, rising-through-descending.

Christ isn't merely one sector of the tapestry of Christian theology. Rather, Christ is interwoven throughout the fabric of every sector. For that reason it's hard to know where to begin and where to stop examining Christology and its impact on Christian identity in a multi-faith world. In a thorough exploration, we would concentrate on key biblical terms, terms that, it turns out, are far more complex, contested, and interesting than most of us Sunday School graduates realize: *Son of God*, *Son of Man*, *Lord*, and *Christ* for starters. And we would look at the ways those terms have been woven into various doctrines and systematic theologies over history. We would pay attention not only to what was affirmed, but also to what was marginalized or ignored. We would ask tough questions about why Greco-Roman philosophical categories gained such prominence in understanding Christ, and we would question whether those categories must forever and everywhere be considered normative.[7]

For our purposes here, though, we can only scratch the surface by considering how a fresh vision of two Christological doctrines can reduce hostility and strengthen benevolence.[8]

---

7. See Mabiala Kenzo, "Evangelical Faith and (Postmodern) Others," in *A New Kind of Conversation*, ed. Myron Bradley Penner and Hunter Barnes (Colorado Springs, Colo.: Paternoster, 2007).

8. I wish that space would allow us to examine many other Christological doctrines in this context. For example, the doctrine of the incarnation of Christ is rich with incentives to encounter the other, as evidenced in the Christmas narratives in which Jesus is honored by "the other" (the Magi) while being persecuted by "one of us" (Herod). The

First, the doctrine of the Deity of Christ is affirmed in the Nicene Creed with these words: "We believe in one Lord, Jesus Christ, the only Son of God, eternally begotten of the Father, God from God, Light from Light, true God from true God, begotten, not made, of one Being with the Father." The process of arriving at each pregnant phrase of these few brief lines was long, agonizing, and fascinating, but it remains largely unknown to the average Christian. In contrast, the average Christian seems to arrive at the doctrine of the Deity of Christ in a simple, quick, three-step process: (1) Define God, using the Bible, perhaps assisted by Greek philosophy. (2) Apply this definition of God to Christ. (3) Work out the areas of apparent contradiction or potential misunderstanding that arise.

In this way, on a popular level many Christians understand the doctrine to mean, "What is true of God is true of Christ," or "Jesus is equal to God," or, put more mathematically (and less theologically), "God = Jesus: Jesus = God." Wise Trinitarians would quickly usher us back to the language of one of the creeds, but again, on a popular level, including on the level of religious broadcasting with its massive impact, this approach often frames the doctrine.

There has been an alternative approach to Christology in the Christian tradition, favored more in the Anabaptist and Quaker communities, and resonant with the Franciscans and the Celts before them. It doesn't contradict traditional or creedal Christology, but it takes another approach to get there: (1) Seek to understand or know Christ (primarily by reading the Gospels in context). (2) Apply this understanding or knowledge to God. (3) Enrich, challenge, adjust,

---

doctrine of Christ's humanity affirms to us that Jesus learned and grew in understanding, and provides examples of him doing so, even from "the other," such as in the story of the Syrophoenecian/Canaanite woman (which I explore in *Everything Must Change* [Nashville: Thomas Nelson, 2007]).

affirm, or correct all previous understandings of God in light of Christ.[9]

So where the popular approach takes a preexisting definition of God and applies it to Christ, this alternative approach challenges preconceived understandings of God and revises them in light of Christ. The assertion shifts the emphasis from "What is true of God is true of Christ" to "What is true of Christ is true of God." Or more simply put, from "Christ is like God" to "God is like Christ."

Again, this might seem like a rather esoteric and trivial adjustment. But consider its importance when we are willing to challenge violent and exclusive conceptions of God in light of the nonviolent and inclusive way of Christ. The impacts of this adjustment are radical and far-reaching, and they suggest not a lower or reduced Christology but an equally or—I would say—an even more robust one. We can trace a similar pattern in regards to a second Christological doctrine.

The doctrine of the incarnation is drawn primarily from the opening words of the Fourth (or John's) Gospel:

> In the beginning was the Word, and the Word was with God, and the Word was God. He was in the beginning with God. All things came into being through him, and without him not one thing came into being. What has come into being in him was life, and the life was the light of all people. The light shines in the darkness, and the darkness did not overcome it....The true light, which enlightens everyone, was coming into the world....
> And the Word became flesh and lived among us, and we have seen his glory, the glory as of a father's only son, full of grace and truth....From his fullness we have all received, grace upon grace. The law indeed was given through Moses; grace and truth came

---

9. I first heard this approach articulated by students of Elton Trueblood.

"If you have seen me, you have seen my father."

through Jesus Christ. No one has ever seen God. It is God the only Son, who is close to the Father's heart, who has made him known. (John 1:1–5, 9, 14, 16–18)

Again, the focus of our investigation prohibits a full engagement with this luminous passage. But please notice three important elements of the text. First, consider the term Word. It's fascinating because of its resonances both in Hebrew and Greek thought. In a Jewish context, the passage evokes the Genesis 1 creation story ("in the beginning...all things came into being...light"), suggesting that the Word is the creative word by which everything springs into existence: "Let there be."

To say that this Word became flesh is to say, among other things, that Jesus embodies the divine creativity that makes impossibilities possible and that makes new possibilities spring forth into actuality. It proclaims something more far-reaching—and hopeful—than the arrival of a new religious leader or a new religion. It proclaims that a new genesis has interrupted business as usual in human history. And what will that new creation entail? Among other things, it will mean a new commandment—that we love one another as Christ loved us. We might say, in other words, that this new creation means an end to the old era of hostility, including religious hostility. "Let there be love," it proclaims.

The term Word—or Logos—is no less powerful in a Greek context. For the Greeks, the logos is the internal logic, pattern, or meaning of the universe. For John to proclaim that this logos has been enfleshed in Jesus would mean, in today's terms, that in his story we see the syntax of history, the plotline of evolution, the deep meaning of the surface events, the unified field theory that explains all data.

True light of the world

Many assume that in using this term *logos*, John is fitting Jesus into the standard Greek framework of Logos, much as some Christians fit

new genesis = Jesus
new commandment = LOVE

Self-giving/servanthood

142 • Why Did Jesus, Moses, the Buddha, and Mohammed Cross the Road?

washing feet etc

Jesus into their preconceived notions of God. But I think René Girard was right when he analyzed the text differently:

> If love and violence are incompatible, the definition of the Logos must take this into account. The difference between the Greek Logos and the Johannine Logos must be an obvious one, which gets concealed only in the tortuous complications of a type of thought that never succeeds in ridding itself of its own violence.[10]

Girard suggests that John is making the same move Paul makes in Colossians when he turns imperial language on its head, or in Philippians when Paul argues that true glory is manifested not in grasping but in self-giving, not in selfish ambition but in servanthood.[11] It is, in fact, the same move Jesus makes later in John's Gospel when he strips and stoops to wash the feet of his disciples. In the conventional Greek understanding, the internal logic of the universe mandates for some to be slave masters and others to be slaves, for some to dominate and others to submit, for some to be male/superior and others to be female/inferior. In so doing, the Greek logos legitimizes a

---

10. Girard, *Things Hidden*, p. 270.

11. The word *grasping* should evoke the taking of the fruit by the first couple, and should contrast with Jesus who "did not think equality with God a thing to be grasped." In this light, Philippians 2 might be more a hymn about the humanity of Christ than the deity of Christ, presenting him not as "existing in the form (or nature) of God," as most translations suggest, but rather as "existing in the image of God"—as the true human, content in being human, not seeking to grasp for more. In his refusal to grasp at deity, he passes the test Adam and Eve failed. When Christians present Jesus as one who demands that others acknowledge his deity (crudely put, "Bow down and say I am God or I will send you to hell!"), they contradict the whole spirit of Philippians 2. To add to the irony: if Jesus truly is the image of God (or "in nature God" or "in the form of God"), then he reveals that God's true nature is not to grasp at deity! That suggests that God is willing to go "incognito"—which might further suggest that God is willing to show up in unexpected places. In other words, if God is humbly manifest in the most unexpected form of a servant hanging on a cross, then perhaps we should expect God to be humbly manifest in unexpected ways in the contexts of other religions, too.

True heart of God = LOVE

Universal logos

world divided between the powerful and powerless, rich and poor, us and them, the civilized and the barbarian, slave master and slave, male and female.[12] In such a divided, dualistic world, hostility, conflict, and violence are...logical.[13] Acceptable. Normal.

But according to John, that logos of power is false. John audaciously proclaims that the true logic of the universe—the true meaning or syntax or plotline of history—has been enfleshed in Jesus and dwelt among us, full of glory, full of grace and truth, uttering one commandment only: love. This logos of love reveals to us the true heart of God and therefore the true hidden logic and meaning of the universe. The false, exclusive, dualist logos of power enlightens only the civilized or the philosophical or the powerful. But in Christ, a universal logos—"the true light that enlightens everyone"—has come into the world.

And so, in a strong-benevolent Christology, Jesus is not lifted up into a preexisting concept of God or a preexisting category of philosophy. No: Jesus presents us with a radically new vision of God, a nonviolent God, a suffering and serving God, descending and disrupting preexisting categories, opening up previously unrealized possibilities. And when this benevolent logos comes, full of grace and truth, we do not welcome him. We reject him. We kill him, in the name of our preferred and familiar logos of hostility and violence. And so a crucified logos beckons us from the darkness of our violent past into the new light of a resurrection morning. Again, Girard captures the drama, with its obvious implications for the formation of Christian identity in a multi-faith world:

The Johannine Logos is foreign to any kind of violence; it is therefore forever expelled, an absent Logos that never has had any direct,

---

12. Paul makes this very contrast in Galatians 3:28.

13. A defender of the Greek logos would say that hostility is not inevitable—if only the subdominant would accept their inferior position. Conflict arises from their refusal to conform to the logos and stay in their place.

full of grace + truth - rejected

Non-violent God revealed in

144 • Why Did Jesus, Moses, the Buddha, and Mohammed Cross the Road?

Christ

determining influence over human cultures. These cultures are based on the Heraclitean Logos, the Logos of expulsion, the Logos of violence, which, if it is not recognized, can provide the foundation of a culture. The Johannine Logos discloses the truth of violence by having itself expelled. First and foremost, John's Prologue undoubtedly refers to the Passion. But in a more general way, the misrecognition of the Logos and mankind's expulsion of it disclose one of the fundamental principles of human society.

...This revelation comes from the Logos itself. In Christianity, it is expelled once again by the sacrificial reading, which amounts to a return to the Logos of violence. All the same, the Logos is still in the process of revealing itself; if it tolerates being concealed yet another time, this is to put off for just a short while the fullness of its revelation. The Logos of love puts up no resistance; it always allows itself to be expelled by the Logos of violence. But its expulsion is revealed in a more and more obvious fashion, and by the same process the Logos of violence is revealed as what can only exist by expelling the true Logos and feeding upon it in one way or another.[14]

This drama is ongoing at this moment, in your heart and mind, and in mine. When we have finally put the old Greek (or Heraclitean) Logos of violence and war behind us, and when we finally accept the new and true Logos of the nonviolent God revealed in Christ, Girard says there will be "incalculable results." In other words, as our understanding of the identity of Christ becomes less Greek and more truly Christian, so will we.[15]

---

14. Girard, *Things Hidden*, pp. 271, 274. What Girard elsewhere calls the Greek Logos, here he calls the Heraclitean Logos, recalling Fragment 53, where Heraclitus says, "War [or violence] is the father of all and the king of all." (See http://www.heraclitus fragments.com/.)

15. Girard, *Things Hidden*, p. 276. Girard acknowledges that the Christian religion has betrayed this essential substitution and has reinstated a God who inflicts violence. He calls this betrayal "sacrificial Christianity"—a theme to which we will return in Chapter 23.

Spirit = power of Creation — directed only by love + compassion

Chapter 17

How the Doctrine of the Holy Spirit Can Empower Our Encounter with the Other

In a very real sense, according to Christian experience and symbolism, the Spirit is given with creation, indeed is the instrument or the power of creation. She is with us from the beginning, grounding and connecting every living being. . . . I can rest in her. . . . Utterly mysterious, totally unpredictable, filled and directed by love/compassion, she is the womb in whom I rest and from which I issue moment by moment.

—*Paul Knitter*[1]

I wanted to crawl under my chair.

It was a few weeks after September 11, 2001, and a group of faith leaders in our community just outside of D.C. pulled together a series of Sunday-afternoon interfaith gatherings. Our gatherings were hosted at a local mosque—fitting, we all felt, so that Christians, Jews, Hindus, Sikhs, Buddhists, and others could experience warm Muslim hospitality in the midst of all the interreligious fear

---

1. Paul Knitter, *Without Buddha I Could Not Be a Christian* (Oxford: Oneworld, 2009), p. 21.

Iman

146 • Why Did Jesus, Moses, the Buddha, and Mohammed Cross the Road?

and hostility of the moment. At our first gathering, we observed the Muslim traditions of removing our shoes and of seating the men in one room and the women in another, connected via CCTV. But our hosts graciously suspended their traditions for subsequent meetings so that we non-Muslims, ("the other,") would feel more at home.[2]

At this particular gathering, the imam invited each of us to take five to ten minutes to address this question: *What, according to my tradition, is my duty to my neighbor of another religion?*[3]

It was a great question and all of us had the best intentions, I'm sure. As I recall, the first speaker was a Sikh from India. Perhaps he became temporarily possessed by the spirit of political animosity between India and Pakistan, the native land of the imam, but whatever the reason, he managed to insult our hosts in his very first sentence, even as he raised a valid concern. "My first duty to my neighbors is not to send them off into another room as second-class citizens, as has been done to the women here today." Awkward!

The next speaker was a Catholic priest, a good friend of mine. He had labored for many hours over a brilliant scholarly paper which he read . . . every word . . . in a perfectly flat monotone . . . without looking up . . . even once. It was full of quotes, quotes from popes, quotes from scholars, quotes from encyclicals, quotes from I-can't-remember-where. His ten-minute paper took twenty minutes to read, and every minute was packed full with good information, but I imagine it felt like an hour for those not fluent in academic prose. I can't remember what he said about my duty to my neighbor of another religion. But I can remember being relieved that his paper didn't insult anybody.

Then came a mainline Protestant minister I didn't know. He also

disrespect by other traditions

---

2. How many Christian churches, I wondered, would have been that flexible with a long-held tradition?

3. As in all stories I tell, a few details of this story have been intentionally changed for privacy purposes, and others may have been unintentionally changed due to my imperfect memory.

read a paper that was filled with a lot of quotes and he also delivered it in an emotionally low-cal monotone. He spoke intelligently of our Christian duty to see Christ in all people, but the illustration he chose was...questionable at best. It's (almost) always good to quote Dietrich Bonhoeffer, and almost always bad to illustrate a point using Hitler. He managed to do both by saying that Bonhoeffer saw Christ even in Hitler. That was when I wanted to be swallowed up by the floor. The two rabbis—one Orthodox, sitting on my left, and one Reconstructionist, on my right—physically squirmed and furiously massaged their eyebrows as if choreographed. *At least he stuck to his ten-minute limit*, I thought, as he sat down. *And at least it can't get any worse.*

It did. The next speaker was an acquaintance of mine, a Pentecostal pastor with a good heart. He started getting emotional, which the people liked as relief from the previous two speakers. The more emotional he got, the faster he talked, and the speed, combined with his Deep South accent, combined with his generous use of evangelical lingo, meant that he was incomprehensible to most of the folks in the room, for whom English was a second language.[4] (He could have been speaking in tongues, and I don't think they would have known or cared as long as he didn't put them to sleep.) Soon he was shouting something to this effect: "I love you! I love you all! And because I love you, it is my duty to you, my neighbors, be you Muslim, Hindu, Jewish, Sikh, or Buddhist, to tell you that you are all going straight to hell unless you repent and receive Jesus Christ as your personal Lord, Savior, Healer, and Deliverer!"

Ah, I thought, so it could get worse. Next he was quoting John 14:6 and John 10:8, implying that all other religions were false and founded by thieves and robbers. At one point, tears streamed down

---

4. Sadly, the two rabbis, whose sensibilities had already been assaulted by one Christian, now experienced another assault that they could understand all too well.

Christian duty = love neighbor

148 • Why Did Jesus, Moses, the Buddha, and Mohammed Cross the Road?

Polite - respecting the "other"

his face as he told everyone how much he loved them and didn't want them to be in hell forever. I looked at my watch. Twenty minutes. Now I was rubbing my eyebrows. "Oh God, let the world just end now," I prayed. After nearly thirty surreal minutes, he wrapped it up, and I couldn't believe what happened next.

Applause! Extended, loud applause! I was so shocked, I can't remember for sure if it was a standing ovation, but I think it was. What? Were they glad he told them they were going to hell? No—I'm quite certain few had gotten beyond his style to capture his content. Were they just happy for it to be over? Maybe in part. Were they responding to his passion, emotion, and conviction? Did the "I love you! I love you all!" come through so powerfully that everything else seemed unimportant? Yes, I'm quite certain that was it.

I won't bore you with the rest of the speakers, of whom I was next to last. (My point was that my Christian duty is to love my neighbor as myself. That late in the game, I knew that the best way I could practice what I was preaching was by being mercifully brief.) Everyone managed to rally by the end of the hosting imam's closing comments, and all considered the gathering a success, and I suppose it was, in the sense that we mostly managed to be polite and respectful of each other in spite of our massive displays of awkwardness, insensitivity, and cluelessness. More than ten years later, and I'm still cringing right now as I remember all this.

In the days that followed, I kept thinking about my Pentecostal colleague. I kept thinking about the applause he received after he spoke. No, I wasn't jealous. But I knew the response was significant, and I wanted to understand it. Here's part of what I gradually concluded: for him to be himself, to pour out his heart, to unleash his emotion—even more, to rouse his emotion, and to do so in the presence of others of different faiths . . . that was just the gift people needed in the aftermath of September 11. People needed to cry and shout and vent, not maintain a monotone of surface calm. They needed to rouse themselves toward something other than hostility or fear. In spite of his theological content, that was what this preacher managed to model that Sunday afternoon. I came to believe that my Pentecostal brother did something magical that day—not for me, because I was feeling so utterly responsible for how things were going, but for the majority who (thankfully) couldn't understand what he was saying. He made space for them to *be* human, to *feel* human, to feel *alive*.

And in that very human connection, he communicated real love for the people in the room. He made eye contact with them, not just his manuscript. He wasn't just faithfully representing a tradition or dutifully fulfilling an assignment as some of us seemed to be doing: he was speaking with fervent, sincere love as a human being to human beings.

In so doing, I think my friend revealed three of the deepest secrets of Pentecostalism: humanity, vitality, and sincerity.[5] When my friend spoke, he wasn't a "human thinking" addressing "humans thinking": he spoke as *a feeling human being* to fellow *feeling human beings* of flesh and blood. He addressed us as human beings who, like him, want and need to stand, shout, laugh, cry, vent, be roused, clap, and... feel alive. And that vitality—so different from the religious gravity that was all too common among us—became a manifestation of good news: the possibility of something beyond routine existence and heads-down survival, the possibility of joyful vitality and conviviality. And when humanity and vitality are focused outward in sincerity

Pentecostal = humanity, vitality — sincerity

---

5. It's hard to argue against the proposition that Pentecostalism has been the most significant Christian movement since the Reformation. In just over a century, the movement has grown from a single gathering on Azusa Street in Los Angeles, California, to a worldwide phenomenon that includes a staggering percentage (estimates range from 10 to 30 percent, with 20 being a good average) of the world's Christians. Today, one in fifteen human beings on the planet identifies as a Pentecostal (or Charismatic) Christian—a category that virtually nobody had ever heard of a century ago.

benevolent spirit God in us

We have our being in the Holy Spirit

and love for others...the condemning content is overshadowed by the spirit, the Holy, vital, loving Spirit.

Pentecostalism in its first dynamic century has helped us see (among other things) what the Spirit can do at the end of long church services with lots of loud singing and louder preaching. In the next century we must discover what the Spirit of God can do outside church services altogether, in the world at large—spreading humanity, vitality, and sincerity in the worlds of business and politics, art and culture—not to mention the arena of interfaith reconciliation. For that to happen, for us to debug and reboot Christian theology as a benevolent rather than a hostile program, we're going to have to give the doctrine of the Holy Spirit—what theologians call pneumatology—a second thought. And a third, fourth, fifth, sixth, and seventh, too.

Our first thought of the Holy Spirit, of course, is the realization that there is a Holy Spirit, and that the Holy Spirit is God-in-us or God-upon-us or God-among-us everywhere and anywhere. Our second thought of the Holy Spirit flows from the first: that the Spirit is ubiquitous—everywhere, always, in all creation. That leads to a third thought, logical and hard to dispute, but too seldom acknowledged: the Holy Spirit preexists all religions, cannot be contained by any single religion, and therefore can't be claimed as private property by any one religion.

That means that Pentecostals don't own the Holy Spirit, nor do Christians, nor do monotheists, nor do theists. According to Genesis, the Spirit was active in creation before there were any human beings, not to mention any religions; according to David, we cannot flee from the Spirit even in the grave; and according to Paul (quoting a Greek poet), all human beings live and move and have their being in the Spirit. So we can say that the Spirit is open-source rather than proprietary, and that people (and macaws and bonobos and tortoises and parrotfish, for that matter) are bumping into the Spirit at every turn, whether they acknowledge it or not. *animals*

That leads to a fourth thought, even more surprising: *what we call the secular is actually the realm or domain of the Spirit.* The secular—literally meaning the world, the realm outside of church control—isn't profane. Rather, properly understood, it is sacred because the Spirit is and has always been active there, evoking light from darkness, order from chaos, fullness from void, life from lifelessness, actuality from potentiality, and potentiality from actuality.[6]

If the secular is sacred, that means the Spirit is at work in what we call secular work in the secular world (a redundancy, by the way). So the scientist studying interstellar dust is investigating the domain of the Spirit, and the Spirit gently "hovers" over her neurons as they fire a hypothesis into being. The same is true of a paleontologist excavating a fossil, an executive developing a marketing plan, a stonemason fashioning a chimney, a father changing a diaper, a mother planning a vacation, an engineer designing a solar panel, and a bookkeeper wrestling with a budget. And that's as true for a Muslim astronomer, a Buddhist paleontologist, a Sikh executive, a Hindu stonemason, a Jewish father, a Jain mother, and an atheist engineer as it is for a Christian theologian. What may differ is not the presence and benevolence of the Spirit, but the awareness and responsiveness of the individual.

These second thoughts lead to yet another: if the Spirit is ubiquitous and all people are encountering the Holy Spirit simply because we live, move, and have our being in the Spirit's domain, we can understand human religions—all human religions, including our own—as imperfect human responses to our encounters with the

---

6. Amos Yong and John Sober Sylvest are exploring these fascinating subjects. See http://www.regent.edu/acad/schdiv/faculty_staff/yong.shtml and http://poj.peeters-leuven.be/content.php?url=article&id=2058666&journal_code=SID/.

Spirit who is present in all creation. That is not to deny the presence of unique divine revelation in any one religion, nor is it to affirm that all religions are the same, nor is it to imply that the Spirit should be credited or blamed for everything going on in our religions. Instead, it is simply to propose that each religion, based on its unique location and history, would have a unique, particular, and evolving perspective from which to encounter the Spirit in a unique way.[7] That would mean that differences between religions would not necessarily mean contradictions. They could simply mean additional data, expressed in different systems of local imagery and language, based on differing encounters with the same Spirit of God, present in all creation across all time. Not only that, but in light of the wildly different local conditions in which they encounter the same Spirit, we might interpret some religious differences in a new light: rather than saying different (contradictory) things about the same thing, various religions could sometimes be saying different (complementary) things about different (complementary) experiences entirely.[8]

What would that mean for Christian identity? It would mean at

---

7. This proposal is neither new nor hard to understand. Wouldn't the Spirit as experienced by the Inuit of the Arctic have a different "feel" than the Spirit as experienced by the desert nomads of Arabia? Wouldn't a desert nomad associate God's grace in a special way with shade and shelter from the unrelenting sun, while an Inuit during the unrelenting dark of winter would associate the Spirit's presence with longed-for sunlight? If different climates would affect their ways of understanding and describing God—one as shade, one as sunlight—wouldn't their different histories do the same? And couldn't these diverse associations with the Spirit be seen as both locally rooted and of universal interest? Couldn't these locally rooted articulations, understood both respectfully and critically as unique phenomena, yield insights to people who have encountered God in different settings? And couldn't those insights be both about the Spirit and about how one's experience of Spirit is connected to one's local environment and local history? For more on these questions, see M. Thomas Thangaraj, *Relating to People of Other Religions: What Every Christian Needs to Know* (Nashville: Abingdon Press, 1997), pp. 15ff.

8. Yes, differences can be contradictions, but they can also be expansions, corroborations, elucidations, connections, corrections, additions, or translations, all contributing to rich and needed conversations.

Unique experiences of Spirit in all religions are gifts to all

least three things. First, we Christians can make a strong claim to have received a real revelation through real encounters with the real Holy Spirit in specific locations and at particular times in creation. Second, we have something unique to offer members of other religions, based on our unique and real encounters with the Spirit. And third, it would mean other religions have something to offer us as well, based on their real and unique encounters with the Spirit. To refuse to receive those gifts would be tantamount to dishonoring the Holy Spirit's work beyond our group's own experience. These second thoughts would prepare us for one more.

If the Holy Spirit is indeed ubiquitous and secular, active in all creation, not just the church, and if everyone in creation can't avoid encountering the Holy Spirit, and if all of our religions potentially contain localized, particular responses to the Holy Spirit[9] (along with lots of other components, such as expressions of rivalry and fear), and if each religion has treasures to give and treasures to receive from the others, then we would expect the Holy Spirit to be moving people in each religion to offer their good gifts to others, and to receive the good gifts offered by others. In other words, we would expect the one Holy Spirit to be moving, working, "hovering" over each religion—and also in the space between religions, inviting people into conversation, exchange, even communion, across the boundaries that have in the past separated them.

And that Spirit-work would apply to us, right now. We would expect that in my writing and in your reading of this book, the Holy Spirit could be at work, hovering over us, seeking to lead us out of our slavery to hostility and conflict and into a good, free land of benevolence and communion.

In a strange, messy, imperfect-but-real way, that's what I believe the

---

9. I am affirming what has often been called "the scandal of particularity," but I am also suggesting that this particularity is scandalously widespread in its dissemination.

Holy Spirit was doing that 2001 afternoon in the mosque. The Spirit moved through all of us, I think. Our shared desire to be together and to communicate intelligently with one another expressed something of the Holy Spirit. But through that Pentecostal preacher—through him, and no doubt in spite of him to some degree—the Holy Spirit conveyed love in an extraordinary and needed way. Predictably perhaps, his words said, *I'm in; you're out. To be in, you must join my religion and believe what I believe.*[10] But his actions and his manner spoke more truly: *I love you. I care about you. I'm here with you. I'm pouring out my heart to you—in spite of our differences. I'm holding nothing back. I'm taking a risk. I'm being real. I love you.* When the people felt that sincere, uninhibited, overflowing, outpouring love—the primary fruit of the Holy Spirit—the walls came down, and they erupted in applause.

Love

actions, manner

I care about you

I'm here w/ you

(In spite of any dif)

Love primary fruit

of the H. Sp.

peace, patience, kindness, goodness, gentleness, faithfulness, self-control

---

10. I wonder to what degree, recalling the conversation in Chapter 6 about our fear of "us," my friend included the "in-out" language more to prove his legitimacy to the members of his church who were present, for whom just showing up at the mosque was a huge step out of their comfort zone. The "I love you" message was what the Spirit was speaking most powerfully within and through his own soul to "the other," and that's what they heard.

harmony - beauty way - good way

Chapter 18

How Faithful Doctrinal Reformulation Can Make Orthodoxy More Generous

Learning from my own intertribal experiences, I had some small understanding that other tribes also used a harmony concept as a foundation for living. I found that each tribe has a word or several words in its own language that broadly represents living in harmony and balance. As far as English references go, some tribes speak of harmony as a way of balance; some refer to the concept as the "beauty way"; while others may talk of a "good way" or "good road" or "a good path." Other tribal groups call it the "blessing way." The majority of Native American people tend to recognize the concept in their own tribes and in other tribes.

—*Randy Woodley*[1]

I have four children, each wonderful, each beloved. One of them is a cancer survivor. From the age of six to ten, he underwent daily chemotherapy, using the best chemotherapeutic agents available at the time to save him from leukemia. During the time of treatment,

---

1. Randy Woodley, *Shalom and the Community of Creation: An Indigenous Vision* (Grand Rapids: Eerdmans, 2012), p. 73.

mutations

his greatest immediate threat was not the cancer, but rather the chemotherapeutic agents themselves. They were unpleasant, to be sure: they caused vomiting, hair loss, throat lesions, extreme lethargy, and mood swings. In addition, they rendered him dangerously vulnerable to common infections. Chicken pox, for example, was potentially lethal. To kill the threat of cancer, chemotherapy threatened to kill him.

As in cancer treatment, so in treatment for religious hostility: the treatment is by no means safe, and it might be considered poison if not for the presence of an even more dangerous threat, which raises an important question: Is Christian orthodoxy so badly infected with so much hostility that it is incurable? Is the patient beyond hope of cure?

Many people answer yes. The only way they see to escape the hostility of Christian orthodoxy is to flee it as a lost cause, to become postorthodox refugees, in either another religion or no religion. Knowing they don't want to stay among a hostile people, they seek a better homeland, one they hope will be less contentious, less aggressive, less hostile. But chances are, once they arrive, the new identity-territory to which they have fled will have derived at least some of its identity-strength through hostilities of its own (including, perhaps, hostilities against Christian orthodoxy!). And once they've settled in that new homeland, they may not find greater resources for reconciliation and peace than the ones they left behind.[2]

That's why I hope a better option has become clear in the preceding chapters: faithfully reformulating orthodoxy by treating its oppositional, hostile, and imperial malignancies. The doctrines themselves don't pose a threat, but rather fast-growing, easy-to-spread mutations of those doctrines. We have to stop those mutations with-

---

2. This scenario recalls the journey of Abraham, who left an empire with all the hostilities it entailed, not knowing where he would be led. In this light, the journey away from a hostile orthodoxy is a truly orthodox pursuit.

out killing the patient (and before the patient goes on a killing rampage), and so we've considered how that might be done in regard to several key doctrines: creation, original sin, election, the Trinity, the deity of Christ, and the Holy Spirit. Many other doctrines deserve similar treatment through similar reformulation. Perhaps, five hundred years after the Great Reformation, we are on the verge of the Great Reformulation.

How, for example, might our atonement doctrines be reformulated in a nonviolent, postimperial, postsacrificial light—thus addressing the real problem of original sin as we have reformulated it here?[3] How might the Bible's apocalyptic passages be reformulated so as to yield a nonviolent eschatology that promotes hope and constructive action for the future? How might we faithfully reformulate those doctrines of heaven, hell, and final judgment so they are no longer malignant? And along with them, how might we reformulate our understandings of the Satan and his minions and their principalities and powers that oppress and possess human beings, driving them to subhuman behavior?[4] How might we reformulate our understanding of the church and its mission so that we could articulate a more robust ecclesiology that will support a strong-benevolent Christian identity in the future?

Clearly, we've already set the stage for these rediscoveries. The doctrinal reformulations we've already considered have sufficient weight to destabilize the status quo and nudge it toward a tipping

---

3. See also Chapter 23. For a short and pithy introduction to the subject of atonement, see Tony Jones's ebook *A Better Atonement*, which is available here: http://tonyj.net/books/.

4. Few areas of doctrine have been more demonic in their application than these—since demonization of the other leads so efficiently to violence against the other. See Elaine Pagels, *The Origin of Satan: How Christians Demonized Jews, Pagans, and Heretics* (New York: Vintage, 1996). The brilliant and courageous work of Walter Wink has done much to "exorcise" and disarm these doctrines, turning them from destructive swords into creative plowshares. See especially *The Powers That Be* (New York: Three Rivers Press, 1999).

Reestablish equilibrium creatively

point. Already the cat is out of the bag, and already these questions are being raised—in seminary classrooms but also in online discussions, in denominational headquarters but also in pub theology groups and emergent cohorts. Perhaps future generations will consider us to be farther along in the Great Reformulation (or the Great Emergence, etc.) than we ourselves realize.

Doctrines don't exist in a static linear outline where you can take out your outdated eschatology module and replace it with a new updated one, leaving everything else intact. Rather, doctrines cohere and interact in a dynamic system in which each part is related to all the others. When you disturb this kind of dynamic system with the right kind, right amount, and right intensity of creative disturbance, the whole system can go through a radical rebooting—what we often call a paradigm shift. On the other side of disequilibrium, the system has the chance to reestablish equilibrium in a creative, robust, generative way.

If the creative disturbance is too limited, other elements in the system will gang up on it and attempt to crush or co-opt the reformulation.[5] Or, in reaction to a successful reformulation, a counterreformulation might be launched, after which the system may reestablish a version of itself that is even more hostile than before. And if the creative disturbance is too great, the system may collapse altogether, leaving insufficient resources for a resurrection of any kind.[6]

Our challenge is to bring the appropriate amount, kind, and pace of creative disturbance to the system, and then to participate in the

---

5. In systems theory, this response would be described in terms of the system seeking to maintain equilibrium. In these terms, we might ask what orthodoxy is. Is it the maintenance of a changeless equilibrium established at some point in the past, or is it the ongoing process of adjusting to constant disturbances to achieve an ever-new, ever-sustainable, and ever-regenerative equilibrium?

6. There is no guarantee that the balanced approach recommended here will succeed, so while we must hope and work for the best option, we must also imagine how to cope with the other options, too—of co-optation, counterreformulation, and collapse.

often messy but always exciting processes of renewal, reform, and refounding, depending on the Spirit of God to guide and energize, to correct and reorient, as the reformulation unfolds.

Whatever we do, we must expect and listen to criticism. We must listen to the critics on the right who tell us that we're proposing too much too fast. We must listen to their counterparts on the left who tell us we're proposing too little too slow. We must soberly consider the dangerous potential consequences of collapse—consequences that are partly in the hands of people like us who propose change from the margins, and even more in the hands of those in the centers of power who have more at stake in defending the status quo. And speaking of the status quo, we also must soberly consider the ways that our religious systems are already fueling the status quo with hostility—between religions, classes, ethnic groups, political parties, and nations, and between human beings and the planet as well, all of which can contribute to the ultimate catastrophic collapses: the destruction of our planetary civilization and our global ecosystem.[7]

These aren't trivial matters! What can we do but speak as best we can, trusting that where we have not spoken strongly enough, others will amplify, and where we have spoken too strongly, others will moderate?

As we play our role in the as-yet-unwritten story, we are acting in good faith upon the doctrines we have already considered. We are trusting that the Creator has built into creation the resources we need for self-correction in this critical moment. We are trusting that original sin, for all its terrifying power, is not more powerful than the more original goodness God has written into the code of creation and of us. We are trusting that God is still calling more and more of us, like Abraham, to leave the Ur of strong-hostile identity and

---

7. I explored these threats in *Everything Must Change* (Nashville: Thomas Nelson, 2007).

venture out, through the barrenness and insecurity of weak-benign identity, into a fertile terra nova where identities can be strong and benevolent.

We are trusting that the doctrine of the Holy Trinity models a kind of glorious one-anotherness that we can learn and into which we can be drawn. We are trusting that Jesus—purely nonviolent, purely benevolent, purely good—truly is the logos that reveals the heart of God and the ultimate inner logic by which the universe arcs toward justice and peace. And we are trusting that the Holy Spirit is drawing us into insight just as others are being drawn into complementary, supplementary, and critically corrective insight. And we are trusting that the Holy Spirit groans within us, as Paul put it, in longings too deep for words, yearning within us for all creation to be liberated from the futility of human hostility and the destruction it unleashes. We are trusting that regardless of the ways the Bible has been abused for hostile purposes, it has unimagined resources for peaceable ones.

If these explorations be deemed unorthodox, we must ask what kind of orthodoxy are we left with? Must we not, in all humility, acknowledge that all orthodoxy is semi-orthodoxy—meaning that none of us can claim to have captured the infinite and inexpressible in our feeble human definitions and expressions? And would that not mean that all orthodoxy is also semi-unorthodoxy, and that every claim to absolute orthodoxy is the least orthodox claim anyone could ever make?[8]

These questions stir a nearly forgotten memory from my childhood. The details are foggy, but I believe I was in the family car, an old Chevy Impala, riding home from church on a Sunday morning. Like any firstborn boy of nine or ten, I was trying to figure out who

---

8. Vaclav Havel's wise words come to mind in this regard: "Keep the company of those who seek the truth—run from those who have found it."

"we" were so I could be a loyal member of "us" and a loyal oppo-
nent against "them." Something was said in the sermon that morning that moved me to ask a question that is central to the identity
of every ardent young fundamentalist: "Who are the liberals, Mom?
They sure must be bad." "Liberals believe in the universal fatherhood
of God and the universal brotherhood of man," she said, as if that
needed no further explanation.

I don't remember anything else, but that brief moment is frozen
in my childhood memory. Why does it stay with me so vividly? The
universal fatherhood of God sounded like a good thing. The same
with the universal brotherhood of man. (We were entirely comfortable with the universal reference of male pronouns back then). I'm
quite certain I didn't argue or even ask another question. But I must
have pondered my mother's reply in my heart in such a way that it
just resurfaced, decades later. That may have been the first moment
when I felt a twinge of identity conflict in my boyish soul, a feeling
that maybe *we* weren't all good and *they* weren't all bad.

We have Jesus to blame for the doctrine of the fatherhood of God,
and for its corollary that we are all sisters and brothers in God's creation. There's no better place to reflect on this doctrine than in the
parable of the Prodigal Son (Luke 15). The parable, it turns out, is all
about identity—after all, what's more primal to identity than one's
family?

As we often tell it, the story climaxes when a runaway boy returns
home feeling disgraced, hoping to reenter the household as a slave,
and the father graciously receives him as a son. But the real climax, I
propose, comes later, when the father slips out of the welcome-home
party to speak with the alienated older brother outside. As the interchange unfolds, it's clear that the older son feels every bit as conflicted and confused about his identity as his brother: "Listen! For all
these years I have been working like a slave for you, and I have never
disobeyed your command; yet you have never given me even a young

goat so that I might celebrate with my friends." Even though he has remained dutifully at home, he sees himself as a slave, not a son, taking orders, putting in his time.

Both brothers, then, not just one, suffer from an identity crisis. Neither sees himself as he truly is: God's beloved child and connected to his brother in one family. The father's prodigal love to the younger son becomes the means by which the older son could discover how loved he himself is . . . if he would "have eyes to see and ears to hear."

But in his alienated and hostile identity, he can't even speak of "my brother." Instead he refers to the returned runaway as "this son of yours." Then the father cleverly, wisely, tenderly turns the phrase, referring to him as "this brother of yours." The primary message of this story, then, is not addressed to rebellious younger sons sowing their wild oats, as we normally suppose. The primary message is addressed to hostile older brothers who feel right and superior and offended, who won't join the party by joining God in welcoming and celebrating "the other as brother." The moral of the story runs something like this:

> You can't maintain hostility against "the other" without also withdrawing from the father who loves both you and the other as beloved children. If you maintain hostility against the other, you stop acting like a son in the same family. You leave your true identity as a son and start playing the part of a slave. When you cut off the other, you're breaking God's heart. God wants you to join God in loving the other as part of one family.

Probably the story should be entitled "the lost son," not the prodigal son, because it comes packaged with two other stories—of a lost sheep and a lost coin. But the lost son, it turns out, isn't the younger son. When the story ends, that son "was lost but now is found." The lost son is the older son. He's the one who doesn't know who he is, where he is, or what he's doing. He's the only outsider—placed there by his own refusal to love. And in this, of course, he is a mirror for the intended audience of this triplet of stories:

> Now all the tax collectors and sinners were coming near to listen to him. And the Pharisees and the scribes were grumbling and saying, "This fellow welcomes sinners and eats with them." So he told them this parable.... (Luke 15:1–3)

Would the meaning become clearer if we altered the text slightly like this?

> Now all the Muslims and Buddhists, New Agers and agnostics were coming near to listen to him. And the radio preachers and heresy hunters were grumbling and saying, "This fellow welcomes non-Christians and eats with them." So he told them this parable....

Could it be that our core doctrines are even more wonderful and challenging than we previously imagined, asking us not simply to assent to them in the presence of our fellow assenters, but to practice them in relationships with those who don't hold them? Could our core doctrines in this way become "healing teachings" intended to diagnose and heal our distorted and hostile identities...restoring a strong and benevolent identity, and unleashing in us a joyful desire to converse and eat with the other? Could our core teachings be shared, not as ultimata (believe or die!), but as gifts (here's how we see things, and here's what that does for us...)? Could each of us examine our heart for traces of the older brother resident there?

PART III
THE LITURGICAL CHALLENGE

Our religious self, like our cultural or social self...takes shape through an ongoing process...of forming a sense of self and then expanding or correcting that sense as we meet other selves. There is no such thing as a neatly defined, once-and-for-all identity.

—*Paul Knitter*[1]

1. Paul Knitter, *Without Buddha I Could Not Be a Christian* (Oxford: Oneworld, 2009), pp. 214–215.

Mirrors daily life (Rhythm)
Rise AM
Sun: Day of "Resurrection"

Chapter 19

How the Christian Year Can Become More Christian

I begin the prayer that Jesus taught us: "Our Father…" Who is included in this word "our"? After that first prayer when I said, "God," there was no way back to unbelief. God was there to stay in my life. After this prayer when I said, "Our God," there was no way back to unbelief either. *The other* was here to stay in my life.

—*Samir Selmanovic*[1]

A few years ago I was invited to preach in an old Anglican church in a rural village in the United Kingdom (further specificity isn't important). Having arrived early, I had a few minutes to wander around the church and read the wall inscriptions that are so typical of old British churches. A large inscription from the nineteenth century arrested my attention. It honored a young man from the parish who had died as a soldier in India, fighting to maintain the British Empire's control of the subcontinent. The

---

1. Samir Selmanovic, *It's Really All About God: How Islam, Atheism, and Judaism Made Me a Better Christian* (San Francisco: Jossey-Bass, 2009), p. 250.

Imperial Christianity

168 • Why Did Jesus, Moses, the Buddha, and Mohammed Cross the Road?

inscription included words to this effect: "He bravely fought and honorably died in service to the crown, the brave son of a conquering race."

My guess is that most members of that parish pay no more attention to the inscriptions on their walls than they do to dust in the corners or cracks in the ceiling. But as a guest, all the while I preached, that inscription seemed to heckle me from the wall to my left. "What if a person of Indian descent came to this church?" I wondered. How would he or she feel to be dubbed "a conquered race"? And how does it feel to be a British citizen, having these words on the wall remind you each Sunday of your colonial past? What does the inscription say to small children as they learn to read, come of age, undergo confirmation? What does the act of ignoring the inscription do to those who ignore it? What would I do with that inscription if I were the priest at this church? Would I try to cover it up? Have it removed? Use it as a teaching opportunity by placing a theological reflection beside it? With all these distracting questions swirling in my mind, I doubt my sermon was very coherent.

The vestiges of Imperial Christianity are not always as obvious as this inscription in stone. But they are no less present in most of our churches. Racism, colonialism, exclusivism, elitism, and other members of the hostility family often hide camouflaged in songs and hymns, devotionals and prayers, sermons and Sunday School lessons. And it's not only what is said that aids and abets hostility: it's what is left unsaid. For example, I remember preaching in a predominantly Tutsi church in Burundi. After I made an appeal for the Twa people, the nation's oppressed minority, someone came up to me and said, "The word *Twa* has never been spoken before in this church. It is as if the Twa didn't even exist. Thank you for reminding us that the Twa too are God's children." I thought of how many real-world hostilities around the world are similarly protected through avoidance and silence in churches today.

Liturgy = order or program of gathered worship

In education, there is something called the null curriculum. It's the between-the-lines curriculum that teaches by what is never mentioned, or by the way the chairs are arranged, or by the way bells ring and meals are served and floors are cleaned and walls are painted (or not). In churches, there is what we might call the null liturgy—the unwritten repertoire of forms and practices that teach without even being noticed. If we are going to reformulate liturgy to reshape Christian identity in the direction of strength and benevolence, we are going to have to address both our explicit liturgy and our null liturgy.

Normally the term *liturgy* is used to describe an order or program of gathered worship, usually on a Sunday morning. It derives from a Greek word meaning "public duty," literally "the work of the people." I've suggested elsewhere that we could better define it as "the workout of the people"—where each liturgical element is like an exercise or apparatus at a gym or health club, designed to strengthen a particular muscle group.[2] Liturgical elements in this broader sense—whether a hymn, a chant, a prayer of confession, a season of the church year, a class or small group, a sermon, or the eucharist understood in this way or that—exercise different faculties of the soul, and in so doing they strengthen, for better or worse, some form of Christian identity.

As in the case of the inscription on that church wall, liturgical elements can harbor vestiges of racism, colonialism, and nationalism that stand in direct opposition to the gospel. When we sing a popular praise chorus like "Show Your Power," we can unintentionally label and objectify the other, as in "for our inheritance, give us the lost." When we faithfully recite a nice, sweet, vague prayer of confession week after week, but never specify what sins we're actually guilty of—institutional racism, complicity with plutocracy, greed, gluttony,

---

2. See my books *Finding Our Way Again* (Nashville: Thomas Nelson, 2008) and *Naked Spirituality* (New York: HarperOne, 2011).

hymn - chant - prayers - season in ch yr - class - group - sermon - eucharist

(1) Christ = offering Himself in love (2) Lamb of God — Sacrifice

(3) Word of God — nonviolent revelation (4) Service

ecological apathy, or cowardice in response to our call to be peace-makers and justice seekers—we are being liturgically formed in a Christian identity that tacitly supports the status quo.

If we want to move beyond both a strong-hostile Christian iden-tity on the one hand and a sweet, sentimental, benign Christian identity on the other, we must grapple with liturgy in this broad sense, starting with the church year. Imagine the positive impact on Christian identity if we conceived of the church year in fresh ways.

(5) Mary - icon of receiving + participating in Birth

ADVENT

tender loving

In Advent, we celebrate the coming of Christ as the prince of peace. We cultivate a longing for peace. We highlight the bright promise of his coming—good news of great joy for all peoples everywhere—against the dark realities of our world: competitive religious suprem-acy, strident neighbor-less nationalism, and the misguided sense of privilege, all flowing from a misguided sense of calling. As we look back to the original Advent, we also see Christ as still coming to us from the future in perpetual advent. In that spirit of welcome, we urge every heart to prepare him room so earth may indeed receive her needed king and the kingdom he proclaimed.

Perhaps we re-tradition the Advent candles around four titles commonly ascribed to Jesus: Christ—meaning the promised libera-tor, who frees us from our endless cycles of violence; Lord—the anti-Caesar, who brings peace not by shedding the blood of enemies but by offering himself in love; Lamb of God—who comes to put an end to the cycles of scapegoating and sacrifice once and for all; and Word of God—who reveals God's character as nonviolent, kind, and rec-onciling.[3] Perhaps in this context, we rediscover Mary as the living

---

3. Or perhaps, as we will suggest in a later chapter, we should focus for one week of Advent on Jesus as friend—friend of all.

Jesus - firstborn of new generation characterized by love, benevolence, non-violence - solidarity with ALL

icon of receptivity to and participation in the new gospel way of life. Perhaps we also rediscover the social, political, economic, and theological foment of Mary's Magnificat. And perhaps we re-tradition the idea of virgin birth as a decisive repudiation of the standard patriarchal systems of violent male dominance, evermore associating the saving power of God with the tender care of a mother's love.[4] Such a celebration would give new meaning to the title *Savior* as applied to Jesus—a fitting focal point for Christmas Eve: Jesus, the firstborn of a new generation of humanity characterized by love, nonviolence, and solidarity with all, comes to save humanity from what it has become.

Jesus = self-giving

CHRISTMAS

On Christmas Day, we would celebrate the birth of the man who repudiated the violent path of obsessive taking (which René Girard called *acquisitive mimesis*) and blazed the new path of generous self-giving. Our mutual gift-giving would then echo the self-giving of God in Christ.[5] And the celebration of Christ's birth could become a birthday party, not just for Jesus but also for the new humanity that transcends and includes all previous identities. Imagine, beginning on Christmas Day, the expansive possibilities of the twelve days of Christmas—rescued from the banality of geese a-laying and lords a-leaping: each day devoted to celebrating a different aspect of the love of God for all humanity, starting with the poor, the vulnerable, the last, the least, and the lost.[6] *birth of new humanity*

---

4. We should also, as Joy Carroll Wallis wisely says, keep Herod in Christmas, remembering the violence of the slaughter of the innocents and all it has to tell us about the destructive power of fear and hostility.

5. Perhaps in this light, we would be more prone to give the more precious gifts of service and presence rather than cheap presents of plastic, cloth, and paper.

6. I plan to explore possibilities in this regard in upcoming books called *Catechesis* and *Subversive Liturgy*. For example, imagine the twelve days unfolding in days of feasting and

Baptism = becoming new + loving in God's image.

LENT

Imagine the possibilities of Lent as an annual season specially devoted to the life and teaching of Jesus, and an annual call to repentance—to examine and change our lives in light of his kind life and teaching of kindness. Perhaps Lent could take shape around a four-year cycle, with year one focused on the Sermon on the Mount, year two focused on Jesus' interactions with individuals, year three focused on Jesus' parables, and year four focused on the meaning of Jesus' signs

God = suffering servant - victim

fasting, with short daily readings and prayers to be shared around a meal; or, instead of a meal:

1. Feast of Christ the King (Christmas Day)—celebrating God's kingdom as a new way of life characterized by good will (benevolence) toward all people.
2. Feast of the Shepherds—celebrating in some creative, communal way God's special solidarity with the poor.
3. Fast of the Holy Innocents—acknowledging the evil of abusive human power that causes children to suffer, and celebrating God's love for children in need around the world.
4. Feast of the Genealogies—celebrating God's work through history, and in each of our own families, bringing us from violence to peace.
5. Feast of the Magi—celebrating God's revelation of messianic compassion in all cultures and among all religions.
6. Feast of John the Baptist—celebrating John's identity as Jesus' forerunner, working on the margins of society, calling all to radical repentance.
7. Feast of the New Year—celebrating all things made new in Christ: New Testament, New Commandment, New Identity.
8. Feast of the Circumcision—celebrating Jesus' identity within the Jewish people, together with his love for all people, reflected in the words of Simeon and Anna (Luke 2:25ff).
9. Fast of the Flight to Egypt—recalling the holy family's experience as refugees by fasting for one meal, and then celebrating God's concern for refugees by eating a simple meal of similar caloric intake as the world's poorest share.
10. Feast of Jesus' Childhood—celebrating Jesus' experience in his Father's House as a boy, and his later proclamation that God's House will outlast the Temple and is meant as a place of welcome for all people.
11. Feast of Jesus' Baptism—celebrating the Spirit descending as a dove upon Jesus, and baptism as turning from old identities of hostility to a new identity as God's agents of peace.
12. Feast of the Epiphany—celebrating God's manifestation in Jesus, in his proclamation of Good News for the poor and outsiders in Luke 4:14–30.

gentiles

and wonders or his Olivet Discourse. Or perhaps one year could be devoted to each of the four gospel writers. Whatever the focus, the purpose would be identity formation as followers of Jesus in his way of peace, justice, and reconciliation.

Love one another-respect-

HOLY WEEK

Again, imagine the possibility of Palm Sunday as we ponder Jesus weeping over Jerusalem for its ignorance of the ways of peace. Imagine us lamenting today's ignorance in today's centers of political, economic, and religious power: *Oh Washington, Washington! Oh London, London! Oh Buenos Aires, Buenos Aires! Oh Harare, Harare!* Imagine if that yearning for peace framed the week to follow, as we hold up our personal, familial, ecclesial, political, economic, and international conflicts to be softened, as it were, by the tears of Jesus. Imagine Monday through Wednesday devoted to specific incidents recorded in the gospel, culminating in Maundy Thursday with Jesus' command to love one another—including stranger, outsider, outcast, betrayer, and enemy. What act could more dramatically embody the opposite of violence than the washing of feet? What attitude could more appropriately express the opposite of hostility than humble servanthood? (We will consider the Lord's Supper in an upcoming chapter.)

Then imagine Good Friday, as we ponder the mystery of God identifying not with the torturers but with the tortured; not with the powerful but with victims of abused power; not with those who scapegoat but with those who are scapegoated. Good Friday thus becomes the great celebration of God's empathy with all human suffering and pain. It exposes all violence as anti-God, and reveals God as the one who identifies with all victims of violence. Pondering the cross and the agonizing road to it, we acknowledge God's self-revelation in Christ as a suffering victim—not as a dominating victor. In our

Jesus - empathy to all human suffering

Good Friday services, then, we defect from the broad and smooth road of violence and domination, choosing the rough and uphill pathway of the cross—choosing to suffer rather than to make others suffer.[7] When we observe the stations of the cross, and especially when we come to the women weeping for Jesus, we hear him saying to us, "Do not weep for me, children of the twenty-first century, but for yourselves and your children." In that spirit, we would return to the tears of Palm Sunday, seeing in the suffering of people today the suffering of Jesus, and vice versa.

Then comes Holy Saturday, a day of silence and stillness, an in-between day that I have often felt should be the day devoted to doubt, the day at which we listen to agnostics and atheists and remind them, and us, that they too have a place among the people of God.

EASTER

Then Easter dawns. The scandal of Easter was not simply that a supernatural event occurred. Minds in the ancient world weren't divided by the rigid natural-supernatural dualism that forms modern minds. In those days miracles were notable not for *defying the laws of nature* (a concept that was unknown until recent centuries), but for *conveying an unexpected meaning* or message through an unusual or unexplainable medium. What was the scandalous meaning conveyed by the resurrection of Jesus? It was not simply that a dead man was

---

7. This reference to Matthew 7:13–14 reflects my conviction that Jesus is not talking about a broad-minded road that leads many to hell and a narrow-minded one that leads a few to heaven, as many seem to assume. Rather, he advocates a difficult way of peacemaking and nonviolence (5:3–10, 5:21–26, 5:38–48, 6:12–13, 7:1–2) that leads to survival and life, and warns of a broad and easy road of violence and hate that leads to the destruction of war, exactly the kind of war that destroyed Jerusalem about a generation later in AD 67–70. This understanding suggests another answer to the question posed in our title: *Why did Jesus, Moses, the Buddha, and Mohammed cross the road? To exit from the superhighway of violence and forge new paths of peace.*

Resurrection = us from violence to peace.

raised. It was *who* the raised man was. Someone rejected, mocked, condemned, and executed by both the political and religious establishments was raised. A convicted outlaw, troublemaker, and rabble rouser was raised. A condemned blasphemer and lawbreaker was raised. A nonviolent nonconformist who included the outcasts—and therefore became an outcast—was raised. What does that mean about the authoritative institutions that condemned him? What does that mean about his nonconformist message and nonviolent ways?

What might happen if every Easter we celebrated the resurrection not merely as the resuscitation of a single corpse nearly two millennia ago, but more—as the ongoing resurrection of all humanity through Christ? Easter could be the annual affirmation of our ongoing resurrection from violence to peace, from fear to faith, from hostility to love, from a culture of consumption to a culture of stewardship and generosity...and in all these ways and more, from death to life. What if our celebration of Easter was so radical in its meaning that it tempted tyrants and dictators everywhere to make it illegal, because it represents the ultimate scandal: an annual call for creative and peaceful insurrection against all status quos based on fear, hostility, exclusion, and violence?[8] What if we never stopped making Easter claims about Jesus in AD 33, but always continued by making Easter claims on us today—declaring that now is the time to be raised from the deadness of fear, hostility, exclusion, and violence to walk in what Paul called "newness of life"? What if Easter was about our ongoing resurrection "in Christ"—in a new humanity marked by a strong-benevolent identity as Christ-embodying peacemakers, enemy lovers, offense forgivers, boundary crossers, and movement builders? What kind of character would this kind of liturgical year form in us? How might the world be changed because of it?

I can imagine Easter opening a fifty-day period during which we

---

8. See Peter Rollins, *Insurrection* (New York: Howard Books, 2011).

meet Jesus in everyone.

Jesus, King of Love

constantly celebrate newness, freedom, change, and growth. As we would retell each year the story of the risen Christ appearing in the stranger on the Emmaus Road, so part of every Easter season for us would mean meeting and inviting to our tables strangers, aliens, refugees, people of other religions or no religion at all, to welcome them as we would Christ, and to expect to meet Christ in them.

During those fifty days, we would observe the feast of the ascension. We would do so without arguing over whether a literal Jesus was literally seen literally rising into literal clouds (have that either way you want it). Instead, we would focus on the meaning of ascension—the *actuality* that transcends *factuality*: that Jesus now reigns for us as the nonviolent king, the servant-king, the king of love. He has already ascended and has already been enthroned, which is to say that we don't need to wait for some future day to start living by his way. We can, we must, begin the insurrection of resurrection now.

PENTECOST

I have always felt that Pentecost is the most underrated holiday. What could be more important than the outpouring of the Holy Spirit on "all flesh"? What could be more meaningful for people being saved from hostility than to celebrate the Spirit who empowers us to "speak in tongues"—to transcend the us-them barriers of language and see all people as one diverse community in God's commonwealth of love? This would be a season to read the Book of Acts—a book that is about boundary-crossing from Pentecost (God speaks all languages, not just ours!), to the early church holding "all things in common" (God reconciles rich and poor!), to the healing of the lame beggar (God welcomes the disabled!), to the resolution of the Jewish-Greek widow controversy (God shows no favorites!), to the baptism of the Ethiopian eunuch (God includes the racially and sexually other!), to

Peter's conversion at Cornelius' home (God calls nobody "unclean"), and so on.

KINGDOMTIDE

[handwritten: Ordinary time]

I prefer this name to "ordinary time"—although the point could be made that living a "kingdom-of-God life" should indeed be ordinary for Christians. (Some may prefer the term *kindomtide*, to shift from a political/patriarchal to a familial/filial image.) If Pentecost celebrates our joyful immersion into the Spirit, this season instructs us in walking in the Spirit day by day. This is the season to focus on the ninefold fruit of the Spirit—strong and benevolent in flavor: love, joy, peace, patience, kindness, goodness, gentleness, faithfulness, and self-control. This is the season to seek Spirit-empowerment as we learn and practice the specific skills and habits of following Jesus' way—active and deep listening, processing pain into forgiveness and reconciliation, feeling and showing compassion, conflict transformation, preemptive peacemaking, serving others, giving secretly, receiving gratefully, returning blessing for cursing, doing good to those who do you evil, withdrawing to pray in solitude. There is plenty here to keep us on the edge of our seats until Advent season begins again.[9]

[handwritten: love, joy, peace, patience, kindness, goodness, gentleness, faithfulness + self control]

"What you're recommending here," you might say, "is a radical revision of the whole church year! Is that allowed? Is it possible?"

"Yes," I would reply, "that is exactly what I am recommending. The deeper question is not whether revision is allowed, but rather whether the church year as it is currently practiced is actually working.

---

9. This is also the season for celebrating the Transfiguration—the day God elevated Jesus over Moses and Elijah, icons of the law and prophets, both of whom—unlike Jesus—participated in religious violence.

Is it producing Christians with a strong and benevolent identity? If not, then how, in these critical times, could we possibly justify not revising it?"

Obviously, this is not the kind of project any one person can accomplish in one chapter or even one book. But great liturgical reformers like John Chrysostom, St. Francis, Martin Luther, John Calvin, Thomas Cranmer, Charles Wesley, Pope John XXIII, and Vincent Donovan have arisen in the past. And I dare to hope and believe that there are, alive today, thousands of women and men, young and old, from the global north and south, east and west, clergy and laity, who have been given the gifts to help us now. If the ancient formula *lex orandi lex credendi* (the rule of worship is the rule of belief) is true, then it is equally true that *lex orandi lex vivendi* (the way we worship is the way we live). If we want to live in greater strength and kindness, then strength and kindness must be more central to our liturgical lives season by season, Sunday by Sunday, year by year.

live in strength & kindness
central in daily lives AND
liturgical seasons

Chapter 20
How Baptism Differs from Sitting on Santa's Knee

Flannery O'Connor conveyed baptism through its exaggeration, in one novel as a violent death by drowning. In answer to a question about why she created such bizarre characters, she replied that for the near-blind you have to draw very large, simple caricatures.

—*Walker Percy*[1]

My second-best educational experience in life (after finger painting in kindergarten) came in graduate school when, under the wise tutelage of Dr. Lewis Lawson at the University of Maryland, I wrote my thesis on novelist Walker Percy, whom I had the privilege to correspond with and meet. In addition to inspiring me by his literary example, encouraging me to write, and introducing me to the term *postmodern*, which would later become so helpful to me, Percy helped me understand the crisis of Christian identity: the Christian today has "cast his lot with a discredited Christendom" and "inherited a defunct vocabulary," he said. What is one to do in such a predicament?

---

1. Walker Percy, "Notes for a Novel about the End of the World," in *The Message in the Bottle* (New York: Farrar, Straus and Giroux, 1980), p. 118.

Bap: Death to old personality + new life

180 • Why Did Jesus, Moses, the Buddha, and Mohammed Cross the Road?

Repenting of all hostility   *to new*

He does the only thing he can do. Like Joyce's Stephen Dedalus, he calls on every ounce of cunning, craft, and guile he can muster from the darker regions of his soul. The fictional use of violence, shock, comedy, insult, the bizarre, are the everyday tools of his trade. How could it be otherwise? How can one possibly write of baptism as an event of immense significance when baptism is already accepted but accepted by and large as a minor tribal rite somewhat secondary in importance to taking the kids to see Santa at the department store?[2]

ceremonial washing

John the Bap - chg. water immer into a spiritual cleansing

As an adult convert to Christian faith, Percy knew firsthand that baptism was in its origin far from a "minor tribal rite somewhat secondary in importance." On an individual level baptism represented, like death, the end of an old identity and, like birth, rising into a new one. On a public level, it represented a rejection of all current forms of religious identity in pursuit of a new kind of identity.

It's surprising how few Christians realize that John the Baptist didn't invent baptism. He revolutionized it. He turned it from a sign of submission to the religious status quo into an act of guerrilla theater that protested the religious status quo.

Luke tells us that John was the son of Zechariah, a priest. The priestly class was centered in Jerusalem around the temple—an opulent monument to religious power, success, and prestige. Prior to entering the temple, pilgrims to the holy city would undergo a ceremonial washing, part of the elaborate ritual apparatus overseen by the priests. Why a washing? Because pilgrims who came to the holy city from faraway places had (along with other contaminations) undergone polluting contact with "unclean" Gentiles. The ceremonial washing in Temple-affiliated baths was, then, a celebration of

---

2. Ibid.

identity—what we might call a conventional or establishment identity: we are the clean and legitimate, they are the unclean and illegitimate, and *we* must be washed clean from all contact with *them*. There was a theological assumption behind this identity: God loves *us* and finds *them* unclean, smelly, disgusting, dirty, unacceptable. The Temple and its baptisms, then, were ritual enactments to bond adherents to this strong-superior identity: *God is hostile to all unclean people, and through our baptism we separate ourselves from all that is unclean.*

When John comes of age, he does not follow his father into the priesthood as everyone would expect.[3] Instead, he turns away from temple and holy city and enters the wilderness. It is highly possible that for some time he associated with one of the Essenic communities like the Qumram settlement, the source of the Dead Sea Scrolls. Members of these hyperpuritan communities felt the Temple system was hopelessly corrupted, having (among many failings) struck a compromise with the occupying Romans. In protest, they created separatist communes out in the desert, far from Jerusalem, and there they set up their own religious apparatus—complete with baptismal pools that would be used several times a day. The message is clear: the conventional establishment is just as unclean as the Gentiles, and by separating ourselves from them, *we* stand apart as the truly, *truly* pure. Day after day, bath after bath, adherents bound themselves ever more passionately to this theological claim: *God is hostile toward all unclean people, and through our baptism, we separate ourselves from all that is unclean.*

These antiestablishment communities in this way positioned themselves as mirror images of the establishment they opposed. If the establishment was oppositional, they were hyperoppositional. If the

---

3. Luke's story of John's birth sets up this father-son tension in a fascinating way.

Qumran

establishment was puritan, they were hyperpuritan. If the establishment required conformity, they were hyperconformist—only to a contrasting hierarchy and regimen. If we are tempted to compare the Jerusalem establishment to Roman Catholicism in Middle Ages, we might see Protestantism as the Essenic counterpart. If we are tempted to compare the Jerusalem establishment to Mainline Protestantism in twentieth-century America, we might see Fundamentalism or early Evangelicalism as the Essenic counterpart. If we are tempted to compare the Jerusalem establishment to Religious Right Evangelicalism in the first decade of the new century, we might see the New Atheism or the Secular Left as its Essenic counterpart. If we critique the former as compromised and institutionalized, we might critique the latter as reactionary and extremist. From a distance, we can see each as a rival whose oppositional, hostile, us-them identity in many ways mirrors that of its opposing double.

Against this backdrop, then, we must imagine John leaving Jerusalem and choosing not to follow in the footsteps of his father in the priesthood. We see him heading east from Jerusalem through the Judean wilderness. But whether or not he stays for a time with the Qumram community, he does not remain with them forever. Instead, he leaves the rugged hill country and heads north into the rift valley above the Dead Sea, and there, on the banks of the Jordan River, he begins to baptize people.

Remember as you see the crowds gather that baptism already has two established (pre-Christian) meanings. For conventional temple adherents, it means separating oneself from Gentiles (people of foreign religions) and conforming to a conventional establishment identity with all its hostilities. For Essenic separatists, it means separating oneself from one's conventional compatriots and taking on a radical, counterestablishment identity with all its hostilities. For both, it means washing away contamination; separation from unclean acts, things, places, and people; the establishment of a distinct and oppo-

The Liturgical Challenge • 183

[Handwritten annotations at top:]
1. Separating oneself for Gentiles
2. Conforming to Cont...
3. Washing away contamination — unclean acts + people

*[Right margin:]* Essenes (1) Sep. fr conv. (3) + being radical

sitional identity. Against that background, what would it mean to be
baptized by John in the Jordan River—far from Jerusalem and the
Temple precincts, yet away from the isolated Essenic communities
as well? What would it mean to be baptized in a public place, in a
natural river rather than a man-made bath, in running—maybe even
muddy—river water?

John defines the essential meaning himself: he proclaims not a
baptism of conformity but a baptism of repentance, which means
a radical, far-reaching rethinking of everything. If one was previously formed by a conventional Temple establishment identity,
one rethinks that way of life. If one was previously formed by an
Essenic antiestablishment identity, one rethinks that way of life.
What might have been considered acceptable before—hating Gentiles, hating priests, hating the poor, hating the rich—now seems
like a sin to be confessed. What might have been considered unacceptable before—reconciling with enemies, showing kindness to
outcasts, putting the needs of people above religious rules—now
seems like a good thing. That kind of repenting would determine the
kinds of sins people would confess as they descended into the Jordan
for baptism.

In Matthew's Gospel, John sees some Sadducees and Pharisees
coming for baptism. (They were not friends, by the way—one might
imagine John addressing American Democrats and Republicans or
British Conservatives and Labor today.) His response is fascinating:

[Handwritten heading:] John: Repentance

You brood of vipers! Who warned you to flee from the wrath to
come? Bear fruit worthy of repentance. Do not presume to say to
yourselves, "We have Abraham as our ancestor"; for I tell you, God
is able from these stones to raise up children to Abraham. Even now
the ax is lying at the root of the trees; *[handwritten: another nation]* every tree therefore that does
not bear good fruit is cut down and thrown into the fire. (Matt. 3:
7–10)

The epithet "brood of vipers" was a common expression of the day, meaning malicious or hostile people.[4] John seems to be echoing Jeremiah 46:22, where Egypt is compared to a viper.[5] Drawing from that allusion, John appears to be saying something very powerful—something about identity:

> You are the offspring of malicious, hostile communities. Like Egypt, you oppress and enslave. Who warned you that you need to change? Yes, you might claim to have a clean, pure identity because you are descendants of Abraham, but that isn't impressive at all. What God is interested in is not hostility but fruitfulness.

The violent image of vipers soon contrasts with a peaceful animal image: the Holy Spirit descending as a dove upon Jesus. So the kingdoms of this world—including religious kingdoms—are viper-like and violent; the kingdom of God is dovelike and peaceful. Baptismal repentance means defecting from the former and identifying with the latter.

In Luke's version of the story (3:7ff.), these words are directed toward not just the Sadducees and Pharisees but the crowds in general, and the crowds ask what kind of fruit God wants to see from them. In every case, the response relates to how they will treat others—not with hostility, not with resistance, but with kindness, generosity, and justice:

Kindness, generosity, justice

---

4. Jesus addresses the Pharisees with the term twice in Matthew's Gospel, in 12:34 and 23:33. In the second instance, the term is clearly associated with violence and bloodshed.

5. If John is indeed echoing Jeremiah 46:22, then it is not God who is holding the ax at the root of the tree—it is another nation. The fire, wrath, and cutting that are coming will indeed be judgment, but judgment inflicted by the Romans, as happened in AD 70.

Repentence means dropping violence + hostility + identifying w K of G doveleke behavior

"Whoever has two coats must share with anyone who has none; and whoever has food must do likewise." Even tax collectors came to be baptized, and they asked him, "Teacher, what should we do?" He said to them, "Collect no more than the amount prescribed for you." Soldiers also asked him, "And we, what should we do?" He said to them, "Do not extort money from anyone by threats or false accusation, and be satisfied with your wages." (Luke 3:11–14)

So for John, baptism is hardly a second-rate tribal rite comparable to sitting on Santa's knee. It is the radical reversal of identities of exclusion and hostility. It is a defection from all exclusive, hostile, and elitist identities—whether they be establishment or antiestablishment in nature. It is a sign that one is repenting of all hostile identities, knowing that those identities can only lead to violent cataclysm. By de-identifying with oppositional identities—by dying to them, one can identify with something new: the kingdom, reign, or commonwealth of God—which is a call not to separation and exclusion, but rather to solidarity and reconciliation, as we have seen again and again.

In most of our traditions, Christian baptism is little different from temple baptism. It represents identification with the clean, the orthodox, the good, the "us." In some, baptism is more akin to Essene baptism, representing identification with the superclean, the hyperorthodox, the holier-than-others, the elite and exclusive "us." What would happen if we rediscovered baptism in this alternative way of John and Jesus: discovering a new identity in the transcendent and inclusive kingdom of God, an identity that locates us in solidarity with all people everywhere?

If we reformulated baptism in this way, what kind of catechism would prepare us for it? How would that subversive catechesis guide us to face and repent of our prejudices, our racisms, our nationalisms, our

Die to the old ways. Rebirth to K of God

Born again

186 • Why Did Jesus, Moses, the Buddha, and Mohammed Cross the Road?

political and economic antagonisms, our hostilities of every sort? How would it help us discover a new identity as people "born again"—not entering an elite human ancestry or exclusive religious pedigree, but passing through water and the Spirit so that we are joined once again to all humankind (and to all creation), to be ever marked by human kindness? How would the history of the last two thousand years be different if this understanding of baptism had been sustained?

Baptism in this sense means far more than immersion into Christianity or a Christian religious institution. It signals immersion into Christ, so that from now on, inside the identity of Christ, we look out at the other through his eyes, so to speak. It is immersion into the kingdom or commonwealth of God, so that we now see all people from the perspective of this new filial citizenship. "In Christ" and "in the commonwealth of God" are far deeper realities than "in Christianity" and "in the Christian religion." Irish theologian/philosopher Peter Rollins captures the difference quite starkly, reflecting on Paul's proclamation that in Christ there is neither Jew nor Greek (religious identity), slave nor free (socioeconomic identity), male nor female (sexual identity):[6]

> This vision of Paul's is often domesticated by those who would wish to turn this radical vision on its head and claim that he really means we must lay down all earthly identities in order to take up another identity, that of being a Christian. All identities are thus rendered impotent in relation to this unique super-identity.

This domesticated understanding betrays Paul's real meaning, Rollins realizes. To truly be "in Christ" does not mean embracing "yet another identity," but rather "lay(ing) down the various identities that would otherwise define us."

---

6. Peter Rollins, *Insurrection* (New York: Howard Books, 2011), p. 165.

Jesus poured Himself out to servanthood to death for us

He then recalls Paul's words in Philippians that call us to share the attitude of Christ, who did not grasp or cling to his exalted identity but rather poured himself out, made himself nothing, descending through humanity to servanthood and through servanthood to death as a criminal and disturber of the violence-based Pax Romana. To follow Christ is to share in his radical divestment of identity. He concludes:[7]

> We can even say that in Christ there is neither Christian nor non-Christian.... The scandalous nature of this radical vision is captured succinctly in the Gospel according to John, where the Christian is described as one who lives in the world (with all of its social, religious, and political divisions) while no longer being of it (not being held fast by them).... When this loss of identity is enacted in a liturgical setting, we may call it a suspended space, for in that location one symbolically lays one's identities at the door.

Could you imagine a baptism that carried this radical and subversive meaning? Can you see how this meaning would turn the site of every baptismal font or pool into a modern-day Jordan River, and every baptizer into a modern-day John the Baptist, and every person baptized into a modern-day agent of the commonwealth of God? Can you see what baptism could be—the laying aside of all hostile identities and the taking up of a new identity in Christ, in which old divisions are replaced by a strong, profound solidarity of human-kindness, shared with everyone?

---

7. Ibid., pp. 167–169.

Chapter 21

How Songs, Prayers, Sermons, and Sunday School Classes Can Save Lives

Onward, Christian soldiers, marching as to war,
With the cross of Jesus going on before.
Christ, the royal master, leads against the foe;
Forward into battle see his banners go!
—Sabine Baring-Gould[1]

I love that old hymn "All Things Bright and Beautiful." You're probably familiar with the chorus if you have much history in Protestant churches...

> *All things bright and beautiful,*
> *All creatures great and small,*

---

1. This hymn was dropped from the Presbyterian hymnal in 1990, and Methodists tried to drop it in 1986, but popular support preserved it in spite of the fact that it reinforces a military model for Christian identity, celebrates "the cross of Jesus" in the conquering ways of Constantine, and renders "the other" as "the foe." M. Thomas Thangaraj offers several examples of similarly un-otherly hymns in *Relating to People of Other Religions: What Every Christian Needs to Know* (Nashville: Abingdon Press, 1997).

All things wise and wonderful:
The Lord God made them all.

Some might say it's a little sentimental, but that's true of a lot of our hymns, especially nineteenth-century ones.[2] Sentimental or not, I love the hymn's five verses because each celebrates the beauty of creation, one of the primary ways my own soul experiences and worships God.

Each little flower that opens,/ Each little bird that sings,/ He made
*   their glowing colors,/ He made their tiny wings.*
The purple headed mountains,/ The river running by,/ The sunset
*   and the morning/ That brightens up the sky.*
The cold wind in the winter,/ The pleasant summer sun,/ The ripe
*   fruits in the garden,/ He made them every one.*
The tall trees in the greenwood,/The meadows where we play,/
*   The rushes by the water,/ To gather every day.*
He gave us eyes to see them,/ And lips that we might tell/ How
*   great is God Almighty,/ Who has made all things well.*

Recently I learned from Peter Rollins that the lyricist, Mrs. Cecil Alexander, penned one more verse to the hymn, one that today's hymnals don't include:[3]

The rich man in his castle,   *ghastly*
The poor man at his gate,
He made them, high or lowly,
And ordered their estate.

---

2. The hymn was composed in 1848 and is a good example of a Victorian parlor hymn.

3. Peter Rollins, *Insurrection* (New York: Howard Books, 2011), p. 107.

As I pondered this verse, I couldn't help recalling various stops in my travels over recent years. I've been inside the castles and mansions of some of the world's rich and powerful—eaten gourmet meals, enjoyed scintillating conversation, slept in the finest beds, and even relieved myself in bathrooms of shocking opulence. And I have walked among the poor outside the gates of the rich... visiting in homes smaller than bathrooms, walking in the fecal mud of crowded refugee camps and squalid squatter villages, sleeping in dingy slums and grim occupied territories where oppression is the norm and the police are just another threat. Having been both inside the castles and outside the gates, if I were asked to sing this verse in church some Sunday, I can only say that I would choke. I would walk out. I don't know if I could ever return to a church where this verse was sung.

Imagine the effects of singing such a verse on the rich—the gratification, the peace, the joy, the sense of <u>divine entitlement</u>. And imagine the effects on the poor—the humiliation, the fury, the outrage, or the resignation. What reaction might Mrs. Alexander have been hoping for?

The verse descends from <u>distasteful to almost blasphemous</u> as I notice how its language inadvertently parodies Jesus' parable of the rich man and Lazarus.[4] For Jesus, the rich man's apathy about the poor man's poverty was <u>a damnable offense</u>. But even the damned rich man wasn't singing about his privilege as something beautiful and ordered by God! If Jesus were present at the singing of such a hymn, I could imagine him pulling the plug on the sound system in protest.

It makes me wonder whether, in Mrs. Alexander's mind, this now-forgotten verse contained the real point of the song. Were all the cute little birds, tiny fluttering wings, pleasant summer sunbeams, and meadow-play just so much sugary distraction to make a nauseating theopolitical, theo-economic message easier to swallow?

---

4. In a beautiful reversal, Jesus gives the poor man a name but leaves the rich man nameless. Luke 16:19–31.

At some point, hymnal editors decided that verse needed to be dropped. On one level, I'm glad they did. It must be a step in the right direction to sanitize our hymns, fumigate our prayers, and otherwise edit out the residue of our inherited prejudices, leaving us with a bright and beautiful church life that is supersentimental and saccharine-sweet. Or is it?

After some second thoughts, I wonder if simply dropping offensive elements like these carries the pungent aroma of cover-up, the stale smoke of denial. Considering our history and its anti-Semitism, imperialism, racism, chauvinism, favoritism toward the rich, carelessness or patronization toward the poor, plundering of the earth, and other expressions of hostility: would it be better if these ugly elements of our heritage could be removed from use but still retained somehow in our corporate memory—if only as an instructive footnote or cautionary appendix to the hymnal?

In that same footnote or appendix we could explain what we've learned, how we've changed, and why we're trying to be different now. In so doing we would acknowledge that what we do in church can too easily serve the interests of the conflicted status quo and the privileged few. We would thus admit that our liturgies can camouflage injustice. We would face the ways our sermons and hymns can baptize hate and bigotry. We would remember how our holidays and sacred rituals can embed a hostile identity in little children for generations to come. And we would simultaneously confess that we have in the past practiced coverup and denial about the dark sides of our history, and declare our commitment to stop doing so in the future. In so doing, we would form in ourselves and future generations a stronger, wiser, humbler, more benevolent identity.

And from there, the next step would be clear: to replace those elements of our hymns, sermons, rituals, and holidays that currently reinforce an oppositional identity with creative alternatives—elements that would help to form in us a strong and benevolent identity as God's creative agents for justice, peace, reconciliation, and hope. So we might replace the "rich man in his castle" verse with something like this:

All who thirst for justice,
Who serve among the poor,
Forging tools for farming
From weapons made for war.

Or maybe this, keeping with the nature theme:

Those who save the planet
From recklessness and greed,
Preserve endangered species,
And tend the soil and seed.

If Christian faith in the centuries ahead is to embody a new identity, it will not be enough to sweeten and sanitize our past. Just as the Bible has faithfully and courageously done (as we'll see in the next chapter), we must preserve the ugly, embarrassing, and contrary voices of our heritage. Doing so will humble us, but also heal us. We must have the humble courage to side with some verses, prayers, and other liturgical resources and against others—not in an oppositional or a hostile way, but in a constructive, identity-forming way. We must understand why Mrs. Alexander, God bless her, would pen such a verse and surround it with such sweetness, and we must then look for ways we are doing the same thing—in our songs and hymns, in our prayers and confessions, in our sermons and classes.[5] We must

---

5. I, of course, must be open to the ways I do it in my writing. In a previous book, for example, I used the word *tribal* to describe hostile clannishness. An African reader (white, from South Africa) pointed out that in so doing, I was inadvertently putting

uncover the null curriculum inherent in all we do in gathered worship.

We must do this for adults, and also for children. In so many churches I encounter, serious liturgical renewal is beginning among young adults, but the kids are being taught through the same off-the-shelf curricula of the past. Many of these curricula are more hi-tech, flashy, and user-friendly than ever, but for all the updates in style and packaging, little thought has been given to the identity they are building in kids.

I was speaking to some staff members from a Christian publishing house recently—more creative, energetic, and committed people would be hard to find. I mentioned my special interest in kids' curriculum for Sunday School and confirmation classes. They showed me their most recent curriculum, built around the life of Samson. I couldn't help but be impressed with the lessons they had drawn from Samson's life. Then I asked, "What do you do about Samson's violence?" They looked puzzled, so I continued, "I mean, we don't want kids to pull down buildings on their enemies, right? So how do we deal with Samson's violence?" Crickets. This question had never crossed my mind until recently, and it was clear it was a new question for them as well.[6]

That interaction prepared the way for a conversation with my friend Tracy Radosevic, a gifted biblical storyteller, and one of her mentors, Tom Boomershine, founder of the Network of Biblical

---

indigenous peoples in a negative light, as if intertribal conflict were more egregious than European "civilized" conflict. Even my use of the term *clannishness* deserves critical scrutiny. Perhaps I should call it *religious nationalism?*

6. The name of this book's U.S. publisher, Jericho, represents a similar tension. The Jericho story concerns what we would call a war crime, complete with the extermination of women and children. The image of bringing down walls that divide, however, can be employed for reconciling rather than violent purposes, thus subverting the original violent meaning.

Stories have violence

194 • Why Did Jesus, Moses, the Buddha, and Mohammed Cross the Road?

Storytellers (a fantastic group more people should know about).[7] I mentioned my concern to Tom: "You're doing a fantastic job of helping kids and adults learn biblical stories, but what do you do about the violence of so many stories?"

Tom had obviously thought long and hard about this. He said he was becoming more and more convinced that we can't tell stories in isolation—especially violent stories. So we can't tell about David killing Goliath (1 Samuel 17), he said, without also telling the story of God not allowing David to build the temple because he was a violent man (1 Kings 5). I had never thought of that kind of pairing before. Ever since our conversation, I keep stumbling across example after example of hostile-reconciling pairings as I read and reflect on the Bible.

For example, we can't tell the story about Elijah (1 Kings 18) calling down fire on the prophets of Baal without hearing Jesus' rebuke of his disciples for recommending the same violent response to the "religiously other" (Luke 9). We can't tell the story of Moses sending people to kill their brothers (Exodus 32) without also telling the story of the Transfiguration, where the nonviolent words and ways of Jesus are honored over those of Moses: "*This* is my beloved son. Listen to *him*" (Mark 9). We can't tell the story of the slaughter of the Canaanites (Deuteronomy 7) without telling Matthew's masterful reversal of that story in Jesus' encounter with the Canaanite woman (Matthew 15). We can't quote "Jacob I have loved, but Esau I have hated," without also telling the story of Jacob's injustices against Esau, leading to Jacob's climactic need to reconcile with his offended brother, leading to Esau's truly amazing grace to Jacob, leading to Jacob's experience of "the face of God" in the very one who was supposedly hated by God (Genesis 32–33). The Bible itself, it seems, has built-in reconciling stories to counteract and disarm the hostile ones, but people who

---

7. To learn more, check out http://www.nbsint.org/.

want to justify hostility pick the hostile ones and choose to minimize the reconciling ones.[8] (More on picking and choosing in the next chapter.)

How we teach our children really matters, for Bible stories no less than Quranic suras can easily be turned into terrorist weapons. Our stories, sermons, prayers, and songs can contribute to liturgies of hostility or liturgies of kindness, forming communities and individuals who translate those liturgies—for better or worse—into their daily lives and into the history of humanity . . . and inhumanity.

---

8. Even Joshua, arguably the most violent book in the Bible, offers resources for the deconstruction of us-them thinking. Rahab (2), an outsider (and a prostitute) is a hero of the story, and Achan (7), an insider, is a villain. The Gibeonites are outsiders who cleverly gain insider status (9). And the narrowly averted Gilead massacre (22:10ff.) explores the danger of hastily prejudging insiders and treating them as outsiders.

Chapter 22

How Reading the Bible Responsibly Can Look Irresponsible (and Vice Versa)

One cannot adhere to the Christian faith without a "decision" in which we take our distance from the "past."

—*Heinz R. Schlette*[1]

I was a relatively unknown pastor and author until *Time* magazine included me on a list of influential religious leaders back in 2005.[2] The brief article recounted something I said during Q & A session at a large Evangelical pastors' gathering the year before. I was asked to declare my position on homosexuality or gay marriage or some related subject. I responded with something like, "The thing that breaks my heart is that there's no way I can answer that question without hurting someone on either side."

---

1. "Religions," in *Encyclopédie de la foi*, ed. H. Fries (Paris: Éditions du Cerf, 1967), 4:59–68. Quoted in Jacques Dupuis, S.J., *Toward a Christian Theology of Religious Pluralism* (Maryknoll, N.Y.: Orbis Books, 1997), p. 52.

2. "The 25 Most Influential Evangelicals in America," *Time*, February 7, 2005, http://www.time.com/time/specials/packages/article/0,28804,1993235_1993243_1993300,00.html.

For all its failings, my not-terribly-inflammatory response accurately reflected a tension I lived in, a tension many of my pastoral colleagues today know all too well. On the one hand, I was the guest of an Evangelical organization that had an official position against homosexuality. I didn't want to be disruptive or inconsiderate of my hosts, who were trying to bring people together in an atmosphere with a low inflammatory quotient. On the other hand, my inherited conservative thinking on the subject had changed, and I was now working to protect gay people from discrimination rather than add to it. Caught in that tension, I aimed for a middle path and tried to articulate the tension I felt. As a result, *Time* judged me a potential paradigm shifter with a "kinder and gentler brand of religion."[3]

A well-known fundamentalist preacher responded to the *Time* article by claiming that in seeking to avoid hurting either my conservative hosts or my gay friends, I was now guilty of "hurting God."[4] He judged me unfaithful to the Bible (as he interpreted it) and to God (as he understood God). His comments stirred up a brief hurricane of controversy in the blogosphere. I and others like me were repeatedly accused of "picking and choosing" the parts of the Bible we liked and ignoring the rest. "If you want to quote the Bible's verses about love and peace, you also have to quote the ones about hell and damnation," they said. "Otherwise you're putting your own authority above the authority of the Bible. So no picking and choosing!"

Some time later, I was surprised to see that one of the world's leading atheists agreed with the "No picking and choosing" rule, albeit for a different reason. By picking the Bible's love verses and soft-pedaling its hate verses, he suggested, moderate believers give

---

3. Later, in settings that seemed more appropriate, I became more outspoken about my own views, although I still endeavor to show respect and sensitivity to my hosts and those who see the issue differently.

4. I am not using the word *fundamentalist* as an epithet here. The person in question has told me on several occasions that "fundamentalist" is what he is.

Interpretation — Objective + ethical

political

198 • Why Did Jesus, Moses, the Buddha, and Mohammed Cross the Road?

cover to extremists. They help maintain respect for the book their less moderate counterparts will use to inspire and defend violence. In order to deprive extremists of this cover, he said, we must decisively throw out the whole book as a bronze age collection of dangerous myths and destructive superstitions.

Just a few months ago, I came across another reference to picking and choosing, one that responded to this atheist's critique. It came from one of my favorite writers, an Irish Catholic philosopher named Richard Kearney:

> So when militant atheists...accuse believers of "picking and choosing," they are actually accusing them of being *responsible* believers. This is what faith is about: making a choice, venturing a wager, discriminating between rival interpretations in order to make the best decision regarding love and hate, justice and injustice.[5]

So there you have the dilemma: picking and choosing is deemed destructive by both a fundamentalist Christian and an outspoken atheist, but praised as responsible biblical interpretation by a Catholic philosopher (one born, not insignificantly, in a country scarred by religious troubles). Beneath the surface of picking and choosing, Kearney realizes, lies the complex art and science of interpretation (hermeneutics, in the language of theologians and philosophers). Interpretation isn't, he makes clear, simply an impersonal, objective, scholarly matter. It is also a profoundly ethical one, and we could say a political one as well. Ultimately, in choosing how to interpret our sacred texts, we pick and choose between "compassion and murder."[6]

---

5. Richard Kearney, *Anatheism* (New York: Columbia University Press, 2010), p. 160. Additional page references to this book will be included in the text hereinafter.

6. Kearney states, "The great stories of Israel are, I am suggesting, testaments to the paradoxical origins of religion in both violent conflict and peaceful embrace. This, in effect, makes every dramatic encounter between the human and the divine into a

hermeneutics = sermons explaining Bible passages

There is no way forward in the pursuit of a strong-benevolent Christian identity that bypasses a lengthy journey through the wild and challenging landscape of hermeneutics.

Hermeneutics is one of the central liturgical practices of the Christian church. Nearly all liturgies include a sermon in which passages of the Bible are read and interpreted. How can we turn this important liturgical practice toward the formation of strong-benevolent Christian identity?

Artist-theologian Derek Flood understands that hermeneutics means far more than either a facile picking and choosing of our favorite texts or an equally facile taking of everything "literally." In an article entitled "Wrestling with Scripture," he begins where we all must: by acknowledging the hostility and violence of many Bible passages.[7] Passages like 1 Samuel 15:2–3 and Psalm 137:8–9 are lying around like loaded weapons waiting for some fearful or angry interpreters to pick them up and use them for genocidal purposes.[8]

---

radical hermeneutic wager: compassion or murder. You either welcome or refuse the stranger. Monotheism is the history of this wager." (22)

7. My quotations here come from an unpublished version of his article "The Way of Peace and Grace," which appeared in shorter published form in *Sojourners* 41, no. 1 (January 2012) (http://www.sojo.net/magazine/2012/01/way-peace-and-grace). Flood also explains his approach in "Does Defending the Bible Mean Advocating Violence?" *Huffington Post*, November 21, 2011, http://www.huffingtonpost.com/derek-flood/defending-violence-in-the-bible_b_1088517.html. This material will appear in expanded form in *Healing the Gospel* (Eugene, OR: Wipf & Stock, 2012). For more on this important subject, see also James Cone's *The Cross and the Lynching Tree* (Maryknoll, N.Y.: Orbis, 2011) and Philip Jenkins's *Laying Down the Sword: Why We Can't Ignore the Bible's Violent Verses* (New York: HarperOne, 2011). See also the introduction to both books available here: http://www.readthespirit.com/explore/2011/12/19/in-season-of-peace-recalling-christianitys-violence.html/.

8. For more on this subject, see Tom Krattenmaker's helpful *USA Today* article available here: http://www.usatoday.com/news/opinion/forum/story/2011-10-09/islam-muslim-christian-violence/50711860/1. He recounts how "an adviser to Israeli Prime Minister Benjamin Netanyahu once gave a journalist this chilling explanation for the prime minister's hard-line attitude toward Iran: 'Think Amalek.'" By mentioning Amalek, the adviser evoked 1 Samuel 15:2–3, where God commands Saul to kill all the Amalekites, *"both man and woman, and infant, ox and sheep, camel and donkey."*

Benevolent Christian identity

Paul edited scriptures

200 • Why Did Jesus, Moses, the Buddha, and Mohammed Cross the Road?

(picking + choosing)

Flood flatly rejects traditional attempts to legitimize passages like these. He instead argues for "a way that allows us to remain faithful to Scripture without needing to defend and promote violence in God's name." The way forward, he says, is to "read our Bibles as the Apostle Paul read his." He then demonstrates how Paul, especially in the Epistle to the Romans, reinterprets his sacred scriptures in the light of God's radical self-revelation in Christ.

Flood graphically displays, for example, Paul's edited quotation of Psalm 18:41–49 and Deuteronomy 32:43 in Romans 15:8–10. Notice what Paul picks to retain and what he chooses to reject:

> For I tell you that Christ has become a servant of the Jews on behalf of God's truth, to confirm the promises made to the patriarchs so that the Gentiles may glorify God for his mercy, as it is written: "I destroyed my foes. They cried for help, but there was no one to save them—to the LORD, but he did not answer....He is the God who avenges me, who puts the Gentiles under me....Therefore I will praise you among the Gentiles; I will sing hymns to your name."
>
> Again, it says, "Rejoice, O Gentiles, with his people, for he will avenge the blood of his servants; he will take vengeance on his enemies and make atonement for his land and people."

The language of divine mercy and promise is retained. The language of divine violence and vengeance is gone.[9] In that simple

---

The ancient historian Flavius Josephus described Saul's action as follows: "He betook himself to slay the women and the children, and thought he did not act therein either barbarously or inhumanly; first, because they were enemies whom he thus treated, and, in the next place, because it was done by the command of God, whom it was dangerous not to obey" (*Antiquites Judicae*, Book VI, Chapter 7).

9. Some might point to Romans 1 as an example of a passage where Paul emphasizes divine retribution. But interestingly, in that passage, the retribution is simply to be "given up" so that "ungodly" people reap the natural consequences of their bad behavior. And then in Chapter 2, Paul masterfully overturns the reader's glee over punishment of "the other," showing that "we" are no better than "they."

move, Paul courageously re-articulates the meaning of salvation. It is no longer "rescuing Israel from peril by killing her enemies," but rather "the restoration of all people in Christ."

Flood notes how a respected professor once "joked that Paul would have surely flunked a seminary class in exegesis." But no, Flood replies, this isn't a case of Paul playing fast and loose with the Bible. Rather, "Paul is deliberately flipping the meaning of these passages...." Paul's rationale becomes all the more clear in Flood's reading of Romans 3:10–18, where Paul weaves together several Old Testament passages to exemplify the core issues of human evil—all relating to hostility and violence, failing to "know the way of peace." (The original passages are cited in brackets.)

> *As it is written,*
> *"There is no one righteous, not even one;*
> *there is no one who understands, no one who seeks God.*
> *All have turned away, they have together become worthless;*
> *there is no one who does good, not even one." [Psalms 14:1–3]*
> *"Their throats are open graves; their tongues practice deceit."*
>   *[Psalms 5:9]*
> *"The poison of vipers is on their lips." [Psalms 140:3]*
> *"Their mouths are full of cursing and bitterness." [Psalms 10:7]*
> *"Their feet are swift to shed blood;*
> *ruin and misery mark their ways,*
> *and the way of peace they do not know." [Isaiah 59:7–8]*
> *"There is no fear of God before their eyes." [Psalms 36:1]*

Flood concludes: "Paul is making a very different point from the original intent of these Psalms. In fact, he is making the *opposite* point—we should not cry out for God's wrath and judgment [on the other], because we are all sinners in need of mercy." He concludes, "This is not a case of careless out-of-context proof-texting; it is an *not asking for God's violence — confess universal*

202 • Why Did Jesus, Moses, the Buddha, and Mohammed Cross the Road?

culpability

artful and deliberate reshaping of these verses...from their original cry for divine violence into a confession of universal culpability that highlights our need for mercy."

In all Paul's letters we find this same pattern, not sloppy proof-texting to buttress Paul's inherited preferences and prejudices, but a consistent pattern of reinterpretation "in Christ," whereby his own inherited preferences and prejudices have been revolutionized. In case after case, hostile and violent sections of quoted passages are simply left out so the meaning is artfully and deliberately reshaped according to "the way of peace," which is the way of Christ. As Flood concludes, "Paul has disarmed Scripture in Jesus' name."

In this, of course, Paul faithfully follows his model. In his very first public sermon in Nazareth (Luke 4:18–27), Jesus similarly "flips the meaning" of Isaiah (61:1–2) by dropping the phrase "and the day of vengeance of our God." Lest anyone miss the "de-hostilization" and "de-exclusivization" of his omission, he then refers to the story of the prophet Elijah who was directed by God to help a Sidonian woman—an outsider of another religion. And then he adds the story of the prophet Elisha helping a Syrian man—another outsider of another religion. You can imagine the panic in the minds of Jesus' neighbors as they process what their homegrown prophet is saying: *What? Is Jesus suggesting that God loves "those people—Sidonians and Syrians"—just as much as "us?" Is this "good news to the poor" universal, for all people, rather than exclusive to members of our religion only? Who does he think he is to betray our elite, exclusive identity like this? This is heresy! Blasphemy! Treason!*

That day in Nazareth when Jesus modeled this deliberately subversive way of reading the Scriptures, he went right to the heart of us-them oppositional identity. No one should be surprised at the response: hostility. The people who spoke well of him a few moments before (Luke 4:22) now want to kill him (4:28–29). (This, no doubt, illuminates the real meaning of Jesus' words, "I have come not to bring peace, but a sword.")[10]

Again and again in the New Testament, when people are confronted for being exclusive, hostile, or violent, they predictably respond with exclusion, hostility, and violence. Consider, for example, the violent response when Stephen confronts the violence of the Sanhedrin in Acts 7. Or consider the incident in the temple (Acts 21–22), when Paul is accused (falsely, it turns out) of defiling their sacred ground by bringing uncircumcised outsiders into it. A mob is about to kill him until some Roman soldiers intervene, and then Paul defends himself. He manages quite a long speech, considering the circumstances, and all seems to be going well until he mentions God sending him to the religiously other. At that, the crowd yells, "Rid the earth of him! He's not fit to live." Accepting "the other" is the one thing that "we" find absolutely unacceptable, time after time.

The more I read the New Testament, the more clearly I realize that this other-aversion is at the heart of what the gospel calls us to repent of. The old era of us-them thinking and oppositional identity is coming to an end, the gospel declares. In Christ, God is calling us to a path of reconciliation.[11] Walking that path requires us to go back and reread our Scriptures and "flip them," faithfully picking and choosing—subverting hostility in the strong pursuit of love.[12] Flood concludes, "Wrestling with Scripture in this way may not be

---

10. For more on this subject, see Peter Rollins, *Insurrection* (New York: Howard Books, 2011), and my book *More Ready Than You Realize* (Grand Rapids, Mich.: Zondervan, 2002).

11. Reconciliation differs from inclusion. Inclusion says we can absorb the other into *us*, while reconciliation means we want to be at peace with the other as the other.

12. I've been tempted to point out to my critics who accuse me of picking and choosing that they do the same thing, the only difference being that they pick the violent and hostile passages for prioritization and choose the inclusive and reconciling ones for marginalization. But I doubt making that point would further the conversation.

accept "The other"—reconcile flip

God revealed in Jesus, who preached inclusion

204 • Why Did Jesus, Moses, the Buddha, and Mohammed Cross the Road?

an expression of doubt at all, but an act of faithfulness to both God revealed in Christ, and to Scripture, whose goal is to point to him (Rom. 10:4)."

True, picking and choosing aren't allowed when you're a lawyer dealing with a legal code or constitution. You can't pick Article I.A.3.b and ignore Article 2.C.7.d. But as I argued in *A New Kind of Christianity*, the Bible isn't a constitution. To read, interpret, and apply the Bible as if it were a constitution is a category error.[13] It's more accurate to say that the Bible is a library filled with diverse voices making diverse claims in an ongoing conversation. Faithful interaction with a library means siding with some of those voices and against others. (But it also means refusing to remove from the library

13. Brian McLaren, *A New Kind of Christianity* (New York: HarperOne, 2010). Too many biblical interpreters today still cling to a form of absolutism regarding the Bible. Either the Bible is valid the way they understand a constitution to be valid, or it is not valid at all. (It should be noted that most constitutional lawyers would reject the simplistic assumptions about constitutions that lie beneath these arguments.) Ultraliberal interpreters, of course, use this logic to critique the Bible and downplay its value. Ultraconservative interpreters defend the constitutional approach as if it were the only alternative, fearing that any loosening of absolutist claims will start a long slide down a slippery slope into the fiery abyss of relativism. The former approach generally produces a benign religion of weak identity, and the latter a strong religion of hostile identity. We need an approach that goes beyond the facile binary of absolutism and relativism. Richard Kearney describes the situation well in *Anatheism*:

"So much depends, of course, on what we mean by God. If transcendence is indeed a *surplus* of meaning, it requires a process of endless interpretation.... The absolute requires pluralism to avoid absolutism." (xiv)

"If the Word was in the beginning, so was hermeneutics. There is no God's-eye view of things available to us. For we are not Gods, and history tells us that attempts to become so lead to intellectual and political catastrophe. Hermeneutics is a lesson in humility (we all speak from finite situations) as well as imagination (we fill the gaps between available and ulterior meanings). Hermeneutics reminds us that the holiest of books are works of interpretation—for authors no less than readers." (xv)

"The acknowledgment of our finite hermeneutic situation saves us, I believe, from both relativism and absolutism." (xviii)

"The absolute can never be understood *absolutely* by any single person or religion." (16)

"For faith means knowing you don't know anything absolutely about absolutes." (170)

those voices you don't side with, as we've already seen. The Bible thus facilitates ongoing, open dialogue and debate, not a totalitarian regime of homogenized propaganda.) Siding with some voices and against others isn't simply picking and choosing according to one's own tastes, then. Nor can it be reduced to a simple matter of objective scholarship or logic. Interpretation is also and always a matter of ethics, a matter of the heart and the conscience. So we can expect hostile people to side with hostile voices in the text; fearful people with fearful voices, and peace-loving people with peace-loving voices. Interpretation will always to some degree manifest the character of the interpreter along with the meaning of the text.

———

Jesus pointed out this ethical dimension of textual interpretation one Sabbath day when he dined at the table of a prominent Pharisee (Luke 14). He boldly defied normative Sabbath restrictions by healing a fellow guest. Then he defended his Sabbath violation by appealing to the basic human kindness of all those present: aren't they all decent enough human beings that they would rescue an ox on the Sabbath if it fell into a pit? He made a similar move in another incident involving a man with a deformed hand in a synagogue (Mark 2:25–3:6). In both cases, the compassionate voice of empathy trumps the accusatory voices of condemnation.[14] The same pattern holds true

———

14. It's highly instructive in this regard to ponder all the passages where Jesus challenges Sabbath conventions. In Matt. 12:8, he shows how he, like David, has compassion on his hungry companions, which reflects both true humanity (as Son of Man or the Human One) and true divinity (because God loves compassion, not sacrifice). In Mark 3:1–6, Jesus heals a withered hand and is angry at the lack of compassion demonstrated by his critics. In Luke 4:33ff., Jesus heals a demonized man and Peter's mother on the Sabbath. In John 5:5–18, he heals a man who couldn't walk for thirty-eight years, and in John 9, he heals a man blind from birth, both on the Sabbath. In Luke 13:10–17, he heals a woman bent over for eighteen years, and when criticized he references the compassion any decent person would have on a thirsty donkey or ox so as to water them on the Sabbath.

in the Sermon on the Mount. "You have heard it said," Jesus says, and then quotes the verses about an eye for an eye, a tooth for a tooth.[15] That kind of retributive justice was once a step up from excessive revenge—ten eyes for an eye, or fifty teeth for a tooth. Now, however, we must take another step up, Jesus says: "But I say to you, love your enemies." Of those eight stunning words, the first may be the most stunning of all.

For Jesus, it is permissible to say, "The Scriptures say...but I say otherwise," if the otherwise takes us in the direction of greater compassion, kindness, nonviolence, and reconciliation. Accusatory retributive justice fades into the past, and a new day of compassionate restorative justice dawns.

Or at least it does with Jesus. It remains to be seen to what degree we Christians today will move forward with Jesus and to what degree we will dig our heels in with the less magnanimous voices in the biblical library.

In our liturgical practice of reading, interpreting, and preaching the Bible, we are repeatedly forced to choose between hostility and hospitality, mercy and condemnation, compassion and legalism, forgiveness and revenge, laying down our lives or taking the lives of others...page after page, reading after reading, Sunday after Sunday. The way we read, interpret, and preach the Bible not only reveals what is hidden in our hearts, but holds the key for changing or reforming our hearts.

Will the Bible be the sword by which we cut off and threaten "the other"? Or will the Bible point beyond itself, directing us to Jesus who offers to his disciples the authority to bind and loose (Matthew 16:19)—or, we might say, to pick and choose? For those who choose the latter approach, the Bible is transformed from the sword of com-

---

15. The "eye for an eye" construction is found in Exodus 21:24, Leviticus 24:20, and Deuteronomy 19:19-21. It echoes language found in section 230 of the Code of Hammurabi.

bat to the scalpel of surgery—for self-examination and self-critique, exposing our own hostility so that we can join God in compassion for all people and solidarity with the other (Hebrews 4:12–16).[16]

Those of us intent upon forging a strong and benevolent Christian identity in our multi-faith world will be carrying our Bibles with (or within) us. We will read and teach the Bible responsibly and ethically, following the strong and benevolent examples of Paul and Jesus. We will pick all passages that advocate hostility, vengeance, exclusion, elitism, and superiority to remind us of where we would be and who we would be if not for Christ. And we will choose all passages that advocate reconciliation, empathy, inclusion, solidarity, and equality to remind us of where we are going and who we are called to be in Christ—a precious identity indeed.[17]

Skim over hostile, vengeful, exclusion, elitism, superiority (JC would)

Advocate: reconciliation, empathy, inclusion, solidarity, equality (JC would)

---

16. When Jesus speaks of binding and loosing, he is not abolishing the law and prophets. Rather, we might say that he is unleashing and fulfilling their true and best intent (Matt. 5:17–19) or spirit (see 2 Cor. 2:6). He thus makes a double declaration of independence—from absolute textual totalitarianism on the one hand, and from absolute moral relativism on the other. He rejects the technical-textual righteousness of the scribes and Pharisees (Matt. 5:20) and argues instead for a kind and compassionate righteousness that refuses to create us and them, insider and outsider, neighbor and enemy (Matt. 5:43-48, Luke 6:27-36).

17. Our doctrine of the Bible, of course, is a subset of a larger doctrine—of revelation. How might that larger doctrine be reformulated in the strong-benevolent Christian identity we are exploring in these pages? How can we cherish the particularly beautiful ways God is revealed within our faith without losing a generosity toward other faiths, and how can we remain generously open to the beauties revealed in other faiths without losing the particular beauties of our own? Even framing the question this way sets us on a constructive path toward answering it.

Altar = sacrificial suffering + atonement

Chapter 23

How the Table Differs from the Altar

Ricouer offers a startlingly refreshing reading of the Eucharist as a celebration of blood-as-wine, transubstantiation being taken as a sign of life and sharing rather than a token of sacrificial blood-letting. The Eucharistic commemoration of the giving of one's life—"Do this in memory of me"—thus becomes an affirmation of the gift of life to and for the other rather than an anxiety about personal physical survival after death. In other words, when Christ said "it is finished," he meant it.

—*Richard Kearney*[1]

I love the eucharist. I am not a stickler for the form it takes. Whether accompanied by robes, choirs, smells, and bells in a lofty cathedral or enjoyed around a simple table in an intimate celebration among friends, I am endlessly enthralled by the meaning and mystery of the Lord's Supper.[2]

But the Lord's Supper has often been the scene of the church's food fight. When Gentiles as well as Jews, the poor as well as rich,

1. Richard Kearney, *Anatheism* (New York: Columbia University Press, 2010), p. 77.

2. Among many helpful books on the Lord's Supper, I recommend Nora Gallagher, *The Sacred Meal* (Nashville: Thomas Nelson, 2009), and Dan Schmidt, *Taken by Communion* (Grand Rapids, Mich.: Baker Books, 2004).

table = hospitality, fellowship, meeting, reconciling ies to God & others.

and slaves as well as slave masters were welcomed to the table as equals, you could predict that trouble might ensue. When neither Jesus nor the apostles wrote a detailed rule book or policy manual for the one right way to conduct the meal, you might expect others would try to fill the void. And because one singular desired outcome for the experience was never nailed down, you could anticipate that debates would erupt about its meaning—although the vitriol of those debates does come as a bit of a shock. Now, it's hard to name the ritual without thinking of the hostile language surrounding it—*ex-communication*, the threat of being *dis-fellowshipped*, the *guarding* or *fencing* of a *closed table*, and so on.

When I just referred to the eucharist as a ritual, I was defining *ritual* as "an act that employs the body to bond to a meaning."[3] But what meaning are we bonding to in the eucharist?

One line of meaning presents the eucharist as a celebration of hospitality, a table of fellowship and welcome, a means of amazing grace, releasing us from bondage to hostility and reconnecting us through the bonds of human-kindness. It emphasizes the table as a place of meeting, of reconciliation, of filial affection, of companionship...the place where God and all humanity "at table are sat down."[4] In this approach, we bond to the gospel of the reconciling reign or commonwealth of God, proclaimed by and embodied in Jesus, which invites us all into reconciliation with God and one another.

Another line of meaning centers on a sacrificial altar rather than a table—a place where God's hostility toward sinners is pacified by body-and-blood sacrifice.[5] In this understanding, we bond not to

3. I explore this understanding of ritual in *Finding Our Way Again* (Nashville: Thomas Nelson, 2008).

4. See the beautiful hymn by Robert Stamps, "God and Man at Table Are Sat Down," which articulates this view of the eucharist.

5. I understand that many people use the term *altar* simply as a name for a piece of furniture, to which I have no objection. My concern here focuses only on the idea of

Jesus' original gospel of the kingdom of God, but to another gospel, the gospel of penal substitutionary atonement, a doctrine that is as precious and central to many Christians as it is problematic or even repulsive to others.[6] The popular idea of penal substitution works like a rather complex equation. God cannot forgive sin without inflicting punishment and shedding blood, the doctrine teaches, so God is obliged to punish all sinners. Because their offense is against an infinitely holy God, their punishment must be absolute, irrevocable, and eternal. All human beings will therefore be damned to eternal conscious torment in hell if God does not provide a substitute upon whom God's infinite wrath can be vented.[7] For those who hold these assumptions, it makes sense to say that God tortured and killed Jesus on the cross so as to be able to vent divine wrath upon a single divine-human representative or substitute rather than all of us.

I grew up with this understanding, and for decades of my life, it satisfied me, inspired piety in me, and troubled me not at all. Gradually, though, the problematic dimensions of the doctrine nudged me

---

pacifying a hostile God with human pain and sacrifice.

6. The doctrine is commonly attributed to St. Anselm. Scholars (such as Gustav Aulen, *Christus Victor*, Wipf and Stock, 2003) debate whether Martin Luther was more committed to penal substitution or an earlier understanding called "Christus Victor." Hymn lyrics by Phillip Bliss, Isaac Watts, and Augustus Toplady have given penal substitutionary atonement a central place in worship for many Evangelicals, and parts of Mainline Protestant and Catholic eucharistic liturgies keep the doctrine alive, albeit subconsciously, in many hearts. Today, some Evangelical authors like D. A. Carson and Albert Mohler tend to identify this theory of atonement with the Christian gospel. Others like Scot McKnight have sought to retain a carefully defined version of it but not as equivalent to the gospel. Others would prefer to purge it from the Christian faith entirely, and still others (I am in this group) urge us to retain the theory as an artifact of theological history but decommission it from contemporary spiritual practice. For three excellent studies on the subject, see Joel Green and Mark Baker, *Recovering the Scandal of the Cross* (Downers Grove, Ill.: InterVarsity Press, 2000); Mark Green, ed., *Proclaiming the Scandal of the Cross* (Grand Rapids, Mich.: Baker Academic, 2006); and Tony Jones, *A Better Atonement* (available via his website, http://www.patheos.com/blogs/tonyjones/).

7. According to the theory, this substitute must have been human so that human sin could be imputed to him, yet he must have been divine so that he could neutralize infinite wrath with infinite merit or grace.

to be more at home with Celtic, Franciscan, Anabaptist, Quaker, Eastern Orthodox, Liberationist, and other perspectives that proclaim the gospel (and celebrate the eucharist) with little or no reference to this atonement theory.[8] I now associate the eucharist not with the altar of sacrifice (as popularly conceived) but with the table of reconciliation and fellowship. This change in understanding, I now see, produces a change in identity—a change that is highly significant in our multi-faith world.[9]

In the altar-sacrifice framing of the eucharist, God is hostile toward human beings, and only Christians are exempt from God's wrath. Having given to Jesus their sin and punishment to bear on the cross, and having received from Jesus his imputed merit and grace, Christians imagine this exchange afresh each time they receive

---

8. Should we see God as incapable of being reconciled to us without violence? Should we understand God as inherently hostile to frail and fallible human beings? Should we conceive of God's retribution as the biggest threat to our well-being? Should sin be defined primarily as an individual legal problem requiring a transaction of forgiveness? Should the deeper and wider existential, social, systemic, historical, ecological, and economic dimensions of sin thus be minimized? Should Jesus' life, teaching, signs and wonders, resurrection, and ascension be marginalized, as if the only thing about him that really matters is his substitutionary death? Should other meanings of Jesus' death also be minimized in favor of this doctrine? Should God be primarily identified with the political and religious leaders inflicting torture and death on Good Friday, rather than with the innocent man being tortured and killed? Should we be sent into the world primarily with an evacuation plan for heaven and an escape plan from damnation, rather than with an incarnation, reconciliation, and transformation plan for our conflicted world? If violence and hostility characterize God's identity, is it realistic to aspire to be better than God by being nonviolent and nonhostile?

9. In *The Prophetic Imagination*, 2nd ed. (Minneapolis: Fortress Press, 2001), p. xx, Walter Brueggemann provides two examples of the impact of this shift in identity. The eucharist, he says (quoting William T. Cavanaugh), helps us identify with a tortured man. In that space, communicants "resist the state's ability to define what is real through the mechanism of torture." The eucharist also helps us resist the numbing effects of consumerism by helping communicants foster a "lively communal imagination that resists a mindless humanity of despairing conformity." This dual resistance—to torture and to numbness—helps us remain more truly human, because "numbness does not hurt like torture, but in a quite parallel way, numbness robs us of our capability for humanity."

the eucharist. The ritual thus reinforces a view of God's identity (as hostile toward sinful humanity and requiring appeasement or satisfaction), of non-Christian human identity (as deserving utter and eternal punishment), and of Christian identity (as being uniquely acceptable and pleasing to God). It is easy to imagine how this view of God, the "us," and the other could be translated into action in society and history.[10]

In contrast, in a table-centered eucharistic understanding, atoning or appeasing sacrifices are simply unnecessary.[11] Nothing need be done to appease a hostile God, because through Christ, God has self-revealed as inherently gracious and kind, seeking reconciliation; not hostile and vengeful, needing appeasement. If we need to speak of sacrifice at all, we speak of it in its root meaning: *sacred gift*. So as we gather around the eucharistic table, we bond to a meaning very different from that of the conventional eucharistic altar; we bond to

10. I should emphasize that I don't think all Christians who hold penal substitutionary atonement share this kind of Christian exceptionalism with its corresponding us-them thinking and repugnance toward "the unsaved." But I do believe the doctrine creates conditions for this exceptionalism to take root in certain circumstances and among people of a certain temperament. Sincere adherents to the doctrine have a responsibility to vigilantly guard against the dangerous though unintended consequences of this Christian exceptionalism.

11. When people begin rethinking atonement, salvation, and the eucharist along these lines, they often wonder, "What then does it mean to say that Jesus died for our sins?" They assume the *for* in that statement means "as a penal substitutionary sacrifice for." It is far more natural, I think, to interpret the *for* more simply. Consider, for example, these two sentences: "I took medicine for my disease," and "I got a ticket for speeding." In the former sentence, the word *for* does not mean "as a sacrifice to appease my disease." *For* means "to help cure my disease." So we understand that Jesus' death intervenes in human history to have a curative impact on our hostility and violence, to turn us toward the ways of peace. And in the latter sentence, *for* doesn't mean "to pay for." It means "because of." Because I was speeding, I got a ticket, and similarly, because we are hostile and violent, Christ died. God didn't torture and kill Christ; *we* did. And that tells us something essential about both God and ourselves. For more on this word *for*, see Marcus Borg, *Speaking Christian* (New York: HarperOne, 2011).

JC = God's sacred love gift to world

He gives Himself to us as ongoing incarnation

the sacred self-giving of a gracious God.[12] As we remember Jesus, from incarnation to crucifixion (and beyond), we see God's self-giving to the whole world in Christ. Christ himself is God's sacred love-gift to the world.[13] At the communion table, then, we manifest God's self-

---

12. The meanings, mechanisms, and functions of sacrifice are more complex (and ambiguous) than most Christians realize. In the pre-Christian Jewish Levitical system, there were a variety of sacrificial offerings (burnt, grain or meal, peace, sin, trespass) offered at different times (daily, monthly, annually, and when needed). Although specific instructions for each sacrifice were articulated in the Bible, specific meanings were not. Even the word *sacrifice*—"sacred gift"—can be interpreted in many ways. Who is doing the giving? Who is receiving? What is the purpose of the gift? What makes it sacred?

For example, when humans give a sacred gift to God, their gift may express repentance and a desire to reconcile and re-bond, as when a husband gives his wife flowers after a spat, a remorseful child brings his mother a picture he has drawn after being disobedient, or a brother offers his alienated brother a "peace offering" in an effort to "bury the hatchet." (The story of Jacob and Esau in Genesis 33 exemplifies this kind of gift.) It may express a vow of love and commitment, as in the sacred gift of a wedding ring. It may express honor and thanks for past achievements, as in a retirement gift or a Nobel prize. Or it may anticipate and honor the expected generosity of another, as in a hospitality gift.

But there's another dimension to sacrifice, as René Girard and others have suggested. Some sacrificial rituals recall the primal practice of scapegoating and killing innocent victims to restore social order or curry the favor of bloodthirsty gods. Over time, through the ministrations of a priestly class, brutal human sacrifice was gradually domesticated and ritualized into animal sacrifice and further abstracted into various kinds of liturgical drama. Sadly, in many strains of Western Christianity, this meaning has been resurrected to frame the eucharist, keeping alive the image of a God who can be appeased only through blood, and (cynics might say) guaranteeing job security for a priestly class who have a monopoly on maintaining favor with this easy-to-anger deity.

James Alison suggests that the Jewish sacrificial system intended to dramatize not humans appeasing God, but God giving life (symbolized by blood) to the world through self-giving (in his lecture series, *The Shape of God's Affection*, available here: http://www.jamesalison.co.uk/; see also http://www.jamesalison.co.uk/texts/eng11.html). The climactic moment of the priestly office was not the priest bringing blood into the Holy of Holies to appease God, but rather the priest bringing blood out of the Holy of Holies to be sprinkled on the assembly, symbolizing God's life-giving vitality being shed abroad in the world. He sees in Temple sacrifice the inversion of traditional God-appeasement (what Alison calls the Aztec approach), and he sees Jesus embodying that inversion through the cross and resurrection.

13. See John 3:16. The cross, in this context, demonstrates not God's hostility against sinners, but rather sinful humanity's hostility against God: when God self-reveals in

He is resurrected in us to go forward &

self give to others in gratitude

giving in Christ. We dramatically receive the sacred gift by eating bread and drinking wine. We take these sacred gifts into ourselves so they nourish us—and more: as food, they *become* us by being incorporated (or incarnated) into our own body and blood. In giving ourselves to be receivers of God's self-giving in Christ, we yield ourselves to the Holy Spirit, to be the ongoing incarnation of Christ, so that his body and blood (separated at death on the cross) are reunited, reconstituted, and resurrected in us. God's sacred self-giving to us then invites us to imitation, to respond in kind through our own self-giving to God, to others, and to the whole world. And so we present ourselves as "living sacrifices" to God, and we continually offer to God the sacred gift of our thankful hearts.[14]

Around the eucharistic table, then, we bond to a love story of mutual self-giving. We celebrate our identity as recipients of God's gracious self-giving. And we respond in grateful self-giving by taking on a new identity as the ongoing embodiment of Christ— sent into the world to show the same love to the other that Jesus demonstrated—whether to leper or Pharisee, poor or rich, Zealot or tax collector, Samaritan or Roman or Syrophoenician or fellow Jew.

This table-oriented eucharist does not minimize Jesus' death. Rather, in "showing forth the Lord's death," we identify with it, and we let our lives be reshaped by it into cruciformity so as to lay down our lives for others just as Jesus did for us all. In this way, we die with Jesus to the ways of this world—hostility, oppression, violence, hate. And we rise with Jesus as well, to "walk in newness of life," to live in the ways of love, liberation, reconciliation, and human-kindness. So

mutual self-giving

Christ, look how we behave! Simultaneously, on the cross Christ demonstrates God's willingness to forgive us sinners, even at our worst: "Father, forgive them, for they know not what they do." And the resurrection further celebrates the point. Jesus doesn't return to say, "Now, go into the world and inflict vengeance on those who murdered me!" Instead, he says, "Go into all the world to preach the good news of God's reconciling love to every creature."

14. See Rom. 11:32–12:2, Heb. 13:15.

Cross = symbolizes God's willingness to forgive

Euch = we bond as a family, nourished by Todre bounty, in love + unity -

the world for us is no longer a battleground; our identity is no longer as warriors fighting with "us" against "them."[15] No: in the eucharist we bond to the good news that life is a table, a feast, a banquet, and we are a family, a circle of friends, being nourished together by God's bounty, the fruit of the vine and the grain of the field, all in a spirit of love, mutual service, and unity.

In this light, the fact that the original eucharist occurred on Passover eve is, of course, highly significant. The original Passover was a meal of hope, and hope was especially important in anticipation of what would happen to Jesus on Good Friday. It was as if Jesus were saying, "Passover was originally a preparatory meal—preparing for liberation from slavery. In the same way, tonight we are celebrating that a new day is about to dawn, a day of liberation—not just from slavery to Egypt then or Rome now, but from all oppressive systems of domination/enslavement, offense/revenge, rivalry/scapegoating, and fear/hostility. Don't be dismayed by the disruption that is ahead. Get ready for your liberation that will arise after the disruption."[16]

This sense of hope and anticipation is especially strong in Luke, where Jesus says, "Know this: I will not eat another Passover meal until its meaning is fulfilled in the kingdom of God...I will not drink another sip of wine until the kingdom of God has arrived in fullness."[17] So just as the Passover marked a new day of liberation

---

15. For more on this change in identity, see Cassidy Dale's brilliant (and free) ebook, *The Knight and the Gardener*, available here: http://knightandgardener.com/.

16. Advocates of penal substitutionary atonement would minimize the larger narrative of liberation from violence and oppression, and would focus on the blood placed on the doorposts of the houses of Jewish families, seeing in this blood an anticipatory symbol of penal substitutionary atonement. In this understanding, the Passover is less about deliverance from human oppression (by the Egyptians) and more about exemption from divine extermination (by the Lord's Angel of Death). Such a reading of the story is certainly possible—and in some settings popular—but it is not the only possible reading, and I find it far more problematic than the interpretation offered here.

17. See Luke 22:15–18. It's interesting to note that the risen Jesus takes the bread with two disciples en route to Emmaus just two chapters later (24:28–35). Luke does not tell

God's agents of reconcil. + love

216 • Why Did Jesus, Moses, the Buddha, and Mohammed Cross the Road?

for the Jewish people, Jesus says the communion meal marks a new covenant—a new covenant of love. Just as Passover was the end of an old identity, as slaves, and the beginning of a new identity, as God's people on a journey, the eucharist celebrates the end of our old oppositional identity and the beginning of our new identity as God's agents of reconciliation and love.

Paul, of course, picks up on this language.[18] The old covenant under Moses was about law, and those laws created an in group and an out group. The in group, identified by circumcision, Sabbath, diet, temple, priesthood, sacrifice, and compliance with a host of other religious laws, is inherently exclusive. For Paul, this law-based exclusivity leads (intentionally or not) to hostility toward the other. In contrast, Paul proclaims a new covenant focused on love, not law, and based on faith, not religious compliance ("law" or "works"). No wonder, then, that Paul so strongly associates the new-covenant meal of communion with unity. At the communion table, the old in-group/out-group hostilities are left behind, and the old walls come down.

---

us whether he also drank wine with them. Although this isn't the place for a thorough exploration of the eucharist in all its rich dimensions, it's worth noting that John's gospel doesn't present the eucharist at all. Where Matthew, Mark, and Luke have Jesus sharing in the Supper with his disciples on the eve of his betrayal, in John's Gospel, Jesus washes the disciples' feet (John 13), providing a model of love and humble service, and pronouncing (Moses-like) a new commandment to love (13:15, 34). John does, however, have Jesus present himself as "the bread that gives life to the world" earlier in his gospel (6). This self-giving of Jesus isn't associated with the Passover at all, but rather with the manna in the wilderness. For John, Jesus isn't a human substitute to satisfy God's wrath, but rather is "food indeed" given to satisfy the hunger of all humanity (6:35, recalling 4:14). "Those who eat my flesh and drink my blood abide in me," Jesus says, the word *abide* resonating with the pivotal passage in John 15, where Jesus images the disciples as branches drawing their vitality by *abiding* in him. The eating/drinking imagery is shocking—seemingly cannibalistic, but there is no hint at all that God needs Jesus' body and blood on which to vent fury: no, it is humanity that needs the self-giving of Jesus, drawing nourishment from him for "life abundant" and "bearing much fruit."

18. In 1 Corinthians 10:1–5, he suggests that as the children of Israel were united in Moses through food and drink (manna from heaven and the water that flowed from the rock), so we are united in Christ through food and drink.

[handwritten: Moses covenant = LAW = exclusive]

[handwritten: Paul's J C ← cov. based on love & faith & unity]

When Paul refers to Christ as the Passover lamb in 1 Corinthians, he doesn't use the image to evoke penal substitutionary atonement theory, but rather to urge the Christians to leave behind all hostilities—as if they were part of the old life under Egyptian slavery: "Therefore let us celebrate the festival, not with the old yeast, the yeast of malice [or hostility] and evil, but with ... sincerity and truth."

Later in the same letter, Paul returns to the eucharist, again emphasizing unity: we share in one cup, and there is one loaf, which means there is now only one body—not us/them, but all-of-us, united in one new humanity (1 Corinthians 10:16-17). He expresses great frustration that cultural and economic differences are still evident even at the eucharistic table (11:17–22), and then again employs the image of one body with many diverse members (12). Our differences, he asserts, can increase interdependence and mutual respect if only we will follow the more excellent way of love (13).

Whether gradually or decisively, in order to move from a strong-hostile to a strong-hospitable Christian identity, more and more of us are finding it necessary to migrate from an altar/appeasement-centered understanding of the eucharist to a table/fellowship-centered understanding.[19] We cannot continue to gather around the altar of sacrifice

---

19. This is the message of the Epistle to the Hebrews, as I understand it. Hebrews is not seeking to explain Jesus inside the framework of blood sacrifice, thus validating that framework (as the epistle is commonly read). Instead, Hebrews argues that in Jesus, the whole idea of sacrifice is put behind us "once and for all" (9:28), because blood sacrifice was never what God really wanted or needed (10:8). God wants far more for us than forgiveness alone (10:18): God wants to change our hearts (10:16) so that we do God's will (13:21)—which is a life of love and good works (10:24). In this, we follow Jesus' example (12:2), who endured hostility—without responding in kind (12:3). In so doing, we "pursue peace with everyone" (12:14) so that "filial love" will continue and we will show "hospitality to strangers" (13:1), always empathizing with those who are imprisoned and tortured (13:3). The old altar mind-set is the mind-set of insiders (13:10), but Jesus has identified himself with outsiders (13:12). So the old sacrificial system is left behind forever, and now, sacrifice (in the sense of sacred gift) remains in two senses only: first, "the sacrifice of praise ... the fruit of lips that confess his name" (recalling Psalm 50, which is itself a fascinating reflection on sacrifice), and second, doing good and sharing with others, "for such sacrifices are pleasing to God" (13:15–16).

with its hostile portrayal of God as requiring violence and bloodshed to be reconciled to us. We instead dare to celebrate the festival of love, the feast of communion, with its portrayal of God as gracious, self-giving, and reconciling.[20] As we do, the communion table will deepen our sense of solidarity with all people, recalling Jesus who loved the outcasts and outsiders and was glad to eat with them, who was not hostile to anyone but was rather a host to everyone. Understood in this way, the table of the Lord fills a unique place in this world: it creates space where we experience a family meal with the other, where *one* and *the other* discover a new identity as *one-another*...Jew and Gentile, slave and free, male and female...where God and all humanity at table are sat down. In this way, we transcend the hostile rival-

20. In these chapters on liturgy, I have not addressed the question of including liturgical elements—prayers, readings, and so on—from other faith traditions. Should Christians, in an effort to build hospitality and overcome hostility, use Hindu prayers, Buddhist meditations, Sufi poetry, Native American or Jewish rituals, and so on? Not, I would say, before developing a strong and benevolent identity rooted deeply in the Christian story itself, and not before thoroughly considering the unintended negative consequences of mixing faith traditions.

Careless cafeteria-style mixing of different traditions can weaken the integrity of each tradition. It can lead to the kind of weak-benign identity we are seeking to move beyond. And it can promote a kind of consumerist commodification and Borg-like colonization (recalling the *Star Trek* TV series). But once a strong-benevolent identity is in place, and once these dangers are faced, gifts from other faiths can, I believe, be warmly welcomed and appreciated, just as Paul did (in an admittedly nonliturgical situation) in Acts 17:28. This subject and the related subjects of interspirituality and multireligious identity are beyond the scope of this book. But these subjects are important and worthy of further discussion, and several Christian communities are experimenting wisely and fruitfully with them (and, no doubt, others are doing so less wisely and fruitfully). For those especially interested in this subject, I would recommend the works of Paul Knitter and Thomas Merton (engaging with Buddhism); Bede Griffiths, Raimon Pannikar, and Anthony de Mello (engaging with Hinduism); Richard Twiss and Randy Woodley (engaging with Native American spirituality); and Mabiala Kenzo and Kwame Bediako (engaging with African spirituality). But again, I think much work must be done first on the development of deeply benevolent, deeply Christian identity. In order to provide genuine hospitality to the other, it helps to have a strong, stable, and healthy home into which the other can be welcomed. And in order to be a good guest as opposed to a freeloader or squatter, it helps to have a strong, stable, healthy home to return to as well.

ries of human politics; we descend beneath the hostile tribalisms of human religions. Scot McKnight says it powerfully: "The single-most powerful political action Christians 'do' is baptism and Eucharist, for in those actions we enter into an alien politics."

As I conclude this chapter, tears fill my eyes and I am once again overcome with awe at the mysteries and hope proclaimed in a simple loaf of bread and cup of wine. I imagine what it could mean if, in the future, each time we arise from the table of fellowship, we do so more deeply bonded with a new identity in Christ, more fully in solidarity with our neighbors everywhere, more profoundly reoriented and reinvigorated to be sent out into the world with a new agenda, a vital, transforming mission. To that mission we now turn.

+ Jesus is the "host" of the meal.

Celebrate each as festival of love, a unified feast from God Jesus who loves us and gives Himself to us still as reconciliation is all. Solidarity w all. A family meal to unite us all. He sends us out into the world to love + serve each other.

24-29
finish
book

PART IV

THE MISSIONAL CHALLENGE

It was granted me to carry away from my prison years on my bent back, which nearly broke beneath its load, this essential experience: how a human being becomes evil and how good. In the intoxication of youthful successes I had felt myself to be infallible, and I was therefore cruel. In the surfeit of power I was a murderer and an oppressor. In my most evil moments I was convinced that I was doing good, and I was well supplied with systematic arguments. And it was only when I lay there rotting on prison straw that I sensed within myself the first stirrings of good. Gradually it was disclosed to me that the line separating good and evil passes not through states, nor between classes, nor between political parties either—but right through every human heart—and through all human hearts. This line shifts. Inside us it oscillates with the years. And even within the hearts overwhelmed with evil, one small bridgehead of good is retained. And even in the best of all hearts, there remains...an un-uprooted small corner of evil. Since then I have come to understand the truth of all the religions on the world. They struggle with the evil inside a human being (inside every human being). It is impossible to expel evil from the world in its entirety, but it is possible to constrict it within each person. And since that time I have come to understand the falsehood of all the revolutions of history: they destroy only those carriers of evil contemporary with them (and also fail, out of haste, to discriminate the carriers of good as well). And they take to themselves as their heritage the actual evil itself, magnified still more.

—*Alexander Solzhenitsyn*[1]

---

1. Alexander Solzhenitsyn, *The Gulag Archipelago* (New York: Harper, 2007), Part 4, Chapter 1.

Chapter 24

How Subversive Friendship Can Change the World

"What a wonderful idea!" the Muslim woman said. "We need to love our traditions and be faithful to our God; but we teach the beauty and goodness of the other religions too."

Her Hindu colleague chimed in, "That is the only way to peace—to be ourselves and to create understanding between all people."

When I reached my car, I realized that I was crying. I had only rarely felt the power of the resurrected Jesus so completely in my soul.

—*Diana Butler Bass*[1]

Christian mission begins with friendship—not utilitarian friendship, the religious version of network marketing—but genuine friendship, friendship that translates love for neighbors in general into knowing, appreciating, liking, and enjoying this or that neighbor in particular. This knowing-in-particular then motivates us to protect our neighbor when he or she is under threat, as a little Rwandan girl understood: just before she was brutally murdered

---

1. Diana Butler Bass, *Christianity after Religion* (New York: HarperOne, 2012), p. 241.

Jesus, friend of sinners

prophet - priest - king - friend

during the genocide, she said to her slayer, "If you knew me, you would not kill me."

Friendliness was so essential to Jesus' identity that his critics labeled him "a friend of sinners," bemoaning the fact that he constantly welcomed the wrong people to the table. Even with his disciples he seemed unwilling to maintain a properly distanced, top-down protocol. Instead, he elevated their connection from authoritarian discipleship to human-to-human friendship. It is far more significant than we commonly realize that the earliest followers of Christ did not call themselves *the Christians*, but rather *the friends*.[2]

That's why I was so pleased to learn that German Reformed theologian Jürgen Moltmann has daringly suggested that the traditional triad of images used to identify Jesus—prophet, priest, and king—is seriously incomplete, as Tony Jones explains:

> To [prophet, priest, and king], Moltmann adds the office of "transfigured Christ" to emphasize the aesthetic dimension of the resurrection. . . . And then Moltmann adds a fifth office: "But the fellowship which Jesus brings men [*sic*], and the fellowship of people with one another to which he calls, would be described in one-sided terms if another 'title' were not added, a title to describe the inner relationship between the divine and the human fellowship: the name of friend."[3]

all humanity

friendship - free choice showing respect & affection

Friendship for Moltmann is a free choice entered into without obligation because of respect and affection. That free choice differentiates being a friend from being a parent, child, sibling, leader, or follower—or a prophet, priest, or king: "friendship is a human rela-

---

2. Luke 7:34, John 15:15, 3 John 15.

3. Tony Jones, *The Church Is Flat* (Minneapolis: The JoPa Group, 2011), p. 169, quoting Jürgen Moltmann, *The Church in the Power of the Spirit* (Minneapolis: Fortress Press, 1993), p. 119.

Highest form of love

tionship which springs from freedom, exists in mutual freedom and preserves that freedom."[4] In radical friendliness to all, Moltmann says, Jesus welcomes all humanity into the divine friendship, and "the many-faceted work of Christ . . . can be taken to its highest point in his friendship," for friendship is "the highest form of love."[5]

By focusing on Jesus as prophet, priest, and king to the exclusion of friend for its first two thousand years, our Christian tradition has no doubt made Christian unfriendliness easier than it would have been otherwise. The next two thousand years could be different if we take Christ's subversive, transformative friendship as seriously as Moltmann recommends.

Since my friendship with that precocious Muslim boy named Aatif, many new friends have come into my life . . . Jews, Muslims, Hindus, Buddhists, New Agers, and others—including lots of atheists and agnostics, too. One of the most dramatic of those friendships began in the aftermath of 9/11/01. Like a lot of churches, our little congregation held a prayer service. While praying, I felt a voice speaking, as it were, in my chest: *Your Muslim neighbors are in danger of reprisals. You must try to protect them.* The next morning, I wrote and made copies of a letter extending, belatedly, friendship toward Muslim communities in my area, and offering solidarity and help if simmering anti-Muslim sentiments should be translated into action. I drove to the three mosques nearby—I had never visited them before—and tried to deliver my letter in person.

The first two were locked tight—no doubt for fear of reprisals—so I put my letters in the mailbox. When I arrived at the third, a TV satellite truck was pulling out. There had in fact been an incident the afternoon before. A Muslim woman—easily identified by her religious dress—was pushed down on the sidewalk, and an angry man

---

4. *The Church in the Power of the Spirit*, p. 115.

5. Ibid., pp. 119, 117.

stood over her and shouted, "You're probably glad this happened." The TV crew had come to get a statement from the local imam about the incident.

As the TV truck pulled out, the automatic gates were closing so I—without thinking—stepped on the gas and rushed my car through the gates. When the imam saw a stranger speeding into his driveway, he ran toward me, motioning for me to stop. I slammed on my brakes, threw the transmission into park, and jumped out, leaving the engine still running. I couldn't have been more intimidating to the poor imam!

I clumsily introduced myself as the pastor from down the street, apologized both for my scary entry and for my failure to visit sooner. I then handed him my letter, which he opened and read as I stood there awkwardly. I remember the imam, a man short in stature, slowly looking down at the letter in the bright September sun, then up into my face, then down, then up, and each time he looked up, his eyes were more moist. Suddenly, he threw his arms around me—a perfect stranger who had entered his property in a less-than-sensitive way. I still remember the feeling of his head pressed against my chest, squeezing me as if I were his long-lost brother.

"It means so much to me that you have come," he said. "Please, please, please come inside." I had never been in a mosque before, much less in an imam's office (which was, in case you're interested, a lot like my own office, except much neater, and all the books were in Arabic). My host welcomed me not with hostility or even suspicion, but with the open heart of a friend. And so that day a friendship began between an Evangelical pastor named Brian and a Muslim imam we'll call Ahmad.

A few days later, the youth group from our church made a colorful banner expressing their desire for there to be friendship between the youth of the mosque and the youth of our church. The banner was covered in their names, each handwritten with a colored marker.

(The imam hung the banner in the back of the mosque, where it remained for months.) The women of our church heard about the Muslim lady who had been pushed down on the sidewalk, and in response they made a list of names and phone numbers, offering to accompany any Muslim women to the store or an appointment if they were for any reason afraid. The mosque began hosting community dinners to which our people were invited along with people from other faith communities in the area, and many of us have warm memories of delicious Pakistani food shared in the basement of their well-appointed mosque.

The friendship between our congregations grew through a series of interfaith dialogues we organized (one of which I described earlier), and Ahmad and I began meeting for lunch every month or so. Ahmad wasn't, back in 2001 and 2002 anyway, much for phone conversations, and he didn't have an e-mail address back then. He followed more traditional and humane ways of staying in touch—by visiting me in person. If Ahmad wanted to talk about something or arrange for our next lunch meeting, he knew one place one day each week where I could be found—Sunday mornings at church. So that's when he would drop by, fully resplendent in his traditional garb.

Some people were, I imagine, a little shocked at first to see a Muslim cleric walking through the church lobby as people chatted over coffee and bagels. But because our congregations had developed a friendship, he was soon recognized and welcomed. Several times, I remember someone coming up and whispering in my ear, "Brian, your imam is looking for you." There was something wonderfully right about Ahmad feeling so at home that he could come find me before or between services on a Sunday to schedule our next lunch meeting.

Both Ahmad and I have moved away since then, and I imagine that contact between the two congregations has waned, which is understandable. But I also know that many people at the church will forget neither the hospitality they experienced from the mosque nor the sense of blessing that came from our friendship, so they won't hesitate to resume contact again when needed. Ahmad and I are on opposite sides of the country now, so we can no longer meet for lunch, but I got an invitation to the wedding of one of his daughters not long ago, after which I called him and we had a great conversation. And he has an e-mail address now, so next time I'm in his new city, I'll e-mail him and do my best to schedule a visit. I know we'll have a great meal, and our friendship will pick up right where it left off.

Imagine what might happen around the world if more and more Christians rediscover that central to Christian life and mission is what we could call subversive or transgressive friendship—friendship that crosses boundaries of otherness and dares to offer and receive hospitality. Imagine what could happen if our experience of communion around the Lord's table on Sundays motivated us, like the Lord himself, to enjoy table fellowship with "the wrong people" all through the week. Imagine the good that could happen—and the evil that could be prevented from happening—if more Jews, Muslims, Hindus, Christians, Buddhists, and others cross the roads and other barriers that have separated them, and discover one another as friends.[6]

The apostle Peter had one such experience in the Book of Acts. Peter had a deeply rooted resistance to otherness...even after three years of daily contact with Jesus, even after the miracle of Pentecost (revealing that God is equally fluent in every language), even after the Spirit transcended boundary after boundary in the early church. It took a vivid dream sequence to convince him to accept hospitality from "the other," a Gentile man named Cornelius. Through their

---

6. Here is an example of one such adventure in friendship: Richard McCallum, "A Rabbi, a Priest, and an Imam...," Yale Center for Faith & Culture, http://www.yale.edu/faith/rp/rp_hope.htm#mccallum. Here is another: the Peace Catalyst International website at http://www.peace-catalyst.net/.

encounter, both Peter and Cornelius (and his household) experienced the Spirit.

Here's what Peter said as the experience unfolded: "You yourselves know that it is unlawful for a [person of my religious background] to associate with or to visit a [person of another religious background]; but God has shown me that I should not call anyone profane or unclean." Then, after hearing more of the story of his hosts, he added, "I truly understand that God shows no partiality, but in every nation anyone who fears God and does what is right is acceptable to God." Peter realized in their encounter that the good news of Jesus subverted and transcended the old laws of insider-outsider, us-them, sacred-profane, clean-unclean.

Even after this experience, Peter slipped back into his old ways, and it took a former Pharisee named Paul to confront him about his hypocrisy.[7] Following Peter's checkered example, the Christian faith has over the centuries repeatedly gained and lost ground in our willingness to participate in transgressive friendship. I've felt the ambivalence myself, knowing that if I befriend "them"—whether they be the denominationally, religiously, sexually, culturally, economically, ideologically, or politically other, some of "us" will be suspicious of me. But time after time, when I dare to risk friendship across barriers, I experience the Spirit just as Peter did with Cornelius. I've come to accept it as axiomatic: *a Christian moves toward the other in friendship.*

Three words capture the heart of that kind of liberating, transformative, and subversive friendship. (First,) it's a friendship of *companionship*—ritualized in the eucharist, to be sure, but actualized whenever we break bread and drink wine (or tea or coffee or whatever) with a friend of another faith. Second, it's a friendship of *conviviality*, not just of coexistence. It's not just a matter of talking together about religion, but more of living together, sharing the gifts

---

7. See Galatians 2:11–14.

of life together—attending one another's weddings and funerals and birthday parties, even sharing in one another's holidays (with appropriate respect and understanding).[8] And third, it's a friendship of *conspiracy*.

The word evokes people whispering in one another's ears, speaking of plans and plots that must be kept secret because one would be punished for announcing them aloud. To whisper such plans requires us to be so close as to breathe one another's breath. And so it was when Ahmad and I sat in a restaurant sharing a meal, or when a rabbi friend and I commiserated about the hardships of congregational leadership on a long drive, or when a Hindu activist confided to me his struggles with the caste system in India, or when an atheist and I took a walk in a park together and shared our common dreams for a better world. In each case, our friendships were conspiratorial . . . seeking to overthrow the current regimes of hostility, opposition, exclusion, fear, and prejudice, not only dreaming of that better world but rehearsing for it, practicing it through the give and take of our friendship. Together we were plotting goodness.

In recent years, I've met people all over the world who are discovering the surprising joys of subversive friendship: two moms, Soraya and Nadyne—one Muslim and one Evangelical Christian—whose children modeled for them the possibility of "playing together" subversively[9] . . . Samir, a former atheist/communist/Muslim who became a Seventh Day Adventist pastor and now helps lead a faith community that comprises subcommunities of many faiths[10] . . . Mark, a former religious-right politician in the United States who realized he had become an anti-Muslim zealot who subsequently became so dedicated to Christian-Muslim friendships that the US government

---

8. Ivan Illich explores this powerful word in *Tools for Conviviality* (New York: Marion Boyars, 2001).

9. See PeaceMoms, http://www.peacemoms.com.

10. See Faith House Manhattan, http://www.faithhousemanhattan.org.

accused him of associating with terrorists[11]...Jeff, formerly a fundamentalist/charismatic Christian pastor who repented from his anti-Muslim ways and now teaches Christians and Muslims to love and understand one another as neighbors[12]...Nita, a Christian woman in a Muslim country who was welcomed into a Muslim feminist group because she, as a Christian and a woman, wanted to share in their struggle against domestic violence.

I've met scores of people involved in these subversive friendships of companionship, conviviality, and conspiracy...but the world needs millions more. So if you aren't already involved in at least one of these friendships, I dare you. It's one thing to say you love humanity in general, whatever their religion; it's quite another to learn to love this or that specific neighbor with his or her specific religion. So, do you have a Sikh neighbor, a Hindu coworker, a Muslim business associate, a Buddhist member of your PTA, a New Age second cousin? Invite them into companionship over a cup of tea or coffee. Ask them questions. Display unexpected interest in them, their traditions, their beliefs, and their stories. Learn why they left what they left, why they stay where they stay, why they love what they love. Enter their world, and welcome them into your world, without judgment. If they reciprocate, welcome their reciprocation; if not, welcome their nonreciprocation. Experience conviviality. Join the conspiracy of plotting for the common good together.

That's what I imagine Jesus, Moses, the Buddha, and Mohammed would do if they met one another along the road. When we cross the road to meet one another as friends, in some way, perhaps, they do, too, through us. Perhaps their story is not yet over but continues to unfold in us.

---

11. See Mark Siljander's website: http://www.marksiljander.com.

12. See Jeff Burns, "Walking with Muslims," Interfaith Youth Core, http://www.ifyc .org/content/walking-muslims.

Chapter 25

How God's Commonwealth of Peace Confronts Earthly Empires of Hostility

The Church, therefore, exhorts her children, that through dialogue and collaboration with the followers of other religions, carried out with prudence and love and in witness to the Christian faith and life, they recognize, preserve and promote the good things, spiritual and moral, as well as the socio-cultural values found among them.
—Pope Paul VI, *Nostra Aetate*[1]

Jesus didn't start a school. Nor did he start a denomination or an institution. If anything, he started what we would call a community organizing movement...a movement supported by a privately funded NGO with an all-female board of directors.[2] He recruited twelve core volunteers to lead the movement. They were a diverse

---

1. *Nostra Aetate*, Declaration on the Relation of the Church to Non-Christian Religions, proclaimed by Pope Paul VI, October 28, 1965, available here: http://www.vatican.va/archive/hist_councils/ii_vatican_council/documents/vat-ii _decl_19651028_nostra-aetate_en.html. The official Vatican translation uses "sons" instead of "children" and "these men" instead of "them."

2. See Luke 8:1–3.

Simon Peter = zealot activist John - mystic poet
matt - tax collector
The Missional Challenge • 233

lot, almost comically so at times—pairing a zealot like Simon with a tax collector like Matthew, or linking an impulsive activist like Peter with a mystic-poet like John. Enhanced by this diversity, their influence extended to a larger network of committed allies that numbered in the hundreds—and eventually thousands.

What did the movement do? They traveled from village to village, much like a political campaign, spreading their message, looking for "people of peace" and networking them together, feeding the hungry, healing the sick, offering hope to the depressed, promising freedom for the oppressed, confronting the oppressors, and conversing with questioners and critics. Sometimes they organized what we might call outdoor festivals—complete with teaching and food for thousands. Sometimes they staged what we would call public demonstrations—a march into Jerusalem, civil disobedience in the temple. Often they engaged in quiet, behind-the-scenes relationship building, meeting with an amazing range of people.

One night they might meet privately with a respected religious leader like Nicodemus or Simon, both members of the Pharisee party. Another evening they might eat with a despised tax collector like Zaccheus or Matthew and their equally despised friends, enemies of the Pharisees. In between, they might spend time with a variety of social outcasts—including foreigners like the Syrophoenician woman, marginal outsiders like the Samaritan woman, and isolated social outcasts like the Gadarene demoniac and a host of lepers and beggars. In short, they were like yeast, kneaded into the dough of society, and by their faithful and active presence they changed the world. What would make them do that ??

After Jesus' death, his disciples continued this same pattern. They extended their travel routes far beyond Judea and Galilee, aiming for "the uttermost parts of the earth." But their pattern was the same: meeting people, spreading their message through word and deed, occasionally stirring up controversy and even a riot or two, all the while recruiting and organizing a wild array of people into groups that would continue their mission after they moved on.

Paul's evangelistic trip to Philippi, described in Acts 16, provides an interesting model of their movement-building work—a model that can inspire and inform today. Paul is accompanied by Silas, Timothy, Luke, and maybe others. They arrive in Philippi—their first engagement with an official Roman colony. The kingdom of God, we might say, is encountering the empire of Caesar for the first time on Caesar's own turf. The Pax Christi is encountering the Pax Romana.

The little team of emissaries meets a group of women on the outskirts of the city, and one of them, a businesswoman named Lydia, hosts them. Soon, they encounter a slave girl who makes a lot of money for her owners as an occult fortune-teller. On seeing the band of travelers, she shouts, "These men are slaves like me, but slaves of the Most High God! They will proclaim to you the way of liberation!"[3]

Paul eventually becomes annoyed (whether at her insistent shouting or at her plight, the text doesn't make clear), and he frees her from the occult spirit, after which she is incapable of continuing her fortune-telling work. This, of course, enrages her owners, who stir up a mob and bring Paul and Silas before the local authorities. Their speech is fascinating:

> These men are troublemakers, disturbing the peace of our great city. They are from some Jewish sect, and they promote foreign customs that violate our Roman standards of conduct. (Acts 16: 20–21)

What might the "foreign customs" in question be? No doubt they are referring among other things to the custom of respecting slaves as

---

3. This translation of Acts 16:17 from *The Voice New Testament* (Nashville: Thomas Nelson, 2008) reflects my conviction that the word *liberation* (recalling the Exodus) is the best one-word synonym for *salvation*.

apostle treated foreign slaves humanely.

Rome-ran on a slave economy, Prison

equal human beings.[4] Few things could disturb a Roman colony more than challenging the slave-based economy upon which the "peace" of the entire Roman Empire depends. The magistrates quickly do the bidding of the powerful economic interests (sound familiar?), breaking their own laws by stripping, beating, and imprisoning Paul and Silas without due process. Upsetting a slave-based economy is a dangerous thing!

That night, Paul and Silas lie in the highest-security section of the local jail. There, severely beaten and chained, they sing songs—probably an act of protest as well as piety, as if to say, *The Romans have imprisoned our bodies, but our spirits are still free to worship the God who liberates slaves!* An earthquake occurs—as if to symbolize the earth-shaking radicality of the liberating message Paul's team proclaims—and the chains and gates of their imprisonment are unlocked again, highly symbolic of their liberating mission. The jailer rushes in, and seeing the open gates, he assumes the prisoners have escaped. He immediately pulls out his sword to kill himself, which reveals the deep fear he experiences as part of the Roman domination system: he would rather die than be thrown into the prison he manages.

When Paul and Silas tell him they haven't escaped—that they are voluntarily remaining in their cells—the man is shocked, falls to his knees in front of his prisoners, and cries out, "What must I do to be liberated?" Not insignificantly, he uses the same word that the slave girl has used.

Paul and Silas say something like this: "You live in the fear-based system of the Lord Caesar. Stop having confidence in him and his system of domination, hostility, and oppression. Instead, have confidence in the Lord Jesus. If you do, you and all those in your household will experience liberation." *Revolution*

---

4. Paul and friends were known to them not as Christians, but as members of a Jewish sect, and Jewish identity was centered in the Exodus—where God was revealed as a slaveholder-confronting and slave-liberating God.

The man is transformed from a hostile jailer into a generous host. He invites the men into his home. He and his family hear the good news of Jesus and the kingdom of God. The jailer washes the wounds his associates had inflicted, and then Paul and Silas baptize the man and his family. (The mutual washing offers a tender and beautiful image.) Finally, they share a meal together. But the story still isn't over. Paul and Silas stage a kind of sit-in at the jail the next day, requiring the city officials to apologize for their injustice before escorting Paul and Silas out of the jail.

So what happens when God's kingdom of liberation and reconciliation confronts Caesar's empire of fear and hostility? Starting with the most marginalized—women and slaves—the gospel proclaims liberation first to the oppressed and then to the oppressors, since both oppressors and oppressed are dehumanized through injustice. Midlevel functionaries (like the jailer) and top-level magistrates are given the chance to defect from hostility and practice a better way of life. The seeds of gospel transformation are sown, and a community to continue the work of transformation has been established. So Paul and his community organizing team move on.

This was what Christian mission originally looked like—without TV or radio, without pianos, organs, or rock and roll bands, without offerings and invitations to walk down an aisle, without national headquarters and retirement plans, and without fiery preaching that inspires hostility against anybody.[5] And this is what we need today.

Imagine teams of unlikely people—Christians, Jews, Muslims, Hindus, Buddhists, people from the whole range of indigenous religions, together with agnostics and atheists—coming together, not in the name of the Christian (or any other) religion, but seeking to walk in the way of Jesus, learning, proclaiming, and demonstrating "the way of liberation."

---

5. . . . although it evokes hostility from some people.

Imagine they begin, as Paul, Silas, and company did, in solidarity with the most marginalized and vulnerable—children, women, slaves, the homeless, refugees, the poorest of the poor. Imagine how their work among the most vulnerable would eventually lead them into confrontation with systems of injustice—the fear-based systems that oppress, exclude, and exploit. Sometimes there would no doubt be sufferings and setbacks, but if, like Paul and Silas, the teams keep faith and refuse to be intimidated, these setbacks will lead to unexpected and even earthshaking breakthroughs. In the process, others will *want to* join them—without threats or promises, but simply because of the beauty, goodness, and truth of their words and actions.

Mission work like this will always involve charity—directly helping those in need: food for the hungry, water for the thirsty, clothing for the naked, shelter for the homeless. But if the hungry, thirsty, naked, and homeless need food, water, clothing, and shelter, what do the oppressed, excluded, and endangered need? Very often, they need new laws and policies to protect them and ongoing reforms to ensure ongoing justice for them. So, charity will also lead to advocacy—speaking and working on behalf of the voiceless and powerless, using the tools of local, national, and global citizenship to work for the common good.

But beyond charity and advocacy, people need opportunity. They need opportunities to learn, opportunities to work, opportunities to move and make a new home. Imagine the role people of faith could have in providing opportunity—classroom teachers and alternative educators, business owners and social entrepreneurs, city planners and civil engineers, immigration lawyers and ethical employers, bankers and venture capitalists. Imagine students learning in new ways, workers being hired into new jobs, and new neighborhoods and social circles welcoming people who have been driven from their previous homes by various forms of hostile, oppositional clannishness.

Sadly, this clannishness has often been reinforced by religion.

Common good of ALL

That's why community organizers working for the common good often must stand in solidarity with people of other faiths to challenge the clannishness of their own faith. They must use their insider status for the protection and benefit of outcasts or outsiders, just as Jesus constantly did.[6]

So we who follow Jesus will discover our true identity not by favoring our fellow religious insiders to the exclusion of others, but rather by going out of our way to serve Muslims, Hindus, Buddhists, Jews, and atheists—doing for people of other religions no less than we would wish people of other religions would do for us. And we will deepen this identity not only by serving others, but also by serving alongside them. In the words of Vatican II, we will "through dialogue and collaboration with the followers of other religions" work for the common good of all, thus advancing the commonwealth of God.

Friendship types: p. 229
- companionship (dining) casual
- conviviality (sharing holidays etc
- conspiracy = (confiding)

6. See, for example, how he saved the life of a woman about to be executed for religious reasons in John 8.

relative reality (relational)
to every truth in other religions.

How *With-ness* Complements *Witness*

Without compromising the absolute commitment inherent to faith, Christianity can be considered as a relative reality; not, however, in the sense in which "relative" is opposed to "absolute," but in the sense of "relational." The truth to which Christianity witnesses is neither exclusive nor inclusive of all other truth; it is related to all that is true in other religions.

—Claude Geffre[1]

It was Good Friday and our worship team had transformed our large gathering space into Stations of the Cross.[2] At each station, participants would engage with an activity to enter into the story of Jesus' final day—kneeling on rocks and gravel, lifting a

---

1. From Claude Geffre, "La singularite du Christianisme a l'age du pluralisme religieux," in *Penser la foi: Recherches en theologie aujourd'hui*, ed. J. Dore and C. Theobald (Paris: Cerf-Assas, 1992), pp. 351–369. Quoted in Jacques Dupuis, S.J., *Towards a Christian Theology of Religious Pluralism* (Maryknoll, N.Y.: Orbis Books, 1997), p. 388.

2. For more on this kind of worship experience, see the Cedar Ridge Community Church website at http://www.crcc.org (with thanks to Bryan Anderson, Betsy Mitchell-Henning, Patsy Fratanduono, and others). For more on worship curation of this sort, see "Meet Mark Pierson, Worship Curator," sparkhouse, http://sparkhouse blogs.org/blog/clayfire/meet-mark-pierson-worship-curator/, and read Mark Pierson, *The Art of Curating Worship* (Minneapolis: sparkhouse press, 2010).

heavy wooden crossbeam, pounding a spike into wood, pondering a picture or statue. One station commemorated Jesus speaking to the daughters of Jerusalem, urging them not to weep for him, but for themselves and their children (Luke 23:26–31). As I stood at that station, I realized I had never before pondered those words, "Do not weep for me." For me, the whole purpose of Good Friday was to weep for Jesus. Why would he say *not* to do so? That soon led to another question: for whom would Jesus have me weep today?

I had recently read an article about the ongoing genocide in Darfur, and as I stood at that station of the cross, I felt that on that Good Friday, Jesus would have me weep for Darfur...for families driven from their homes, for children bereft of parents, for girls subjected to brutal rape, for elderly people living in fear. In the following weeks, my concern for Darfur wouldn't go away. A vision took shape. I shared it with friends at Sojourners (http://sojo.net), and together we developed a public demonstration we called Worship in the Spirit of Justice. We chose five significant locations in Washington, D.C., and there we staged public worship on consecutive Sundays. One week we gathered in front of the Lincoln Memorial, one week in front of the Capitol, one week near the National Press Club, one week near the White House, and one week near the Sudanese Embassy. At each location we sang, prayed, read Scripture, preached, and worshiped God as the God of justice, the God who cares for all people—whatever their race, religion, economic status, or nationality.

One week we invited a rabbi, David Saperstein, to preach, and everyone agreed he was our best preacher. He preached from Leviticus 19:16, "Do not stand idly by while your neighbor bleeds," explaining how the Holocaust must move us to speak out against not only anti-Semitism, but against violence and genocide against anyone anywhere.[3] Each week we had Sudanese people share their moving and unforgettable stories of survival, some of them Christians who had suffered in Southern Sudan, others Muslims who had suffered in Darfur.

Although our speakers included Christians, Jews, and Muslims, we didn't describe our gatherings as interfaith worship. No, it was explicitly Christian worship. But we discovered that explicitly Christian worship can be explicitly hospitable to Jews, Muslims, and others.

I'm certainly not against interfaith worship, and I think there's a vital need for multi-faith worship as well.[4] But I am especially interested in worship in one's tradition that practices hospitality to the other. So as a Christian, I can welcome Hindus or Buddhists to be guests in Christian worship. They can participate or observe, as their consciences will allow, knowing their presence does not imply understanding of or agreement with everything that goes on. Similarly, if I am invited as a Christian to be the guest of Muslims or Jews in worship, I can joyfully accept the invitation, participating or observing as my conscience will allow, knowing that my presence doesn't mean I fully understand or agree with everything that is said or done. (The fact is, we Christians all share this understanding when we attend any explicitly Christian gathering, too. How often do we

---

3. Leviticus 16:19 is rendered variously in different translations, but this was the rendering from which the rabbi preached.

4. By "interfaith worship," I mean a setting where all participants assume they are worshipping the same God, using different language and ritual systems to reach out toward the One who surpasses them all. So Christians might chant Hindu prayers, or Muslims might sing Christian songs—not affirming the literal content of the words, but seeking the deeper realities to which the words point. By multi-faith worship, I mean a setting where each participant worships according to his own tradition, in the company of others who worship according to their traditions. In this context, Christians participate in the Christian parts of the service and respectfully observe during other parts.

working with "others"- solidarity for a common good.

242 • Why Did Jesus, Moses, the Buddha, and Mohammed Cross the Road?

fully understand and endorse every single word of every single prayer, song, or sermon, even within our own congregation?)

In the years before the 2001 terrorist attacks, I wouldn't have considered "with-ness" to be an important dimension of Christian worship or mission. I believed in *witness*, not *with-ness*. I believed in *speaking to* and *working for* people of other faiths, not conversing and working *with*. But since 2001, I've been convinced that Christian identity involves both *witness*—graciously and confidently sharing our unique, Christ-centered message, and *with-ness*—experiencing solidarity with people of other faiths, worshipping in one another's presence and working together for the common good.

As I've spoken out on behalf of with-ness, some of my critics have responded quite aggressively—one even accusing my friends and me of being an ally of Al Queda![5] But I've learned that the best way to "turn the other cheek" as a writer and speaker is simply to dust myself off, get up, and write or speak again. Instead of defending myself by responding to the last criticism, I try to move forward to the next project in my mission.

So in that spirit, after a season of protracted and intense criticism from some of my fellow Christians, a few years ago I felt I was being called to go even further in with-ness. I wasn't sure what that would mean, so I prayed for guidance. The answer came when I was speaking at a church in Michigan, where my friend Rob Bell was pastor. After one of the services, an enthusiastic woman named Nadyne came up front, waited patiently in a rather long line, and then told me that she had developed a deep friendship with a Muslim woman named Soraya. They formed a group called Peace Moms, and she wondered if I'd like to join her the following summer in participat-

---

5. Frank Pastore, "Why Al Qaeda Supports the Emergent Church," Townhall.com, July 22, 2007, http://townhall.com/columnists/frankpastore/2007/07/22/why_al_qaeda_supports_the_emergent_church/page/full/.

with-ness = respect

ing, as a Christian, in the Muslim fast of Ramadan with her friend.[6] Instantly I felt the Holy Spirit speaking deep inside me: *This is it. Do this.* "I'm in," I said.

As the month of Ramadan approached, I called my Muslim friend Eboo Patel, explaining my desire to be in public solidarity with Muslims and asking him if he would be my "sponsor." He wasn't comfortable with the word *sponsor* and expressed some valid concerns about the way I was using the word *solidarity*, but gladly offered to be my friend and advisor through the fast—to extend hospitable *with-ness* to me.

In terms of community organizing, you might say my fast became, along with a personal spiritual discipline, something of a demonstration or nonviolent action in protest of religious clannishness, fear, and hostility.[7] I blogged about my experience several times during the month, and most of the responses were deeply moving and encouraging. A number of Christians felt moved to join in the fast, many of them reaching out to local mosques, making their first Muslim friend, and experiencing warm hospitality for the after-sundown fast-breaking meal. Some amazing spiritual and social breakthroughs occurred. I received notes from Muslims around the world as well, nearly all positive, saying, "We have never heard of a Christian having respect for our religion. Thank you," or "We only hear about Christians insulting our prophet or disgracing the Quran, never about them respecting us and joining us in our fast. Thank you."

My journey into with-ness had begun several years earlier. I

---

6. See the PeaceMoms website at http:// www.peacemoms.org.

7. I walked a fine line between wanting to be public about the fast for the sake of demonstrating with-ness in relation to my Muslim friends, yet not wanting to fall prey to the hypocrisy Jesus warned about—fasting "to be seen by people." You can read my blog posts about the experience by going to http://www.brianmclaren.net and searching "ramadan 2009."

Common good — saving love

244 • Why Did Jesus, Moses, the Buddha, and Mohammed Cross the Road?

was attending a conference on religious violence where a Muslim scholar delivered a sparkling and informative lecture. I came up to her later with a long list of questions, which she answered patiently and brilliantly. We exchanged e-mail addresses, and some time later I received a note from her that said something like this: "After meeting you, I Googled your name and the words *Muslim* and *Islam*. I read about all the times you have stood up for Muslim people. I was moved by the ways you have shown sincere love for us. I also read the harsh things your fellow Christians said and wrote about you for doing so. I want to thank you for your courage. You have risked your reputation as a Christian to protect Muslims from prejudice and violence. This work saves lives." That was moving enough, but then came her last sentence: "You are a true Christian."

I would have been honored if she had said to me something parallel to what one of my Buddhist friends once said to me: "I know you aren't a Buddhist in name, but you are one in heart." I knew this was the highest compliment that friend could give me, and I was touched. But this woman's words struck me even more powerfully because, I think, she wasn't trying to include me in the clan of Islam. Inclusion of this sort can be a form of colonization, asserting that one's own clan includes all good people, albeit anonymously. Instead, she was affirming me in my otherness. And she was saying something not just about me, but about Christ and the kind of Christianity he would want there to be. She saw that the true way of Christ is to show solidarity with the other—to work, not for the good of one's religious clan alone, but for the common good, the good of all, with saving love.

A Christian friend of mine, Cindy, discovered the power—and cost—of with-ness. She was born with one arm fully formed and the other partially formed. While doing graduate research in East Africa, she learned that in many places in Africa, children born with physical disabilities like hers are hidden away, considered cursed by God or demons, a shame to the family. If Cindy had been born there, she probably wouldn't have been allowed to go to primary school, much less graduate school.

She immediately felt a calling from God to do something for African children with disabilities. She went home and began raising funds to help pay school fees and get needed support and supplies for these children.[8] Her motivation flowed from her Christian faith, and most if not all of the donors to her new charity were fellow Christians.

Cindy made a decision that her fledgling organization would serve all children, whatever their religion. They would involve qualified adults as educators and administrators, whatever their religion. If Christians and Muslims could work together for needy children, that would be an asset, not a liability, in her mind. But over time, Cindy experienced pushback for her stance. Some of her Christian donors saw her work "less Christian" because she made service and education, not religious conversion, her primary aim. But Cindy couldn't back down. Backing down would be a betrayal of her true identity as a follower of Christ as she understood it.

I think of another friend we'll call Mike who went to a Muslim-majority country specifically to convert Muslims to Christianity. After some time there, he got a sick feeling: he felt he was serving neither God nor the best interests of the people around him, but was instead serving the colonizing agenda of the religious clan that sent him. So he changed the direction of his work. He started mobilizing Christians and Muslims to work side by side in helping the poor. "Something happens," he told me, "when we work together for the poor. We all change. I know that both the Christians and the

---

8. You can learn about Cindy's work—and find out how you can support it—at http://www.kupenda.org/.

Interfaith dialogue = collaboration for the good of "others"

246 • Why Did Jesus, Moses, the Buddha, and Mohammed Cross the Road?

Muslims feel they are encountering God in one another, and together we are encountering God as we join God in serving the poor."[9] He discovered that *witness* led him to *with-ness*.

Meanwhile, similar things are happening among people of other religions. I think of a prosperous Hindu engineer named Sailesh who left his lucrative high-tech career because he developed a passion to do something about the global environmental crisis. He is developing important technological breakthroughs to help people in poor countries to improve their lives without adopting the consumptive, environmentally destructive ways of the West. He told me, "I am doing this as a Hindu, but I feel I should not move forward unless I have Christians and Muslims and others working alongside me."[10]

I already mentioned Eboo Patel, my co-faster when I participated in the fast of Ramadan. Eboo formed an organization—Interfaith Youth Core—designed to bring young people of different faiths together to serve.[11] He knows that talking together is important—but that interfaith dialogue becomes much deeper in the context of multi-faith collaboration. Words are good, but actions are better—especially actions that bring us together solving problems that affect everybody. And when one of our biggest global problems is hostility between religions, this kind of mission-with is doubly important.

What Soraya and Nadyne, Eboo, Cindy, Sailesh, Mike, and so many other people are doing is a lot like what Jesus did: bringing together unlikely people to serve and heal together, to liberate the oppressed and their oppressors together, and to model, in their col-

---

9. For reasons of privacy, I am leaving out a lot of interesting details. I should add that I know of several separate stories like this one, unfolding independently in several Muslim-majority countries.

10. For more on Sailesh Rao's work, and for information about his excellent book *Carbon Dharma*, for which I wrote a foreword, see the Climate Healers website at http://www.climatehealers.org.

11. See their website at http://www.ifyc.org.

laboration, the kind of harmony and human-kindness the world so desperately needs. Their shared commitment—to interfaith collaboration for the common good—doesn't make them all Christians, but it does make them all a little more Christ-like. I'm sure I'm not alone in wondering what good having the former label is without having the latter quality of character and behavior.

Jesus = brought unlikely people together to serve others.

Tax collectors
lepers,   etc,
prostitutes

Chapter 27

How Mission Can Reorganize Organized Religion

The eschatological fullness of the Reign of God is the common final
achievement of Christianity and the other religions.

—*Jacques Dupuis*[1]

I mentioned earlier that I was in East Africa a few months after
intertribal violence had rocked Kenya. Shortly after returning
home, I was listening to a conversation between a Kenyan and an
American. The Kenyan explained the background for the outbreak,
the tensions among Luo, Luhya, Kikuyu, Maasai, and others of the
fifty-odd tribes in the country. The American asked, "Which tribe
are you from?" The man hesitated for a moment and replied. "I
could answer your question because I am not ashamed of my tribe.
It is part of who I am, and I know who I am. But at the risk of
sounding rude, I would rather not answer, and let me explain why.
In reality, in every country, there are only two tribes: the haves and
the have-nots. It is enough to say that I am from the haves, and I

---

1. Jacques Dupuis, *Toward a Christian Theology of Religious Pluralism* (Maryknoll,
N.Y.: Orbis Books, 1997), p. 390.

friendship — service to needy

because we love God ↑. *Commandment*

want to use the advantages that have come to me by accident of birth on behalf of the have-nots, whatever their tribe. So although I am from one tribe, I exist to serve people of all tribes."[2]

Like that man, I know who I am. I am a Christian. I love my heritage and thank God for it. But my identity as a Christian can never be a barrier, a wall, a reason for apartheid. Rather, my identity as a follower of Christ requires me first to move toward the other in friendship, and then to move *with* the other in service to those in need. In so doing, both the other and I are transformed from counterparts to partners. This is good news for both the haves and the have-nots. The haves suffer dehumanization—a loss of human-kindness—when they hold themselves aloof from their fellow humans, just as the have-nots suffer when the haves hoard wealth and opportunity at the have-nots' expense. The gospel calls both to discover salvation in encounter with the other, in the love of God.

What might this renewed sense of Christian identity and mission mean for our collectives and institutions known as "organized religion"? The term, of course, has a lot of detractors. I often ask those who speak critically of organized religion what they're more critical of: being organized or being religious. They most often reply they have problems with both. Then I'll explain that the word *religion* is based on the root *lig*, meaning "to bind or connect together" (as in *ligament*), so *religion* means reconnecting or rebonding broken relationships—with God, with neighbor, with stranger and enemy, with nonhuman life, with all creation. Generally their eyes get a little brighter and they realize that sounds like a good thing. But what about the organized part?

I might then suggest that the problem isn't organization, but the purpose and effectiveness of the organization. What if religious

---

2. His words echo those of Paulo Freire: "Washing one's hands of the conflict between the powerful and the powerless means to side with the powerful, not to be neutral."

communities were well-organized to bond broken relationships—between the haves and have-nots, for example? Suddenly, the idea of organized religion has a completely different feel.

Try imagining what might happen if our religious communities started organizing for the common good, for holistic or integral mission—mission that integrates witness and with-ness. Imagine that the leaders of our various faith traditions actually began meeting with one another—not merely for something called "interreligious dialogue," but to become friends, to share their personal values and spiritual experiences, to seek mutual understanding, to practice the neighborliness and hospitality toward the other that their traditions preach. And then, from there, imagine that they started setting an example—say one day a month or two weeks a year—working side by side modeling with-ness, collaboration for the common good, on behalf of those in need. Imagine the Pope and the Dalai Lama, a televangelist and a Muslim imam, a leading rabbi and an Orthodox Patriarch, side by side, serving meals in a refugee camp, distributing mosquito nets, digging wells, or assisting dentists in providing dental care to a poor village.

Now imagine that these religious leaders devoted say a month a year to meet together...dreaming, praying, and working for the well-being of all. (Some might say they couldn't spare that much time, since the internal demands of their organizations wouldn't allow it. But shouldn't the external demands of the future of humanity and the planet have some demand on them, too?) Imagine if they led their various religious communities to sign treaties or agreements of nonaggression and mutual protection—if they decided to boldly move ahead in peacemaking when nation-states shrink back. Imagine that they showed up in person when one of the presidents or prime ministers or party leaders supposedly under their care spoke or acted in hostility toward others, bringing the power of their religion to bear on the powerful for a change. And imagine if their top-level example were then to inspire religionwide acts of friendship and collaboration worldwide, getting the haves to see the have-nots as their sisters and brothers, fathers and mothers, sons and daughters.

Imagine if organized religion organized billions of people and trillions of dollars to tackle the challenges that our economic and political systems are afraid or unwilling to tackle—a planet ravaged by unsustainable human behavior and an out-of-control consumptive economy, the growing gap between the rich minority and the poor majority, and the proliferation of weapons of all kinds—including weapons of mass destruction.

"Wow," people frequently say when I propose these possibilities. "If they did that, I might become religious again." Some quickly add, "But I won't hold my breath. It'll never happen."

It wouldn't be impossible to prove them wrong, since with God all things are possible.

This possible impossibility is, I think, what Jesus meant when he claimed that the kingdom or commonwealth of God was *at hand*. It was not *out of reach*, impossible; nor was it *in hand*, already attained. It was simultaneously in reach and not yet seized, a gift already fully given, and not yet fully received, opened, and enjoyed.[3] Jesus embodied this truth to the edges of Judaism and beyond, and the apostles spread it "to the uttermost parts of the earth": God's commonwealth was a table where the Pharisees and prostitutes were equally welcome,

---

3. I have written two books on the subject of the kingdom of God: *The Secret Message of Jesus* (Nashville: Thomas Nelson, 2006) and *Everything Must Change* (Nashville: Thomas Nelson, 2007). Yet the subject continues to open up new dimensions to me. It is only in the sense mentioned here—a gift already fully given but not yet widely opened and enjoyed—that I subscribe to the *already/not yet* formula so common in some theological circles. The typical use of the formula does not, in my view, take into account the already-present-ness and already-given-ness of the kingdom inherent in Jesus' declarations that the kingdom is *at hand* and *among* (or within), and especially in his earth-shaking words of Luke 4:21: "Today, this Scripture *has been fulfilled* in your hearing." I see the kingdom as fully present and available, even when we fail or refuse to adjust our lives to it.

the chief priests and the Samaritans, the Sadducees and the Roman centurions, the poor homeless leper and the rich young leader, Onesimus the slave and Philemon the slave master, Gentile and Jew, male and female, one and all. A new religion called Christianity (that conflicted term, of course, didn't exist yet) wasn't the point; the kingdom or commonwealth of God was the point...for Jesus, for Paul, and for all the apostles.

What did Jesus mean by the term kingdom of God? He himself resisted defining it, preferring to tell what it was *like* rather than what it *was*, enlarging it for imaginative encounter through symbol and story rather than shrinking it for rational encounter in formula or proposition. He surely meant something far bigger than any religion should or could contain. He meant something that his movement (later called, for better or worse, *the church*) was to seek, to receive, to enter, and to participate in...not to own, control, commodify, or rule. He meant, among many other things, a profound transcendence of dualisms in a larger, unitive harmony, a unitive harmony that Christian mystics—and mystics of every religion—point to again and again as that which cannot be defined or even fully named.

To get a feel for the dimensions of that unitive harmony, we might ask—both playfully and reverently: what could be bigger than God?[4] The commonwealth of God, we might answer, in that it contains all of God and all of creation. And all of creation contains all of humanity, with all our languages and cultures—and religions. So in this way, Jesuit theologian Jacques Dupuis concluded his monumental *Toward a Christian Theology of Religious Pluralism* with the resonant—and profoundly Christian—words with which we began this chapter.

Organized religion is not an end in itself. It organizes for a purpose. So "organized Christianity" must, from this generous and emer-

---

4. Thanks to Samir Selmanovic for this way of framing the question.

gent Christian perspective, organize to receive, experience, celebrate, and live the commonwealth of God. This gift has already been given and so is already present, but we have yet to awaken to it, receive it, open it, and enter it fully. We have, for two thousand years, been exploring its frontiers, as it were, but it beckons us to venture deeper in. The deeper we enter, the more we feel welcomed home, experiencing the profound belonging that Jesus called "My Father's house," in which there is no hostility, only hospitality. There we experience God's welcoming embrace of us, but not only of us: of all the others, too. So in the Apocalypse, when the seventh angel blows his trumpet, loud voices do not shout, "Everyone has joined our religion, or been destroyed." No, they shout, "The kingdom of the world has become the kingdom of our Lord and of his Messiah!"

When we have that vision of the *telos* toward which we are moving, our attitudes change and our identity changes. We anticipate what Pierre Teilhard de Chardin called a "marvelous convergence," and our anticipation inspires participation. We work and pray for that marvelous convergence. We sing and dialogue for it. We even organize for it. And in so doing, we see, receive, and enter the gift that has already been given to us in, through, and with Jesus: yes, the kingdom, kindom, reign, dream, beloved community, regenerative economy, sacred ecosystem, or commonwealth of God.

Chapter 28
How Evangelism Is Like a Windmill

Do not leave others where they have been. But do not try to bring them to where you are, either, as beautiful as that place might be to you. Rather, invite them to go with you to a place neither you nor they have ever been before.

—*adapted from Vincent Donovan*[1]

It was an idyllic day—a perfect breeze, sunny skies, windmills turning with a rhythm at once natural and humane. I had been to Holland many times, but this was my first visit to the windmills. My host Sam and I climbed up into the belly of one of these engineering marvels.[2] As we watched the wooden gears turning in perfect calibration, Sam started telling me about the inhumanity of the system in which the windmills played so important a part. Peanut oil squeezed from imported Indonesian peanuts provided a painful

---

1. Adapted from Vincent Donovan, *Christianity Rediscovered* (Maryknoll, N.Y.: Orbis Books, 2003). My Muslim friend Eboo Patel expresses the same sentiment in *Acts of Faith* (Boston: Beacon Press, 2007): "We need a language that allows us to emphasize our unique inspirations and affirm our universal values. We need spaces where we can each state that we are proud of where we came from and all point to the place we are going to.... We have to save each other. It's the only way to save ourselves" (182 ,180).

2. Sam is a gifted leader, author, and blogger. You can learn more about his work at http://www.samlee.org.

metaphor for the crush of colonialism on the Indonesian workers who planted, harvested, and packed the peanuts for processing in Holland. There was no consciously malicious intent in all this, Sam explained: Dutch shipbuilders, traders, and windmill operators were simply making a living using the means of wealth production at hand. But much injustice can occur with little or no conscious malice, so we both felt at once the beauty and agony of the windmills as the huge gears turned and groaned around us.

It's nearly a cliché in many circles to say that the old evangelism— evangelism as we knew it—was, like the windmills, an unwitting accomplice in the story of European colonialism and empire. Protestants from Northern Europe raced against Catholics from Southern Europe to convert and educate "savages" and "heathen" around the world. Their conversion usually meant being co-opted and domesticated so they would become docile, cooperative producers of goods and services in the Northern or Southern sectors of the Euro-American economic system. The benefits to the Euro-American colonizers were obvious: profits from cheap raw materials and equally cheap cooperative labor. The "benefits" to the colonized were far more complex and ambiguous.[3]

This evangelism-plus-domestication was often undertaken on a completely unconscious level. The missionaries of the colonial era— including my own grandfather and grandmother—were sincere and good-hearted to the point of enormous personal sacrifice, motivated by a sincere desire to save souls for heaven. No malice was in play. But neither the naivete nor the sincerity of the colonial-era missionaries could nullify the unintended consequences of their work, some of which were tragic—whether those dimensions were social, economic, cultural, psychological, or political.

---

3. I explore some of these ambiguities in *Everything Must Change* (Nashville: Thomas Nelson, 2007).

Some missionaries felt a growing ambivalence about these impacts as they watched them unfold over time, and some became outspoken critics of the economic, social, and environmental exploitation inherent in the colonial system.[4] For most, though, civilization and development were seen as unmitigated blessings from heaven. In many ways they were blessings. Girls began to be educated along with boys, for example, and hospitals saved uncountable lives. But the costs and losses have been immeasurable, too.

Since nearly everyone these days is aware of these costs and losses, I imagine that many readers will assume there is no place for evangelism in this emerging understanding of strong-and-benevolent Christian identity. "You have your religion and I'll have mine" seems to be a step away from the evangelistic abuses of the past. But while taking a step from harm to harmlessness might be good in some ways, it's not good enough. We must rise to higher ground, from benign to benevolent, from harmlessness to human-kindness. When we do, we will make a surprising discovery. Just as there is a great future for windmills beyond their morally compromised use in the age of colonialism, there is a great future for a new kind of evangelism, although it will be so different that it may well need a new name.[5]

Nobody has conveyed this new/renewed dimension of Christian mission more poignantly than a Catholic missionary named Vincent Donovan. His experience "on the mission field" forced him to face the dark sides of the colonial-era missionary project, and the words that opened this chapter capture his transformed vision.

This shared journey is not the call to convert from your religion to mine. It is, rather, the invitation for both of us to seek a deeper

---

4. Predictably, Protestants often saw the ugliness of Catholic missionary colonialism, and Catholics often saw the ugliness of Protestant missionary colonialism.

5. For more on the subject of evangelism, see Doug Pagitt's winsome and insightful *Evangelism in the Inventive Age* (Minneapolis: sparkhouse press, 2012).

conversion that begins in our deepest religious identity and transforms all of life. Whatever our religion, this conversion transforms the way we see us-ness and otherness. We still cherish our distinctive religious identity, but we abandon what my friend Samir Selmanovic calls *religious supremacy*. We are converted from hostility, from seeing the other as a threat to be feared, pitied, eliminated, or refashioned into our image. We are converted into hosts and guests, practicing and receiving hospitality, sharing our treasures as gifts. Karen Armstrong said it well:[6]

> Sometimes it's the very otherness of a stranger, someone who doesn't belong to our ethnic or ideological or religious group, an otherness that can repel us initially, but which can jerk us out of our habitual selfishness, and give us intonations of that sacred otherness, which is God.

The shared escape from "habitual selfishness" and this shared listening for "sacred otherness" is not a claim by or for any religious institution or tradition, including one called Christianity. Instead, it makes a proposal to members of each religious tradition, inviting them to turn away from all hostile identities and turn toward God and neighbor, stranger, outcast, outsider, and enemy.

In so doing, this proposal celebrates a joyous opportunity for everyone, whatever their religious affiliation: the opportunity to encounter the God who loves everyone and every created thing. But according to Jesus, the genuine encounter with God never ends there. It always leads to a fresh encounter with the other as well. So our proclamation isn't simply a matter of pointing others to God: it

---

6. From an interview with Bill Moyers, available here: http://www.pbs.org/now/printable/transcript_armstrong_print.html.

is about inviting others on a shared journey to *and through* God to the neighbor, the other, the enemy—and, we might add, to all living creatures and the creation that sustains them.

In this way, the old language of saving souls grows more meaningful than ever: it is our mission to save souls from the dehumanizing effects of hostility to God and other; souls, yes, and the bodies on which souls depend. And the human societies on which bodies and souls depend. And the natural ecosystems on which bodies, souls, and societies depend. And this precious planet on which everything depends. So more than ever, we are engaged in the sacred mission of salvation—including salvation from the disastrous effects of misguided, distorted, dysfunctional religion, beginning with our own. This saving mission calls every individual—each soul, if you will—to make a saving decision: the choice to live not for our own selfish interests alone, and not for the groupish interests of our clan or caste or civilization alone, but for the common good, the good of all creation.

That term *common good* and its cousins, *commonweal* and *commonwealth*, are, I am increasingly convinced, excellent synonyms for Jesus' term *kingdom of God*. Similarly, Jesus' word for this radical turn from selfish and groupish interest toward the common good was *repent*. And here Christians face a special challenge, because Christ's good news calls *us* to repentance before it calls anyone else. It calls us to repent of the many ways our Christianity has become an oppositional clan or hostile caste or supreme civilization that demands loyalty due only the commonwealth or kingdom of God.

Clans and castes and civilizations are part of our history. They are a given in human society. If we abolished them all today, new ones would emerge tomorrow. And they have a real value: they conserve shared memory, they preserve shared values and virtues, and they serve as the "identity tents" in which generation after generation of children learn to move beyond *me* to *we*. But when our clans, castes, and civilizations teach generation after generation of children to hold oppositional identities, rendering them hostile toward other people who have been raised in their respective identity tents, then our clans and castes and civilizations must be repented of, including our Christian clans and castes and civilizations.[7]

That is a great gift of a multi-faith world to Christians: in challenging us to repent of our clannishness, caste-liness, and cultural exceptionalism or supremacy, our multi-faith context challenges us to become better—meaning more Christ-like—Christians.

Although this new approach to Christian mission is indeed warm, it is not fuzzy or fizzy, the spiritual equivalent of the old Coke commercial about the world singing in perfect harmony. It is frank, pointed, and even confrontational about discordant forces among and within us that won't yield to harmony even when enticed by a cool sugary drink. It warns us what to expect if we don't change our ways—not a fiery torture chamber after death, but a death trap in this life: war, hate, violence, and fear; famine, disease, floods, and drought; hunger, riots, refugee camps, and crime. Because it is willing to challenge the status quo of oppositional identity, it requires a lot of guts and resilience, because there are few things more dangerous than approaching with open hands an angry gang with clenched fists.

Surprisingly to some, in deepening our engagement with the love of God, this new era in Christian mission may require us to speak again of the wrath of God. But it is not the wrath many of us encountered in our religious past, the divine mascot of *us* who is ready to bark, bite, and devour *them*. If we speak of an angry God at all, we will speak of a God angry at indifference, angry at apathy, angry at racism and violence, angry at inhumanity, angry at waste, angry at

---

7. Speaking as an American, it's interesting to reflect on the ways that denominationalism relates to clannishness and caste. For example, consider these terms: Scottish Presbyterians, British Evangelicals, Dutch Calvinists, Italian Catholics.

destruction, angry at injustice, angry at hostile religious clannish-ness. That anger is never against *us* (or *them*); it is against *what is against* us (and them). It is not out to destroy us; it is out to destroy what is out to destroy us. If we compare it to a fire, it is not a fire that consumes good things. Only an evil fire could consume good. The holy fire of God can consume only evil things—things that would be better off not existing. And since human beings bear the image of God, their humanity can never be considered an evil thing. The greed, pride, fear, craving, and hostility that infect humanity—*they* are the evil thing—and they are what God loves to save us from.

So that is the salvation we must proclaim, including salvation from dysfunctional religion itself. That's why God's good news is nei-ther a call to convert from one religion to another, nor an injunction against the freedom of religion that would restrict people from con-verting if they so desire.

So if a Muslim or Hindu community is destroying Muslims or Hin-dus, if it bores them with irrelevance, wastes their time and energy with meaningless and pointless rituals, if it turns them against others and obstructs the common good, I hope a Christian community will open their doors wide and offer sanctuary and healing. How could anyone turn them away? How could anyone refuse them water for baptism? How could anyone refrain from breaking out the bread and wine and welcoming them to the table?

But the same must be said when Christians are being destroyed, bored, wasted, or turned hostile by their Christian communities, and other communities (often agnostics or atheists) offer them sanctuary. That's why this saving mission vigorously supports religious freedom, including the freedom to change religions and the freedom to be nonreligious, multireligious, or spiritual-but-not-religious.[8]

---

8. The subject of multireligious identity is a fascinating and important one, but beyond the scope of this project. For a good introduction, see Paul Knitter, *Without Buddha I Could Not Be a Christian* (Oxford: Oneworld, 2009).

Contrary to some accusations, we advocates of this emerging missionality do not downplay Jesus. We celebrate Jesus more than ever. But instead of holding Jesus hostage as the private property of the Christian religion, we dare proclaim that God has already offered Christ as a gift to the world ("For God so loved the world that he gave..."). Christ does not, then, belong to any single religion, especially our own. No, Christ already belongs to everyone everywhere. As the Christmas carol puts it, "Let every heart prepare him room and heaven and nature sing." And so we challenge every religion—including all forms of Christianity—to prepare him room and sing.

We are not saying, "Take Jesus and custom-design him to fit into your existing culture or religion," even though that's exactly what we Christians have done repeatedly throughout our history. Instead we say, "Welcome Jesus into your community and watch as he turns your water into wine, trades your temples of stone for temples of humanity, turns over the tables of your religious-industrial complex, and invites you to be born again, not as a one-time experience but as an ongoing transformation. Welcome Jesus and watch everything change."

So this emerging missionality is neither universalistic, exclusivistic, nor inclusivistic in the traditional sense. Those old terms are framed within assumptions (about original sin and hell, about God and vengeance, etc.) that we have come to acknowledge are part of the problem. We aren't taking new positions framed within old approaches: we're seeking a new approach altogether.

But at the same time, our saving message is indeed exclusive in the sense that it excludes hostility, injustice, apathy, and violence. And it is inclusive in the sense that everyone is welcome to participate, regardless of religious label. And it is universalist in the sense that it will not rest until everyone who wants to can and does experience the abundant life of shalom, humility, kindness, and justice that God desires for all. We want to share the treasures of Christ universally, with everyone, everywhere, in every religion.

But sharing is never a one-way street. It is always about receiving as well as giving. In generosity, we freely share our treasures with people of other faiths, *without requiring them to convert*. And in that same spirit, we gratefully receive the treasures generously offered to us by other faiths—*without needing to convert*. So we Christians generously share our treasures with others, and we receive the gifts generously offered to us by Jews, Muslims, Buddhists, Hindus, agnostics, atheists, and others. We don't force everything we have on them: giving is not imposing. Nor must we receive everything they may offer. The freedom to say "No, thank you" or "Not right now" is essential to human dignity and generosity.

We never forget that there is a difference between a guest and a thief, just as there is a difference between quotation and plagiarism. The former respects the right to privacy and property and the latter doesn't. So the new evangelism encourages generous sharing of spiritual treasures but doesn't condone their theft, pirating, or misappropriation. It sees the importance of each faith maintaining its own identity—and believes that can be done without hostility and with generosity.

Meanwhile, in this emergent missionality, we respect the freedom of people of any religion including our own to be hostile. We understand that hostility is often an unchosen reflex or unconscious habit, not a chosen response, so we don't insult, shame, or condemn people for practicing the kinds of religious hostility we are seeking to provide an alternative to. The very act of insulting, shaming, or condemning others for hostility would be hostile and therefore inappropriate, not to mention absurd. And besides, we have learned from our own mistakes that religious people engage in hostility not because they are inherently hostile, but because they perceive things they love are under threat. Their aggression often boils over from a loving defensiveness.

So our new approach demands a great deal of us: graciousness, understanding, empathy, nonretaliation, nondefensiveness, and patience when wronged. In fact, it requires us to rejoice when unfairly persecuted, rejected, and slandered, because we know that it is only from the position of vulnerability, when we stand at risk of being misunderstood, excluded, and misrepresented, that we can embody and speak the good news. (Mustn't our good news come in risk, not power; in weakness, not strength; as apparent foolishness, not with worldly coercion; with rough edges, not slickness? If we employ power, domination, persuasion, and slickness, wouldn't we be conquering, colonizing, and selling, not evangelizing?)

Finally, our saving mission respects privacy and avoids pressure. We know that people need time to reflect, privacy to come to themselves, and space to consider turning around and choosing a new path. Yet we also know that choices must be made, convictions confessed, regrets acknowledged, costs counted. So we urge people, as soon as they are ready, to speak out and confess where they stand, who they are becoming, where they are going, how they believe, and why. With both patience and urgency we invite people to 'fess up, sign on, join in, and come out of the closet. This requires courage and grace—the courage to differ, and the grace to do so both gently and firmly.

So we constantly issue what we might call an *alter call* instead of an *altar call*. We do not invite people to another religious altar where another hostile deity can be appeased by another list of protocols, thus engendering another set of hostilities. No, we invite people to alter their understanding of God, to come to know God as revealed in the human-kindness of Christ... to discover a God who needs no appeasement but who seeks to bring all things into joyous reconciliation. In light of this altered experience of God, we invite people to alter their self-understanding as well, discovering a new identity that alters everything—leading to a conversion so deep it fills with new meaning old, spent, clichéd terms like *born again, saved, converted, confirmed, baptized,* or *catechized.*

Because the cost of embracing a strong and benevolent Christian identity is so high, we must provide lots of support for those who respond... support through fellowship, support through teaching (knowledge) and training (know-how), support through ritual and symbol, support through guided practice and mentoring. But since we are still young and inexperienced in this new identity, we have a long way to go in learning how to provide this support, and each of us must take whatever little we have learned and pass it on to others, even as we look for others who can pass more on to us.

This book represents my sincere and highly improvable contribution to that process. I conclude with my *alter call* to you, inviting you to become, even now, not only a believer, but an evangelist in this way of holding Christian identity in a multi-faith world.

Yes, sailing ships were used to transport slaves, and yes, windmills were part of the colonial economy. But the wind can't be held responsible for the uses toward which it was put.

So I invite you to feel and enjoy the wind of the Spirit that flows around and within you at this very moment. I urge you to unfurl your sails and welcome the Spirit's power in your life. I bid you rejoice that the wind of the Spirit blows everywhere and can't be contained in anyone's box, no matter how big or small, old or new. And I point you to Jesus, this strong and kind Galilean man who was filled with the Spirit, who walked the way of peace and bids us to follow. Let us who identify ourselves as Christians boldly follow Jesus into new territory to explore new possibilities we have never even dreamed of before. Let us, with him, cross the road in order to encounter the other, and in so doing, encounter the Other.

Chapter 29

How a Hindu Can Help Christians Discover Their True Identity in a Multi-faith World

The tremendous question presses itself upon us: Will the present Christian Church be big enough, responsive enough, Christlike enough to be the organ through which Christ will come to our multi-faith world? For mind you, the Spirit of Christ is breaking out beyond the borders of the Christian Church. Will the Christian Church be Christlike enough to be the moral and spiritual center of this overflowing movement of the Spirit? Or will many of the finest people in our multi-faith world accept Christ as Lord and master of their lives but be forced to live their spiritual lives apart from the historic Christian Church?

—*adapted from E. Stanley Jones*[1]

My friend Rob Bell stirred things up a while back with a book called *Love Wins*. You wouldn't think that would be such a controversial proposition for Christians, but Rob suggested something daring: *if love has the final word, hell and damnation can't.*

1. E. Stanley Jones, *The Christ of the Indian Road* (New York: The Abingdon Press, 1925), p. 63. Here are his actual words, with the phrases I altered in italics: "The tremendous question presses itself upon us: Will the present Christian Church be big

The book raised questions similar to the ones we raised in Part II of this book, questions about some of our long-held theological assumptions that may have outlived both their practical usefulness and their biblical credibility. You could almost hear the theological gears clicking in some readers' minds: *If Christianity isn't a plan for avoiding hell, why be a Christian?* and *If we lose threats of hell, our religion loses its reason for existence.* The idea that there could be even better, stronger, more compelling reasons for Christian faith than hell-avoidance didn't seem to cross many minds, and even fewer seemed to "get" the alternate vision of Christian faith that Rob was proposing. Many couldn't get past the first page, where Rob challenged an assumption that many Christians share: *because Mahatma Gandhi died a Hindu, not a Christian, he is in hell at this moment.*

Gandhi's eternal destiny, it turns out, troubles Christians on both sides of the hell debate—upsetting some that he might not be granted access to heaven and upsetting others that he might. As different camps of Christians continue to debate and speculate about Gandhi's post-mortem fate, it seems appropriate to let Gandhi get a word in edgewise ... through a conversation he had with a Christian missionary named E. Stanley Jones.

Jones (1884–1973) was a professor at Asbury Seminary before becoming a Methodist missionary to India. In India he became friends with Gandhi, and years later, he wrote a biography of Gandhi that inspired Dr. Martin Luther King Jr. to commit himself to nonviolence in the civil rights movement. Jones wrote many other books

---

enough, responsive enough, Christlike enough to be the medium and organ through which Christ will come to India? For mind you, *Christianity* is breaking out beyond the borders of the Christian Church. Will the Christian Church be Christlike enough to be the moral and spiritual center of this overflowing *Christianity*? Or will many of the *finest spirits and minds of India* accept Christ as Lord and Master of their lives but live their *Christian* lives apart from the Christian Church?" The complete text is available here: http://www.scribd.com/doc/46133550/The-Christ-of-the-Indian-Road/.

as well, and his most famous, *Christ of the Indian Road* (1925), sold over a million copies.[2]

The life and work of E. Stanley Jones serve as a beautiful example of the strong and benevolent Christian identity we have been advocating in these pages. Like other great Christian missionaries in India,[3] Jones neither watered down his deep commitment to Christ, nor did he set out to knock down the world's third-largest religion so he could replace it with Christianity. He looked for a way that Christ could enter, incarnate himself within, and bless Hinduism just as he had done in sectors of Judaic culture, Greco-Roman culture, Celtic culture, Anglo-Saxon culture, and many other cultures through history.[4] He envisioned a time when a new movement of Indian followers of Christ would model a new, non-Western kind of Christian faith, one that respected the Hindu roots in which it grew and one that brought blessing to its Hindu and Muslim neighbors.

Gandhi's relationship with Christian faith was long and complex. Although he never joined the Christian religion, he loved Christ and wanted Indian culture to welcome what Christ had to offer, as his famous interchange with E. Stanley Jones made clear. Jones asked, "I am very anxious to see Christianity naturalized in India, so that it shall no longer be a foreign thing identified with a foreign people and a foreign government, but a part of the national life of India and

---

2. The complete text is available here: http://www.scribd.com/doc/46133550/The-Christ-of-the-Indian-Road/. Johnny Baker blogs about the book in a series beginning here: http://jonnybaker.blogs.com/jonnybaker/2005/10/christ_of_the_i.html.

3. Examples would include Lesslie Newbigin and Bede Griffiths. Important Indian Christian leaders like Raimon Panikkar (whose father was Indian, but was born in Spain) and Anthony DeMello should also be noted.

4. For example, Jones noted what he called "five living seeds" in Hinduism: (1) spirit is the ultimate reality, (2) there is a sense of unity running through all things, (3) there is justice at the heart of the universe, (4) freedom should be passionately pursued, and (5) there is a tremendous cost in living a truly religious life (*Christ of the Indian Road*, p. 173).

contributing its power to India's uplift and redemption. What would you suggest we do to make that possible?"

Gandhi replied, "I would suggest, first of all, that all of you Christians, missionaries and all, begin to live more like Jesus Christ." Reflecting on Gandhi's statement, Jones commented, "He needn't have said anything more—that was quite enough. I knew that looking through his eyes were the three hundred millions of India, and speaking through his voice were the…millions of the East saying to me,… 'If you will come to us in the spirit of your Master, we cannot resist you.'"

Gandhi continued, "Second, I would suggest that you must practice your religion without adulterating or toning it down." And again, Jones commented, "The greatest living non-Christian asks us not to adulterate or tone it down, not to meet them with an emasculated gospel, but to take it in its rugged simplicity and high demand. But what are we doing? As someone has suggested, we are inoculating the world with a mild form of Christianity, so that it is now practically immune against the real thing."

Gandhi then said, "Third, I would suggest that you must put your emphasis upon love, for love is the center and soul of Christianity." Once more, Jones observed, "He did not mean love as a sentiment, but love as a working force, the one real power in a moral universe, and he wanted it applied between individuals and groups and races and nations, the one cement and salvation of the world."

Gandhi concluded: "Fourth, I would suggest that you study the non-Christian religions and culture more sympathetically in order to find the good that is in them, so that you might have a more sympathetic approach to the people."

On these four points, the Hindu leader and the Christian missionary were in full agreement. We might call them four cornerstones or four foundations for Christian identity in a multi-faith world. But I think it would be better to imagine movement rather than stasis, so we can think of them as four pistons in an engine or four wheels on a car. They can help us take what we've learned in this book, translate it into action, and live it on the global multi-faith road as Jones sought to live it on the Indian road.

As Gandhi said, Christian identity in a multi-faith world must be marked first and foremost by *Christ-likeness*—so that we experience spiritual formation in Christ-like character, Christ-like vision, and Christ-like virtues and values.[5] Second, Christian identity must focus on unadulterated, undiluted Christian *practice*—full-bodied, caffeinated, high-proof devotion in action.[6] The third mark of Christian identity hardly needs to be said in light of the first two: to emphasize *love* as "center and soul" of our faith, love for God with all our heart, soul, mind, and strength, and love for neighbor, stranger, outcast, outsider, and enemy. And fourth, we must approach other religions and cultures—and the people who inhabit them—with what Gandhi called "sympathy," but we might better call understanding, respect, human-kindness, or *benevolence*.[7]

---

5. On Christ-likeness, Jones said, "Here is a new and amazing challenge, for this [movement of people following Christ] outside Christianity is going straight to the heart of things and saying that to be a Christian is to be Christlike. This means nothing less than that ancient rituals and orders and power at court and correctly stated doctrine avail little if Christlikeness is not the outstanding characteristic of the people of the churches. If Christianity centers in the Christian Church in the future it will be because that church is the center of the Christ-spirit" (*Christ of the Indian Road*, pp. 63–64).

6. I know that for many, Christian faith is still seen primarily as a doctrinal system rather than a way of life, elevating assent to certain doctrinal statements above the practices, character, and virtues of Christ-like living. But that assumption is being questioned and modified on many fronts, thanks to the work of people like Ruth Haley Barton, Richard Foster, Dallas Willard, Cynthia Bourgeault, Shane Claiborne, Diana Butler Bass, Mindy Calliguire, and many others. In a practice-oriented faith, doctrine still matters—but it is subsumed within a practice: *doctrine* is defined as the never-ending practice of seeking to understand and articulate the mysteries of faith, in conversation with others, and mindful of the past, the present, and the future.

7. It is in this context that deep resonances among religions can be seen and appreciated—the nongrasping, for example, of Philippians (2:4–7) and the Buddhist idea of detachment; the "single eye" and nonjudgmentalism of Matthew (6:22–23 and 7:1) and the non–dual seeing of Hinduism and Buddhism; the conjugal imagery of the

If you are a Christian, you already know that some Christian communities will not help you practice this kind of Christian identity animated by these four driving forces. Some will pile on strictures and baggage and qualifiers and burdens and arguments that will tie you down, hold you back, and do you in. Others will require you to imitate their hostility as a proof of your orthodoxy. These kinds of communities will frustrate you, and you will frustrate them.

That's okay. We shouldn't be surprised. This is to be expected. This is exactly why the good news of Jesus Christ is so needed—good news of reconciliation, proclaimed in word and deed. Because thankfully, while some groups constrict and others fight and still others wrinkle, shrink, and wither, many communities of faith are coming alive in a fresh, new way. They are becoming more and more committed to developing more and more Christians with this kind of joyful, peaceful, contagious strong-benevolent identity. And more good news: if you can't find this kind of faith community, you can form one. You really can. It might be as simple as inviting a few friends over for dinner (or gathering online) to read and discuss this book and books like it together.[8]

Everyone is crossing roads. Many, like the religious leaders in Jesus' paradigmatic story (Luke 10:25–37), cross the road in fear and

New Testament (Ephesians 5:32 and Revelation 21) with the similar imagery in much Sufi and Hindu poetry; the dynamic tension between unity and diversity in both Trinitarian and Hindu conceptions of the Godhead, and so on. These resonances do not argue for throwing all the religions into a blender, pressing puree, and then making the simplistic assumption that "they're all the same" or that their differences "don't matter." But, recalling our considerations of the doctrine of the Holy Spirit, these resonances suggest that within God's creation, upon which God's Spirit hovers (to use Genesis 1:2 language), glimpses and experiences of the mysteries of God are ubiquitous. And they suggest that sincere people of differing religions can approach one another with what Gandhi called "sympathy" (or human-kindness, or benevolence), not suspicion, and in a spirit of generosity, not hostility.

8. I hope to recommend and provide additional resources to help both existing and newly forming faith communities of this kind in the future. Check for links at http://www.brianmclaren.net on the page for this book.

prejudice to avoid contact with the other. But some, like the good Samaritan, cross the road in compassion and solidarity, moving toward the other to touch, to heal, to affirm human-kindness. In that spirit, we have begun crossing the road, and on the other side, we are discovering the other as neighbor, and God as loving Creator of all.[9] This crossing forever changes our identity. Each page that we have turned has been a small step in embracing that new identity, in making room for it to be born within us.

For all our progress, we still have a long way to go. We have only begun to face and trace the darker threads of our history and to own them and integrate them with the brighter hues in our tapestry of faith (the historical challenge). We are just beginning to reformulate and celebrate our doctrine as a healing teaching rather than an exclusive litmus test (the doctrinal challenge). We are neophytes when it comes to reinvigorating our liturgy for strong-and-kind spiritual formation (the liturgical challenge). And we have a long journey ahead in reframing and practicing our mission in a politically conflicted, ecologically precarious, economically unjust, and spiritually diverse world (the missional challenge). But to be crossing the road at all is great progress in comparison to being huddled defensively on our opposite corners, glaring from a distance in fear, pride, isolation, and ignorance. So, just as Jesus introduced an outsider—a despised Samaritan—to teach his companions about the greatest commandment, a Hindu has given us a final word in these final pages.

Let's also hear the voice of a Muslim, born under apartheid in South Africa. While many of his peers veered into Islamic radicalism—some of them later joining the Taliban—Farid Esack pioneered Islamic liberation theology, working nonviolently with Christians, Hindus, and others to overcome apartheid and gender inequality, and to pursue

---

9. Here is another answer to the question, *Why did Jesus, Moses, the Buddha, and Mohammed cross the road? To discover the other as neighbor, and to show solidarity with those on the other side.*

justice, peace, and the common good. Here is how he concluded his book on the rediscovery of a strong-benevolent Muslim identity:

> These are but some of the many issues that we know little about and need to address. It is not going to be easy. What we do know is that our world has become small and the dangers threatening it, multifarious.... Humankind, especially the marginalized and oppressed, need each other to confront these dangers and the challenges of liberation. Let us hope that, because of, and not despite, our different creeds and worldviews, we are going to walk this road side by side. Let us hope that we will be able to sort out some of the theological issues whilst we walk the road.[10]

Our varied histories have brought us to a crossroads. We can stand our ground here on our opposite corners and defend the frigid distance between us. Or we can cross the road. With outstretched hands, smiling faces, and open hearts, we can move toward one another, meet in the middle, and walk side by side beyond the limits of our old suspicious, segregated spaces. We can reject the mutual hostility by which we have defined ourselves, respect the different gifts we bring one another, and inject fresh hope into the global human equation through the unexpected factor of human-kindness. Walking together, we can face our common threats and seek the common good, forging a future that would have been impossible any other way. In so doing, as Farid Esack said, we will all feel like beginners, for we will all have to acknowledge how little we know.

---

10. Farid Esack, *Qur'an, Liberation and Pluralism: An Islamic Perspective of Interreligious Solidarity against Oppression* (Oxford: Oneworld, 1997), p. 261. The quotation continues, "All of us...participate in the shaping of the cultural and religious images and assumptions that oppress or liberate the Other, and thus ourselves." Esack's words suggest a final answer to the question asked by the title of this book: *Why did Jesus, Moses, the Buddha, and Mohammed cross the road? To walk side by side and together sort out the theological issues that too often turn their followers into enemies rather than friends.*

Becoming like little children is not such a bad thing. If we are humbled to the point of beginning anew and seeing afresh, maybe, just maybe, our identities will be transformed by grace so that we will reflect more fully the One in whose image we are created. Perhaps this encounter with the other is the crossroads to which God has been leading us all along. Perhaps this choice now—to move forward or to hold back, to open arms or to clench fists, to identify ourselves by opposition and hostility or to identify ourselves by hospitality and solidarity—perhaps this is our defining moment.

So imagine, then, Jesus, Moses, the Buddha, and Mohammed crossing the road to encounter one another. Imagine us following them. What will we discover together in that crossing?

Surely, it will be holy and humbling in that sacred space. Surely there will be joy, grace, and peace. Surely justice, truth, and love. We will find hospitality there, not hostility, and friendship, not fear, and it will be good—good for our own well-being, good for the poor and forgotten, good for our grandchildren's grandchildren, and good even for the birds of the air and the flowers in the meadow and the fish out at sea. "This is very good," God will say. And we will say, "Amen."

Acknowledgments

First, thanks to those who read this book and made important suggestions, especially Sailesh Rao, Paul Rauschenbusch, Jeff Burns, Michael Hardin, Paul Nuechterlein, and Rabbi Or Rose. Where I followed their advice, the book is better; where I didn't, it's not their fault. Thanks to Joy Madeiros of Oasis Trust (http://oasisuk.org) for a stimulating conversation eight or nine years ago that planted a seed for this book. Thanks to all who guided me to important scholarship, especially Sheila Bravo, Amanda Henderson, and Samuel Ewell. Thanks to Michael Hardin, Tony Bartlett, James Alison, Suzanne Ross, and others who have helped me more deeply appreciate René Girard. Thanks to Carl Medearis, Rod Cardoza, Bart Campolo, and Jeff Burns, for their friendship, conversations, and connections related to this book. Thanks to Ted Durr and Imam Shamshad Nasir and other friends in the D.C. area who rose to the occasion after September 11, 2001. Thanks to Jeff and Janet Wright for introducing me to Israel/Palestine, and to Bowie Snodgrass and Samir Selmanovic for pioneering multi-faith community. Thanks to Rabbi Shawn Landres, Mark Braverman, Marc Ellis, Michael Lerner, Eboo Patel, Soraya Deen, and Nadyne Heinert for all you've taught me.

Thanks to all my colleagues on the speaking circuit, especially Jay Bakker, Nadia Bolz-Weber, Tony Jones, Doug Pagitt, Phyllis Tickle, Gareth Higgins, Frank Schaeffer, Diana Butler Bass, Marcus Borg, Dom Crossan, Jim Wallis, Pete Rollins, Bart Campolo, Shane Claiburne, and Tony Campolo. In your diverse ways, you are itinerant evangelists of a new Christian identity.

Thanks to booksellers and all in the publishing industry who are steering a course through choppy waters. Thanks to bloggers who use the new media to alert people to good things in the old. Thanks to Wendy Grisham, Katherine Venn, and everyone at Jericho, Hodder, and Hachette: you are a pleasure to work with, and I am so grateful to be on your team. (And special thanks to Joanna Davey for the brilliant title brainstorming!) Especially enthusiastic, heartfelt thanks to Kathryn Helmers and everyone at Creative Trust, whose guidance and support mean more to me than I can say, and to Luci Neuman, Joe and Suzanne Stabile, and all my colleagues at Life in the Trinity Ministry, for giving me a professional home. Thanks to Kyle Bennett, John Ineson, and the people of St. Mark's for great pastoral care.

Thanks to Grace, whose companionship makes everything in life better, and thanks to my parents for raising me in the first half of life, and to my kids for raising me in the second.

Thanks to all of you who will read this book and translate it into kind, generous, road-crossing action, each in your own creative way. Thanks to all of you who will recommend this book to friends, both those you know will love it and those you suspect might hate it, but still should read it anyway.

And finally, thanks be to God. Each book I've written has stretched me and matured me in the writing of it, and that's especially true for this one, which gives me reason to hope that the same will be true for all who read.

For more information and additional resources, including a downloadable group study guide, please check out http://www.brian mclaren.net.

About the Author

Brian D. McLaren is an author, speaker, activist, and public theologian. After teaching college English, Brian was a church planter, pastor, and networker in the Baltimore-Washington, D.C., area for over twenty years. He is a popular conference speaker and a frequent guest lecturer for denominational and ecumenical leadership gatherings in the United States and internationally, and is Theologian-in-Residence at Life in the Trinity Ministry.

Brian's writing spans over a dozen books, including his acclaimed *A New Kind of Christian* trilogy, *A Generous Orthodoxy*, and his most recent titles, *Naked Spirituality: A Life with God in 12 Simple Words* (2011) and *The Girl with the Dove Tattoo* (2012). A frequent guest on television, radio, and news media programs, Brian is also an active and popular blogger, a musician, and an avid outdoor enthusiast. Learn more at his website, www.brianmclaren.net. Brian is married to Grace, and they have four adult children.

P. 61 threatening

Interprete
Scriptures (OT)
w kindness not
hostility

Healing on Sabbath: Jesus
Compassion trumps condemnation
Basic human kindness

Scriptures say
eye for eye = love your enemies
     no revenge (p. 206)
But JC says

Read responsively, Compassionately
+ ethically!

Friendship - p. 223